ROBERT DOWNEY JR

For Mum and Dad

First published in the United Kingdom in 2010 by
Portico Books
10 Southcombe Street
London
W14 0RA

An imprint of Anova Books Company Ltd

ISBN 9781906032876

A CIP catalogue record for this book is available from the
British Library.

10 9 8 7 6 5 4 3 2 1

Printed and bound by WS Bookwell, Finland

This book can be ordered direct from the publisher at
www.anovabooks.com

ROBERT DOWNEY JR

The Rise and Fall of
The Comeback Kid

BEN FALK

PORTICO

Contents

Author's Note

'Robert Downey Jr is a genius.' It's a phrase I came across a lot during my research for this book. Most people were referring to his acting across more than 50 films and television shows. Others were talking about his singing, or his piano playing, or his poetry. Some even mentioned it in conjunction with his intellect, though while the following story will prove him to be an immensely intelligent individual, I have found no official certification to that end.

Having lived and worked in Hollywood myself, I can attest to the fact the word 'genius' is one that's bandied around a great deal in showbiz circles. Not just about Kubrick or Brando, but about the guy who came up with the marketing campaign for *Transformers*, or the Beverly Hills orthopaedist who does all the A-list stars. In other words, its frequent usage often renders it meaningless. As a cynical entertainment hack with more than a decade in the (posh hotel) trenches, the mere mention of the term immediately sends my hackles rocketing skywards.

But you know, having spent more time than one man is supposed to spend studying another man if he doesn't plan to ask him out on a date, the whole genius thing doesn't seem so far-fetched when you're talking about Robert Downey Jr. To watch his transformation into a vivacious yuppie-turned-pathetic addict in *Less Than Zero*, his Oscar-nominated performance as Charlie Chaplin or more recently his laconic, charismatic turn as an industrialist-cum-superhero in *Iron Man*, it's no surprise that he's frequently tapped to play the more highly evolved on-screen characters.

Robert chose not to participate in this book. He was scheduled to write his own autobiography in 2006, even took the advance, but returned it two years later when his comic book caper became an international blockbuster and set his career onto an even more stratospheric path.

It makes sense, considering a great many young viewers of *Iron Man* don't know Robert's history – his peculiar upbringing, his struggle with drink and drugs, his tabloid-friendly tussles with the law and his trail of great performances in not-so-great films.

But for more long-held fans – and I count myself one wholeheartedly – it was precisely this history that endeared us to the actor. Not because we wished to revel in his misery, but because we were fascinated by his journey, how a man who could keep churning out brilliance on-camera could be imploding so spectacularly off it.

Many showbiz journalists like to pretend to themselves they know their subjects. That when an actor says hi and smiles at them, it is because they're mates, not simply because the film company has forced them to sit in a junket room and talk to a group of random people from all over the world in a bid to drum up publicity for their movie.

I am not Robert's friend or acquaintance. I have met him at various promotional functions, talked to him a couple of times during my job as a hack, but should I walk up to him on the street, he wouldn't have the faintest clue who I am. I'm not going to pretend I know exactly who Robert Downey Jr is. What I have attempted to do within these pages however, is get as close as I possibly can to finding out. The writing of this book has been as much of an exploration for me as I hope the reading is for you.

I've talked to former colleagues, old friends, even innocent bystanders who happened to come into his orbit. It's testament to the charm of the man that they all have something to say about him, even if the meeting took place more than 30 years ago. I've also covered pretty much all the films he has been in, but I have missed out some. Put it down to authorial licence – some I simply consider too insignificant an entry on his CV often because it was a tiny cameo, others I have missed out because I don't want the book to just be a long list of *everything* he's been in. You've got the Internet. You can look it up if you want to (and there's a complete filmography at the back of the book should you desire to delve deeper). What I have included are the films and shooting experiences I believe most important to his life and career, as well as when I have had access inside those experiences from a first-hand perspective.

Similarly, addiction is a difficult disease to dissect, especially if you can't tap directly into the mind of the person experiencing it. But Robert has never tried to hide his flaws and many other people were present during those troubling periods. As such, this book makes some attempt to uncover the truth behind the headlines.

Perhaps most pleasingly, despite all the setbacks and what is probably the sign of a true star, Robert Downey Jr has never been swayed in the belief of his own talent. He's often called the greatest actor of his generation. No-one believes that more than Robert himself.

I hope you enjoy the life I have been privileged to spend many months glimpsing into. Whatever happens in the future, you can be damn sure Robert has . . .

Ben Falk
February 2010, London.

Introduction

He stood on the stage of the auditorium. He was happy, naturally, holding the 2010 Golden Globe statuette for Best Actor in a Comedy or Musical in his hand and looking down on the sea of stars and their plus ones. Let's face it, there was a lot to be happy about. The gossip columns put his latest pay packet at a staggering, if unsurprising, $25 million per movie. *Sherlock Holmes,* in which he plays the title role, had broken 2009 Christmas holiday box office records and landed him this prestigious award. The sequel to his biggest hit *Iron Man* was due out in less than four months. Not bad for someone who before ten years ago was in prison, addicted to hard drugs – one bad choice away from death. The journey that Robert Downey Jr had taken, from a hospital in New York's Greenwich Village to the podium at the Beverly Hilton Hotel in Los Angeles was worthy of a movie in itself.

The bright lights of the Hilton seemed worlds away from a solitary, rat-infested cell in the city's Twin Towers jail, where he had once languished after violating probation and was beaten by other inmates. And even further from the California Substance Abuse Treatment Facility and State Prison at Corcoran, where he served time in 1999 and 2000. Those orange jumpsuits wouldn't have looked good on *any* red carpet.

It had been a heady ride. Born to permissive filmmaker parents, he grew up amidst the underground movie scene of the late Sixties and Seventies. It gave him a taste of the high life, but affected him so deeply that he has never really got over it. It was bohemian enough that it was his own father who gave him his first joint at the age of just eight.

Acting has always been in his blood. He made his screen debut aged five playing a puppy in his dad's movie *Pound*. After dropping out of high school in Santa Monica before graduation, he returned to New York to try and make it on his own. He was hired and fired from seminal comedy show *Saturday Night Live* at 20 and met his first great love, future *Sex And The City* star Sarah Jessica Parker, whom he dated for seven years before they broke up over the spectre of his drug abuse. He paid his dues in teen pics like *Weird Science* and *Back To School,* before showing his ability as a cocaine user in the cinematic adaptation of author Bret Easton Ellis's cult novel *Less Than Zero*. He called the role the 'Ghost Of Christmas Future'.

But while he wowed the critics and impressed his peers, he couldn't find box office success and soon his rebellious teen partying transformed into full-blown addiction. 'It's like I've got a shotgun in my mouth and my finger's on the trigger and I like the taste of gun metal,' he said in court after several arrests, including being busted in his car in 1996 for possession of heroin, cocaine and a Magnum handgun. A month after that, he broke into his neighbour's house and fell asleep in a child's bed. This so-called 'Goldilocks' incident has become part of Hollywood folklore.

He's worked with director greats like Oliver Stone and Robert Altman, is best friends with Mel Gibson, but is still remembered for the letter Jodie Foster wrote begging him to seek help after he smoked heroin throughout the filming of her 1995 movie *Home for the Holidays*. A week after being released from Corcoran Prison, he was hired as the love interest on TV show *Ally McBeal*, only to get fired after two more drug/police episodes, the second of which found him wandering barefoot under the influence in a Los Angeles alley.

His drug arrests have threatened to ruin his career, previously making it incredibly difficult to insure him on set. He only starred in 2003' s *The Singing Detective* after producer Mel Gibson paid his bond, with insurers also withholding 40 per cent of his salary for *Gothika* until the film's completion in case he relapsed. But despite an ex wife (whom he married after just 42 days and with whom he has a now-16-year-old son) and the rest, he managed to get through it and turn his life around. Much of that was thanks to the new love of his life, second wife Susan Levin, who he met on the set of *Gothika* in 2003. He stuck with sobriety, practised martial arts, attended Anonymous meetings and continues to take a daily regimen of herbal supplements and vitamins. Though a struggle, it has worked. Films like well-received action-comedy *Kiss Kiss Bang Bang* and drama *Zodiac* continued to pour in and he finally committed his long-held musical aspirations to disc with a full-length album in 2004.

Then in 2007, he was a left-field and controversial choice to play the lead in comic book movie *Iron Man*. The rest, as they say, is history. Or should that be the future. With *Iron Man* taking over half a billion dollars at the worldwide box office, it has become a bona fide superhero franchise. *Sherlock Holmes*, directed by Guy Ritchie and co-starring Jude Law, was another commercial smash in 2009 – and the reason he was invited onto the dais at the Golden Globes where his impromptu speech brought the house down. The same creative team will gear up for a sequel at the end of 2010.

As a man, he is by turns brazenly honest and shrewdly

enigmatic. Musing on his chaotic, jail-tinged 45 years, he recently said: 'I have a sense of destiny that you are led to the things you are supposed to do,' he says. In other words, Robert Downey Jr has been through hell – but now he's back.

Junior

'Was acting a burning desire of mine? People tell me it was.'

(1995)

When Robert Downey Jr was seven, he watched God beat up his mother. This was, mind you, after the Almighty had slit his throat. Unsurprisingly, it was upsetting. 'It could have been too much to expose him too,' said his father, experimental film-maker and director Robert Downey Sr, whose movie *Greaser's Palace* (1972) they were making. 'It was traumatic for him to see that kind of violence.' Junior, who was basically cheap labour since Dad's films were always low budget, didn't seem to his father to enjoy the process at that stage. After shooting one scene he refused to do another take, telling his father he had done it right the first time and there was no need to do it again. After the laughter from the crew subsided, Junior agreed to do it one more time, but a bird flew into shot. This time he refused point-blank, saying he wanted to go back to the house the family was staying in. Like in hundreds of films before and since, a little actor ego-massaging was required. The only difference this time was Downey Sr took his son behind a wagon and gave him a quick smack. Junior did the scene again. The pair subsequently joked about it, Dad realising that even then his son had a sense of thespian spontaneity, of keeping it fresh. Not for the last time,

Robert Downey Jr was unable to hide the fact he was easily bored.

Downey Sr had taken his family with him to Santa Fe, New Mexico, where he was shooting the avant-garde, spoof spaghetti western. His wife Elsie, Junior's mother, was also in the film, while older sister Allyson hung out around the set. It was a wild ride, an improvised Biblical parable starring amongst others little person Hervé Villechaize (*Man with the Golden Gun*) and 'Hey, Mickey!' singer Toni Basil as a Native American who rides a horse topless.

'There was no set,' she remembers. 'We were out in the desert.' She had been recommended for the role by Downey Sr's friend Jack Nicholson. 'Downey had been talking to Jack about people who could physically move and let me tell you, I was happy to do any recommendation from Jack Nicholson.'

Santa Fe in 1972 was an interesting place, 'far out' as the hippies used to say. In fact, Downey Sr – a self-confessed drug user and committed kook – was, to many observers, one of the more normal people around.

'There were a lot stranger people around than him,' remembers Texan oilman George Dreher, who along with some friends picked up some part-time work on the film. 'He was really kind of laid-back, even though he was doing all these crazy things. He was driving a real old car, a 1930s Sedan. One guy on the set was always working on it. During the breaks, he had a guy who was giving him a massage, keeping him relaxed. I think he kind of looked at it as his chance to be as avant-garde as he was ever going to get, but due to the times and the area he shot it, he seemed pretty normal on a relative scale.'

Basil explains, 'I think if you understand that style of working, his style of film-making that's not so scripted, it's not kooky. If you're not familiar with it, I think it can be difficult.'

Having shot his death scene in the mountains, Downey Jr

certainly didn't seem very interested in watching his dad at work. 'He wasn't out and about,' says Basil. 'Once I was over at the house where they were editing and I saw him. Years later, I was in an elevator and he was in there and said, 'Hey, Toni, I want to introduce myself, I do know you.' I said, "You do?" and he was like, "Yeah, I was there with my father when you were shooting the film." I didn't put it together!'

As with any life story, it's crucial to examine the environment from which they sprang. Rarely is that more true than with Robert Downey Jr. 'You should do a lot of research on what it was like to grow up with his father during that period in history,' says Stuart Kleinman, a producer who worked with Junior on 1995's *Home for the Holidays*. 'I would say growing up in the experimental film world of the sixties and seventies can't have been easy.'

Robert Downey Sr was born in Tennessee in 1936, the son of a four-times-married Irish model-cum-magazine editor called Betty McLoughlin and Jewish–American Robert Elias. They split when he was young and Betty took up with Jimmy Downey, a close friend of 'Moon River' composer Johnny Mercer, with the family moving to Long Island, New York. Tall, slim and good-looking, young Robert Elias Jr was kicked out of three prep schools before deciding he didn't much fancy the quiet life. At the age of sixteen, he faked a birth certificate using his stepfather's name and enlisted in the army for three years. He soon began to show his free spirit, getting drunk and fighting with his lieutenant. He and a couple of friends also mocked-up a Soviet attack on Alaska and he abandoned his post to attend a local dance. All of which meant he spent eighteen months of his three-year tour in the stockade. He later admitted he didn't mind prison so much, as it helped with his creative juices. While inside he wrote a novel that would never be published, but gave him a taste for fiction.

While he was not a particularly good soldier, he was an excellent sportsman, boxing to a high standard and playing baseball for the army, once pitching against New York Yankee Hall-of-Famer Yogi Berra. Folklore has turned that encounter into Downey striking out the great man. In fact, as Downey remembered ruefully, Berra smashed him for a triple and he was sent swiftly back to the stockade.

After being dishonourably discharged at the age of nineteen, he briefly played semi-professional baseball in Pittsburgh and Georgia, before heading back to New York, intending to make a career in the arts. His future took off when he started working with avant-garde editor Fred Von Bernewitz in 1960 – he began to write off-Broadway plays, got a few small acting jobs (including being an extra in *The Andersonville Trial*, starring George C. Scott) and supported himself by waiting on tables. It was during the run of his theatrical effort *The Comeuppance* that he met short brunette beauty Elsie, a bohemian and aspiring actress, who was the daughter of Pennsylvanian Fay Ford. He proposed to her on their third date at a baseball game. The two of them worked part-time shifts as cleaners at the Charles Theatre on New York's Avenue B, where they let anyone show their movie as long as it made it to the projection booth. While doing *The Andersonville Trial* he had had to wear a Civil War uniform and when his friend, a cameraman called William Waering, suggested they make a film, Downey dreamed up a comedy about a Civil War soldier wandering around modern-day New York. That became the silent half-hour short *Balls Bluff*, which he showed at the Charles, the first time a reel of his film had been given a public airing. The scenes also eventually made their way into 1968's anthological *No More Excuses*.

In the early sixties, the alternative film movement was in full swing and it suited Downey Sr's tastes to a T. Directing was never his favourite discipline – he preferred the writing and the editing, the latter of which he called another form of rewriting. The critics often dubbed his work 'plotless', but the film-maker preferred to say he was creating 'non-plot', a particular challenge in itself. As Toni Basil witnessed on *Greaser's Palace*, the emphasis was on the visual imagery rather than simply the words, and later Downey actively railed against the more traditional film-makers who were regarded – initially at least – as being progressive, like George Lucas or Peter Bogdanovich. The former he accused of pointless nostalgia, the latter of openly stealing from John Ford. Meanwhile Downey himself told *Postscript*: 'I wouldn't know a narrative if I saw one. And that's a good thing.'

Comedic writer/director Tom Schiller, who was a big fan, worked with him in the eighties on an abandoned TV project and summed up his qualities. 'He was honest, funny, surprising and collaborative,' says Schiller. 'He was totally open to trying anything and making stuff up as we went along. He didn't take anything too seriously and the results were hilarious. It was easy to improvise and have fun. He had a funny take on the world.' That was certainly true, with most of Downey's ideas stemming from what he called 'my own fantasy notions of whatever Elsie and I talk about'. He was heavily influenced by Preston Sturges and Fellini, while revelling in *The Battle of Algiers* and, later, *The Harder They Come*.

He first made a splash with *Babo 73* (1964), a shortish comedy that targets American politics and follows the perils facing a newly elected president. It was, said the *Village Voice*, 'the freshest (which is to say, the most blatantly infantile) of Downey's early films . . . The mode is a shambling, lackadaisical slapstick in which the Free World's leaders wander aimlessly, constructing toy missiles and waving toy flags.'

Meanwhile, away from the cutting room, the Downey family was finally expanding. Daughter Allyson arrived in 1963, born at

Bellevue Hospital in New York, and Downey Jr arrived two years later (after *Babo 73*) in Greenwich Village on 4 April 1965. His birth in a nicer hospital to Bellevue was paid for by *The Sweet Smell of Sex* (1965), a would-be porno Downey Sr had to write, direct and deliver in a week. The producer baulked at the lack of sex and concentration on comedy, but the film ran in the 42nd Street cinemas.

After Robert's arrival there wasn't much time for respite, with the release of his parents' first official collaboration, *Chafed Elbows* (1966), a typically offbeat satire of everything from social mores to the welfare state in which a boy marries his mother. Elsie played all the female roles – while pregnant with Robert. It cost $25,000, $5,000 of which was raised via an advert in the *Village Voice* proclaiming, 'Walk soft and carry a blank check.' The *New York Times* recognised the potential in Downey Sr's work, even if he hadn't quite found his voice. 'One of these days,' it wrote, 'Robert Downey . . . is going to clean himself up a good bit, wash the dirty words out of his mouth and do something worth mature attention in the way of kooky, satiric comedy. He has the audacity for it. He also has the wit.' Elsie also attracted praise for her inventiveness and comic timing.

The *Times*' prescience was revealed in 1969 when Downey released *Putney Swope*. This cult classic, which lampoons everything from the advertising world to racial politics, has found a niche in the independent film world and has since been lauded by modern-day auteurs like Paul Thomas Anderson and mainstream helmers like Brett Ratner. Starring Arnold Johnson, it tells the story of a token black executive at an ad firm who is accidentally put in charge, replacing his Waspy colleagues with his militant 'brothers'. It wasn't beloved by everyone. *Variety* said: '[it's] only intermittently funny and the satire is mostly shallow and obvious. Director Robert Downey's sense of the ridiculous is employed in a spotty, punchline kind of comic usage. The sharp individual parts do not build to anything and the film, as a piece, is more often dull than exciting, less revealingly witty then merely clever.'

Still, with a low budget, *Putney Swope* was a success. Clever stunts helped its box office, like hiring the actor who played an on-screen flasher to stand in the lobby at the end of screenings at the Cinema II Theater wearing only an overcoat, pretending to flash the audience. It made the list of *New York* magazine's ten best films of the year, helped to usher in the blaxploitation genre and, most importantly, is credited with breaking Robert Downey Sr into the ranks of recognised American auteurs. In retrospect, the film was lucky to get made at all. Costing $200,000, it had been funded by an industrialist who wanted to invest in movies but remain anonymous. Arnold Johnson wasn't the first choice as the lead. But Downey's pick, L. Errol Jaye, had pulled out when the Screen Actors Guild intimidated him over the picture's non-union production. Johnson was hired a week before shooting started and couldn't remember many of his lines, meaning his director ended up over-dubbing him himself. Locations were hard to come by, so people slept on the set, including the boardroom of Chase Manhattan Bank, and Downey hired anyone and everyone, including a tramp he paid ten dollars and a bottle of wine.

He was famous. It's frequently reductive to boil a group of different film-makers' work down to a 'movement', but Downey Sr's style was steadily adopted and adapted by other young film-makers eager to try different things. People like Jim McBride made 1967's *David Holzman's Diary* and *Glen and Randa* in 1971. Meanwhile, Brian De Palma (soon to take off along with the rest of the so-called American new wave auteurs of the seventies) was making *Greetings* (1968) and 1969's *The Wedding Party*.

Tours of the lecture circuit followed, as well as TV directing gigs, anything he could do to support his family and subvert the mainstream a little at the same time. Robert Jr remembers his father being away a lot. By 1970, he decided the time was right for his son to grace the screen – not, he later admitted, that Junior was especially itching to get in front of the cameras. *Pound* (1970), an adaptation of his own stage play *The Comeuppance*, featured eighteen actors and was set in a New York City dog kennel. Allegorical in nature, each performer played a different breed of canine, hanging out as they wait to be adopted and/or put down. The cast featured many of Downey Sr's regular repertory company, including Antonio Fargas (better known as Huggy Bear in TV's *Starsky and Hutch*), Stan Gottlieb and Lawrence Wolf. This method he learned from his hero Preston Sturges, who frequently used the same actors from production to production. When Downey showed it to the studio who financed it, they were nonplussed, thinking they were going to watch an animated movie. They stuck it on a double bill with a Fellini film, gave it an X certificate (just before it was cool to do so) and basically forgot all about it. The writer/director wasn't entirely convinced by his achievement, arguing that turning a play into cinema is an almost impossible job. The lack of backing didn't help its chances. Still, like all Downey's work, it had its moments. The *Village Voice* wrote: 'Social commentary served with inspired lunacy may be found . . . Part wacky comedy (with plenty of jailhouse humping), part existential allegory, *Pound* betrays its stage-play roots with too much actorly grandstanding but is peppered with ecstatic funk-powered freak-outs.'

Little did anyone seeing the film realise they were watching a future Oscar nominee's debut performance. Aged only five, Robert Jr played a puppy who confronted Lawrence Wolf's Mexican Hairless, his immortal first cinematic line being: 'Got any hair on your balls?' Looking cute in a T-shirt, with wide brown eyes and sandy-brown hair, Robert looks slightly embarrassed and entirely guileless when he speaks, staring at Wolf's shiny, bald pate. He later joked he deliberately spoke the words with a slight lisp, 'a little accent I was doing'. It may not have been one of the great child performances, but Robert's film career was off and running.

Growing Up

'When my dad and I would do drugs together, it was like him
trying to express his love for me in the only way he knew how.'
(1988)

Sadly, perhaps the most infamous fact about Robert Downey Sr
is not related to his celebrated, cult filmography. Rather, it is that
barely a year after Jr's wrathful deity experience, at the age of
eight, Downey Sr gave Junior his first marijuana joint. It was
1973, hippies were all around and he believed he was a hypocrite
for not sharing something he did readily. Little did he know how
important that spliff would turn out to be. It – and the addictions
that followed – almost destroyed his son.

There were always drugs in the Downey household. Robert
Jr even called it a 'staple in life'. Though he essentially loved
his family, his father comes across as a patriarch, a travelling
showman, a man who stirred his tea with the handle of a hammer
and dominated the room, but at the same time was an addict, a
self-absorbed agitprop stoner more concerned with creative
endeavours than being a proper, responsible parent.

Nevertheless, while life in the Downey household was peculiar,
it was entertaining. Writers, poets and painters, as well as people
like counter-culture activist Abbie Hoffman, floated through on a
regular basis. Films were projected on a white sheet in the sitting

room. Downey Sr would pretend to be Sturges the family dog and go into long monologues about what was inside his head. Junior remembers wandering around Greenwich Village on his father's shoulders, taking in the life around them. They would go to the movies and often leave after the opening credits, because Downey Sr didn't think much of what he was seeing. The arts were encouraged and by the age of seven Junior was already playing jazz tunes on the piano at home.

One thing the Downeys did do was travel. Robert Jr said that every time he came home and told his father he had made a new friend, Dad would tell the family to pack their bags. They flitted between New York, Woodstock, Connecticut and California. It played havoc with Downey Jr's schooling, moving between educational establishments and missing chunks of term time. It led to feelings of inadequacy on Junior's part and a desire to cover up his perceived scholastic shortcomings by being the centre of attention. There was even a brief sojourn in London just after *Putney Swope* came out, picked apparently because Downey Sr thought they needed to go somewhere more boring than New York. Robert Jr did find it dull, telling interviewers he attended Perry House School in – as far as he remembers – Chelsea, where he was encouraged to learn ballet. Further research does not unearth any school remotely resembling Perry House in the West London area, but wherever it was, he does recall standing in the corner of the room for most of his lessons. He told the *Biography Channel*, the teachers were to blame, criticising his American accent and grammar and punishing him unnecessarily. '[They] would say, 'Robert?' and I'd say, "What?". Then they'd say, "Don't say what, say excuse me." And I'd say, "Huh?" However brief, I didn't enjoy England's education system. The teachers seemed awfully uptight.'

The family returned to America and older sister Allyson was sent to boarding school while Robert remained at home. While in Connecticut in 1973, Robert made friends with a young man called Richard Hall, who later became the musician Moby. Hall described them as best friends, adding, 'Parents used to smoke pot together. Haven't seen him since.' Downey Sr directed a live television production of playwright David Rabe's *Sticks And Bones* for CBS, for which the channel was unable to sell any advertising due to its anti-war leanings. Then in 1975 *Moment to Moment* was released – a scattergun effort, almost a series of sketches, written by Elsie (credited as L. C. Downey) and her husband and starring Leonard Buschel. Despite fitting into the general framework of Downey Sr's previous work, the film didn't reach a wide audience. The heat generated from his earlier work was fading and financing was difficult to come by. The director was doing more and more cocaine, using it as an excuse to stay up all night writing, and was also smoking grass. He'd sit at his typewriter at night and his son would join him in his pyjamas and ask his father why he wasn't allowed to join in. Struggling with the feelings of hypocrisy and somehow unable to simply tell him he was only a kid and therefore unable to deal with the consequences, he gave in and they would do some together. Years later, he beat himself up over how he handled the situation, calling himself a 'jerk' and a 'schmuck'. But if Junior's hours beside his old man's scripts led to anything positive, it was his increased desire to actively follow in his parents' professional footsteps. Having watched them make a few films, and in spite of his original reluctance, the acting bug was starting to make Robert itch. As he recalled in a interview with the *Chicago Sun-Times*: 'With Dad, I didn't have a choice about acting. My sister would look at me funny, I'd turn around and smack her and there'd be a 16mm camera filming it all. To me, it just kind of seemed like a day-to-day thing.' His sister believed there was a sense of Robert achieving the things his father always really wanted to achieve –

proper success and fame. It was obvious to his parents from when they were young that Robert was special and they were hard on him, pushing him to do better.

Though Robert says he has had no official training as an actor, he and his sister did attend what is now considered to be one of the most prestigious theatre camps in the country. In 2010, Stagedoor Manor is a recognised breeding ground for future Disney and musical theatre stars – a super-professional entertainment complex housed in the grounds of an old resort hotel by the picturesque Loch Sheldrake in the Catskill Mountains of New York State. Set up by Carl and Elsie Samuelson in 1975, its alumni include Natalie Portman, Zach Braff of TV's *Scrubs* fame and actress/singer Mandy Moore. In the seventies it was a little more rough around the edges, though no worse for it. The '76 camp- was actually called Berkshire Showcase and was temporarily in residence on a camp site in Windham, New York. Richard Allen also attended that summer and noticed a very different Robert from the timid kid who had muttered his *Pound* line almost under his breath.

'He was a real character,' remembers Allen, 'walking around in sunglasses with a cockiness most kids his age – or any age – rarely possess. He and Allyson were very mature, much cooler than most of the mainly suburban kids who populated the camp.' Allen was sixteen at the time and, as such, more interested in the thirteen-year-old Allyson, who was beautiful and developed and, as fellow alumnus Jeff Blumenkrantz says, had 'a great personality, laugh and smile'. She was also fiercely intelligent in a much more linear way than Robert ever has been. 'We were talking about Shakespeare and she said Shakespeare was retarded,' laughs Allen. Initially, he thought it was just the rantings of a typical kid, but Allyson proved to be anything but. 'It turned out she had some intellectual argument about why she didn't like Shakespeare and I remember being very impressed. They were both more cynical and worldly than the average kid their age.'

Some of that may have been due to the fact that this was one of the first times the pair of them had been away from home without either the left-field guidance of their father or the arty love of their mother. The other kids at camp knew Downey Sr made weird, out-there films, but not many teenagers had had the opportunity or the desire to watch *Putney Swope*. 'I do remember [Downey Sr and Elsie] coming up to camp and it seeming like two hippies [being there],' says Allen. 'By 1976, there weren't supposed to be hippies any more! It seemed like they were having this hippy upbringing ten years too late.' As to whether the children showed any signs of discontent with their family situation, he continues, 'I did get the feeling he wasn't so serious. She seemed affected by how unusual her upbringing was, whereas he was a little boy. He acted more like a little boy would. She was going through growing pains, having a more complex reaction. Certainly there was a sense of a complex life. She was in the hands of some very erratic [people]. I don't think they were great parent material.'

Robert and Allyson were close that summer, not simply in the sense they hung out together, but rather because they were kindred spirits. At home, they had something of an adversarial relationship, though not much worse than most siblings. The furthest she went was trying to cut off his finger with a pair of scissors. Richard Allen spent a lot of time clumsily flirting with Allyson, but didn't know how she felt. One day, Robert turned to him and said, 'Do you like my sister?'

'He was trying to help her,' says Allen. 'It was like, "I know my sister likes you, do you like her back?" I didn't think it was sarcastic.' When the session came to an end, Allyson asked her would-be suitor if they could be pen pals, a suggestion he warmly accepted. 'She would write from Arizona somewhere, because they were on location there,' he says. 'I didn't write back, because I didn't really have a place to write back to. I remember hearing down the road that she was very angry and hurt I didn't write back to her.'

He continues, 'I remember [her letters] were clever, thoughtful, sensitive and opinionated. She was having a response to her crazy family. It wasn't like, "I'm so famous, you should be here with me," it was more, "Oh my God, stuff is going on here." Teen angst.'

Despite their personal issues, Robert and Allyson indulged fully in and relished the camp's jam-packed theatrical programme. The students were encouraged to write and perform their own material and, incredibly, although he was barely in double figures, Robert directed a play during the last week. 'I think because his father was a director, I assumed he'd be following in those footsteps,' says Allen. 'When his name came out later that he was acting, it wasn't shocking. It was like, well he was charismatic and obviously he went beyond the connection.'

The two of them returned the following year for the first official unveiling of the camp in its new Loch Sheldrake site. The Downeys were mainly living in Woodstock and Robert's confidence was higher than ever. 'Robert used to rub it in everybody's faces his dad was a producer and director,' remembers fellow camper Dina McLelland. 'He wasn't a nice kid. He had an attitude of being better than everybody else because of who his dad was.' According to McLelland, like the year before, the other kids may have understood Robert's creative background, but Robert Downey Sr meant nothing to them and thus neither did the attitude. They were far more impressed with Jenny Goldman, whose father was screenwriter William Goldman, or the daughter of Martin Charnin, co-creator and lyricist of the musical *Annie*. 'I didn't know who his dad was,' says McLelland. 'I do now. But someone kept saying, "Oh, he thinks he's all hot shit because his dad's a producer/director type." And I was like, "Have I seen any?"'

Robert and his sister were still close – obviously the ructions at home had made for a tighter sibling bond. But McLelland says Allyson never seemed aloof. 'She'd also go walking round and hang out with him a lot. [But] Allyson didn't have that same feeling. Being a little bit older, I think she was a little bit wiser. He was just trying to impress people. I think he probably had friends, but he wasn't the most popular person. If I remember right, he kind of isolated himself in some ways.'

Deren Getz thinks differently. He was sixteen that summer, an aspiring magician who came to the camp because it had some well-known teachers on the circuit. He found Robert, despite being a theatre kid, was drawn to him and his small gang. 'We had rooms of three people,' recalls Getz, 'basically a room full of beds. We used to hang out in the room and we liked to take flash paper and make smoke. We even made little movies of this effect. Just five kids and a counsellor.'

Life at Stagedoor was pretty full-on. There were about 200 kids there and they were woken up early with an announcement or a recording of Reveille. There were classes in the morning, a break for lunch, then more classes. After that, you had some time off during which you could play tennis, swim in the pool or hang out with your friends. After dinner, you worked on the shows you were involved in. There were public shows every fortnight that you auditioned for in the first couple of days after you arrived, showing off your ability to tap-dance, sing or do a monologue. 'The magicians had more freedom,' says Getz. 'It's possible he enjoyed that.'

But, like when he had directed a play in 1976, Robert revelled in the performance aspect of the camp, appearing in musical *The Red Shoes* as Nels, the cobbler's assistant. That show turned out to be perfect practice (and a good indicator of his skill) for his later efforts playing Charlie Chaplin. 'Oleg the ballet instructor was really intense about getting the dancing right,' says Deren Getz, who also appeared as the evil magician. 'We realised, the day before the show, that we had never rehearsed Act Two! And then that no one other than me knew their lines for the second act either. So we decided we were going to choreograph the second act in the manner of clown boxing, which my friend Jon Koons had taught me. We did the whole second half in slapstick, a Chaplin-type thing.'

He continues, 'Robert also did a play with us that Jon and I wrote called *A Shakespearean Tragedy*. It was a comedy revue, like early *Saturday Night Live*, *Monty Python*, that type of thing. Theatre of the absurd – he was into it.'

'I remember him being a decent actor, even as a kid,' admits Dina McLelland. '[But] there wasn't anything that stood out that said this is someone who's going to go places. There were plenty of others who outshone him in a heartbeat.'

However, in the summer of 1977, Robert Downey Jr was embracing his performing instincts and showing off the brazen confidence in himself and his talents that permeated his later life. And, not for the last time, he didn't always get away with it. 'It's not like he wasn't put in his place a couple of times,' laughs McLelland. 'I remember him mouthing off to some kid and the kid put him right back down in his place.' As an actor, Junior was becoming a man.

Dysfunction and High School

'Mediocrity is my biggest fear' (1989)

Perhaps Robert's attitude was a reaction to his home life, perhaps it was merely a confidence instilled through artistic encouragement, though most amateur psychologists would say acting up outside the home is a sure sign something's going wrong within it. His parents had been together for fifteen years when things fell apart. They were fighting a lot. Robert remembers an incident in a hotel room when his father threw a milkshake and it stuck to the ceiling. As the young man recalled it, the globules of ice cream slowly dried to form what looked like a brown nipple above his head. The fury with which the milkshake had been hurled, almost as if it was some kind of weapon, stuck with him. He later admitted he used the image to tap into feelings of anger and sadness when acting.

By his own admission, Downey Sr was struggling with drugs. 'In the 1970s, I was a mess . . . it was a disaster,' he told *Postscript*. 'Coke is such a waste of time. A total waste of time.' He was barely working. There were little bits here and there, writing for *The Gong Show Movie* (1980) and developing an uncompleted film called *Jive*. But something had given. 'The first thing you gotta have if you are going to make movies this way is a good old lady, or it's impossible,' he explained to writer Joseph Gelmis. Elsie had got a lot out of the relationship, but put up with a lot. They had often borrowed money, banking on the fact Downey Sr would get another job and his salary would be able to pay off the debt. The electricity and telephone were cut off a number of times. Both parents were increasingly hands-off. Downey Jr remembers visting his sister in Vermont by himself at the age of just thirteen.

Still, when the proper split finally came his mother was, according to her son, stunned. Downey Sr moved to Los Angeles and Allyson moved with him, against the better judgement of her brother. Sensing Elsie needed someone to lean on, Robert Jr stayed in New York. They moved into a small apartment, on East 48th Street between 5th and Madison. It was in a depressing five floor walk up – after all, the movie business had never been particularly lucrative – and there were bars across the windows. They didn't have an oven and, while he was keen to comfort his mother, Robert started avoiding the place. Instead, he spent most of his time going to the cinema to watch *The Rocky Horror Picture Show*, hanging out with his friends in Washington Square Park and occasionally stealing his mum's money. He started experimenting with more drugs, changing from a self-confessed 'pot-head kid' into someone who enjoyed the harder stuff. He spent much of his teenage years going back and forth between Los Angeles and New York.

'For a teenager, it was rather confusing,' said Robert. 'Always on the move, hanging out with this group here and that group there . . . due to the drugs I was taking, I was completely inaccessible . . . I was not dealing with my life in an effective manner. Instead, I was creating a separate reality from the one in which I now live and was dealing with that reality the best I could.' Allyson has suggested he acquired a sense of no self-esteem, though it's difficult to pinpoint exactly why and when this began. More than likely it was accumulated, because his parents – while loving their children – were more focused on themselves and their goals than those of their kids.

The late seventies in New York was a heady time. Punk was breaking out, but Robert preferred the more melodic, mellow tunes of Genesis and Journey. Early Van Halen was about as rocky as it got. Increasingly, the young man found himself out of sync with the Big Apple. Much to the amusement of his classmates, his mother used to pick him up from school in a quilted cape, and the coastal, more tranquil vibe of LA – which also meant a reunion with his father – became more and more enticing. Robert Sr's house was bigger and more luxurious. It looked like it was owned by an artist, with hand-crafted fixtures, brass pieces, sculptures and a pool with a giant mural painted on the bottom. His name and profession meant something there, the home of cinema. Robert Jr's desire to become a professional actor was getting stronger and he understood Hollywood was where the action is. What's more, he would be the cool East Coast kid with the funky haircut and edgy clothes. No one knew him there, he could be anyone he wanted to be. The time had come to go west.

He enrolled at Lincoln Junior High for the eighth grade. It was a feeder school for Santa Monica High, fourteen blocks from the Pacific Ocean, near the Interstate 10 freeway. Downey Jr is vague about the dates of his high school attendance as are his friends. But he's listed in the student index for the 1979-80 school year, 9th grade. It was chaotic. Punk rock, skateboarding, cocaine, hundreds of single-parent families and hot weather all combined to create quite the 'scene'. The Santa Monica Civic Center used to put on huge gigs for three dollars. Things felt like they were in flux. Those who attended school with Downey Jr have a vast array of different memories. One, who appears to have met a similar person to the one that walked nonchalantly into Stagedoor in 1977, rather bluntly states: '. . . in short, he was arrogant and pretentious. Not the brightest bulb, but the cockiest of them all. He had no qualms of saying he was going to be a movie star – his dad told him so. I'll give him credit for accomplishing a path he had set when he was only thirteen or so.'

Most of the students there were so-called Southsiders, latch-key kids with a lot of time of their hands. Robert had a bit of money and lived on the North side. He was, says another former pupil, similar to the Estevez kids (a.k.a. Charlie Sheen, Ramon and Emilio Estevez), all of whom were sons of Martin Sheen and also attended the school. They were 'shadows around the school who lived in their own world, never connecting with their classmates'. One female student remembers it differently, though the sense of self-belief remained intact. 'He was outspoken, had a lot of confidence and was popular,' she says. 'I was quiet, not part of the popular crowd, so at the end of the school year, when Robert offered to sign my yearbook, it was sort of shocking.' However, he wrote something scandalous and she remembers that 'at the time it was not very funny. I literally had to hide the book from my father.'

In autumn 1980, for 10th grade, he transferred along with many other Lincoln graduates to Santa Monica High School, known locally as Samohi, on the other side of the freeway, further towards Venice Beach. One former pupil describes it as 'part beach club, part barrio'. Robert's dramatic side came out when fellow pupils assumed that because he was from New York he must be tough. Playing the role required of him – a habit he was wont to do – he took to riding around on his bike by the ocean with a knife tucked into his sock, like someone out of teen bestseller *The Outsiders*. In fact, he was a theatre geek and choral regular. Chris Bell was a year older than Robert and remembers him coming to the school. 'He was just this new guy in class from New York,' says Bell. 'We had these auditions for a show – an evening of science-fiction one-acts. Everyone got up in front of the group and made up information about the character that they were going for. I just remember he went on a roll, it was hilarious, he just started making up all these strange facts about the doctor he wanted to play. We were really rolling in the aisles. We did the show together, an adaptation of an Isaac Asimov short story. It was about a robot that was getting involved with a doctor and this relationship stuff. He played the scientist and I played the robot and we just hit it off. He was very funny and we just had the same sense of humour. We became good friends, mostly from goofing around all the time and joking. He was always quite off the wall.'

Bell's grandmother lived near Downey Sr, who was often visited by his brother Jim, a writer on *Saturday Night Live*. Bell ended up spending a lot of time at Robert's house. They would hang out at home watching movies like *The Shining*, which was one of his favourite films. They ate a lot of scrambled eggs and would drive around in Robert's first car, listening to Stevie Wonder records, going to coffee shops, singing along to musicals. Robert had seen *Hair* on Broadway as a youngster and was a big fan. They would stop at fast-food joint Jack in the Box to get Jumbo Jack hamburgers with Colin Kellaway, whose father was a jazz pianist.

'We all went camping once in the Angeles Crest Mountains,' recalls Bell. 'That was a fun time. I was the only one that was very serious about camping. I remember waking up in the morning in my sleeping bag outside and everyone was in the car waiting for me to leave the woods. Colin had some kind of airgun and we'd go off shooting at things.' Downey Sr – who walked around in flares and open-chested shirts with lots of gold chains – mostly left them to it. 'He gave Robert a lot of freedom,' says Bell. 'His house was a fun place to go because his dad was rarely around so everyone could just hang out.' Robert avoided talking about his mother. 'He didn't talk much about his mom,' says Bell. 'I didn't even know much about his sister. He was very excited to be in LA.'

Meanwhile, in maths class he helped future Porno For Pyros guitarist Peter DiStefano with his homework, and in drama club he won the awards for 'Most Likely to Succeed in Theater' and 'Biggest Flirt'. He had a well-toned, tanned body and an open, amused face. 'He used to go around the dressing room with his shirt off flexing his muscles and stuff,' says Bell. He was also noted for his style. 'We used to refer to him as Studley Moore,' grins one student, who was in the madrigal group with him, where he sang baritone or bass in traditional a cappella songs by old-fashioned, untrendy people like sixteenth-century composer Thomas Morley, a far cry even from Phil Collins. 'Everyone talked about how Robert had the nice shoes. He wore Crayons and his fashion sense stood out. There was a little bit of a mystique about him.'

The blond hair had made way for his trademark black and, although he could have done with an eyebrow pluck, he did well with the ladies. 'It seemed like he was always chasing women,' says Bell. He had a relationship with Heidi Kozak, and school hottie Amber Gilbert showed interest, sitting around the swimming pool showing off her bikini body. Robert later remembered the thrill of driving down Sunset Boulevard in Amber's car together. Like any teenager, he was excited when he got a yes from the opposite sex. 'We used to go to the Santa Monica Place [shopping mall], which was brand new at the time,' remembers Bell. 'He asked Kelly McReynolds to a dance and she said yes. He proceeded to get up and walk through the fountain inside the mall, which was a large round pool with a jet of water shooting up in the centre. He walked right through it. We were kind of amused and horrified at the same time and he was immediately hauled away by the mall security. We had to wait about 25 minutes for him to be released and told not to come back into the mall again. That story encapsulates a lot of qualities in being his friend – fun, very extravagant and wild. But you also have to sort of pick up the pieces that come with it. There's a problematic side to that. There were definitely some over-the-top moments.'

Robert has spoken of himself as being something of an outsider, though friends to all those normally labelled high school outcasts. 'He started off quiet in class, but ultimately he did have a lot of confidence,' says Bell. 'He was sociable, but he didn't take on a lot of friends, there were just a few of us in the inner circle. And it's not like we were cool. Robert didn't go after popularity. He was very worldly because he'd travelled a lot. I never thought of him as a kid so much as just a wicked guy.'

But when Bell returned to see how the school was getting on the following year, things had changed. Robert's new best friend was a kid called Reed, a long-haired dreamer who continually wore a Rolling Stones T-shirt and caused a stir with some show-stopping comment about the word 'climax' in English class. 'I consider my time with him to be much more innocent,' says Bell. 'Before the drugs, before things got too jaded and dating was very new. I was never one to party too much in terms of drugs but I knew he was starting to hang out with people who were a little more on the dark side. That was never appealing to me. It's amazing when I look back at all the drugs that were in high school, at our disposal.'

They had always drunk though, leading to one of Robert's most infamous incidents. 'We were at a party of a friend of ours in Santa Monica and I had my mom's car, this old Mercedes,' says Bell. 'We had been drinking and I remember a few of us went to go and sit down for some reason to get away from the party, to chat. We sat in my mom's car. He was sort of looking quite out of it and he goes, "I just want to sit here for a little bit," so I left him there. Suddenly we're in this party and someone said, "I just saw Robert two blocks down the street being arrested!" and we're like "what?!" He'd driven off in my mom's car.' Rumours flew that he had wrecked it, but actually there was no damage. 'I got the car back and I remember his dad was very upset. A group of us had to go down to Santa Monica Police Station and that's where I got my mom's car keys back.' Downey had driven off drunk, got lost and stupidly chosen a policeman to ask directions. He ended up with his first DUI. Years later, Bell met up with Robert in New York and overheard him on the phone to Reed, saying how he was now hanging out with Chris Bell. Reed was shocked because he thought he would still be upset about the car. 'Obviously they had made it into a big story,' says Bell.

Relying on his innate intelligence to coast through school, Robert would escape from the grounds by climbing over a twenty-foot-high chain-link fence after arriving in the morning. He and his friends would go to a nearby German deli, tell the guy behind the counter they went to University of California Los Angeles (UCLA) and buy Grolsch or Spaten beer before heading over to Douglas Park and getting drunk. Sometimes they would return at the end of the school day to take part in the drama and musical programmes. The madrigal group was serious stuff, an elite group that won local competitions, rehearsed five times a week and performed two dozen concerts a year, presided over by a teacher with the nickname Killer. 'The choir people were flat-out geeks,' says a fellow member. 'By participating in chorus at all, he was putting himself at risk, socially.'

There wasn't much money to spend on school issues, but students remember funds being injected into the creative pursuits at Samohi. 'We had a great auditorium,' says one who was there at the time. 'When we did *Oklahoma!* we had a full pit orchestra.' Robert has said that performing in the legendary musical was one of his favourite memories of high school. Samohi was packed full of kids with long-term acting aspirations, including the afore-mentioned Estevez brothers and Rob Lowe, though according to someone present: 'I don't think the Brat Pack was assembled on campus.' Even if he has since said he thought his theatre arts teacher was jealous of him, Robert was well coached in dancing, singing and acting, performing in *Detective Story* and playing Captain Absolute in *The Rivals* by Richard Sheridan in the round. For *Oklahoma!* Ramon Estevez taught him how to tap-dance outside Zucky's deli.

'Robert was amazing on stage,' says Bell, 'even back in high school. He just commanded presence, more so than anybody. I almost feel like his film work has done him a disservice. He's better than Hugh Jackman when it comes to song and dance on stage. He could have gone a different route. Some films are better than others but he doesn't really have the impact that he has on stage.' His friend remembers Robert already had a lot of industry contacts and believes he auditioned for *The Outsiders*. 'He was promised this big career,' says Bell. 'We were all very happy for him.'

What is it that a lot of future stars say? Those beautiful, successful, rich stars?

'School wasn't for me.'

'I decided I would be better off learning in the real world.'

'The educational system was stifling me.'

'When I was a teenager, no one understood me.'

Yeah, right. What they really mean is most people that good-looking aren't clever enough to pass the requisite exams and, quite frankly, a quick hop onto the pages of a catalogue, or the set of a TV show – where people write down what they've got to say for them – seems far more pleasant than sitting through another round of double chemistry. For Robert Downey Jr, his sense of urgency was nothing to do with intellect, rather a lack of any concept of delayed gratification. He was in the eleventh grade, playing truant more and more. Graduation was close, but his mind was made up when his father had to return to New York for work. Allyson had returned east some time before to attend boarding school in Vermont, where she graduated top of her class and subsequently moved to Washington Heights in New York, sharing an apartment with a girl fifteen years her senior. The friend remembers her disappearing for long periods at a time. 'She couldn't find herself, what to do for a living,' she says. 'I don't think she really wanted to be in the theatre, but she would have made a wonderful actress. She could be theatrical and dramatic. She was alive, a brilliant girl. I miss her making me crack up, she was very funny.' She remained far more critical of the Downey clan than her brother. 'We never really spoke about it, because they kept it hush-hush,' says her friend. 'I don't think she had such a good childhood.' Whenever someone brought it up, 'she said, 'Let it be'.' She was very protective of Downey and in turn, he was generous with her. 'If she was in trouble, I don't know if he would be there in person as much as he would make sure it was taken care of,' says her friend. 'If she called for help, he would help her.'

Junior himself had to decide whether to hang on in Los Angeles independently, or head back to the East Coast under the aegis of his father. It was a no-brainer. The counsellor called him into their office and told him they wanted him to stay at Samohi, making up the work in summer school. Robert quit instead.

'She's like, "We'll call your father about that",' said Robert. 'She called my dad and he's like, "Sure, whatever he wants to do, as long as he gets a job and is productive." And I said, "I told you so" and walked out of the school.' He briefly worked at a

Thrifty's pharmacy in Santa Monica, doing inventory work and doling out ice cream to the customers. 'I remember going home at the end of the shift and washing my arms and hands as much as I could because I smelled of cow,' Downey said. He and his friends ran what he dubbed a counter scheme there, where he got his friends to come in buy something expensive, only to charge them much less and take a cut for doing so. Moving back east and eschewing further education wasn't a difficult choice. Though interested in non-fiction, history and the arts, college never seemed like a viable option to the teenager. 'What am I going to major in,' he said, 'tap dancing?'

Chris Bell got a phone call from his old friend out of the blue in 1987. 'At that time he'd just finished his stint on *Saturday Night Live* and he was definitely the "star",' he says. 'He already had a string of movies and was definitely successful, but he was still the same guy. There's a very private side to him. I think most of his friends only got to know this one side of him that was funny, personable, very nice. I'm not suggesting he has a dark side but there is a very private side – we didn't talk about his family, even his dad, other than the funny things. I'm sure he went through a lot of angst with the parents and that whole broken-family situation but I don't think he ever shared that with too many people, if anyone. The whole drug situation, I think that's part of that, an escape. When I see him on television, that really captures the way I remember him – he'd always put on voices, he'd always put on characters, he didn't take things too seriously.

'He was always able to maintain a great love of life but I can also see that he obviously had his demons. He would over-compensate because, when I think about the drugs, that to me indicates that there was something missing.'

Breaking In

'It doesn't matter whether or not you can act. If you can go into a room and make these sweaters want to have you around for six or eight weeks, that's what'll really get you a job.' (1998)

So, at the age of seventeen, it was back to Manhattan. And this time, he was on his own, Downey Sr respecting his wish to drop out, but refusing to help him residentially or financially. He lived on 84th Street, working as a waiter at the hip Soho restaurant Central Falls and going out on mostly fruitless auditions. He would annoy casting agents by being facetious. When they asked him how he was supporting himself, he would say, 'My spine.' He spent time as a shoe salesman and briefly as a living art exhibit in a window display at the legendary nightclub Area. The theme and thus the décor of the club changed regularly and Downey was part of 'Future'. He wore an orange jump suit and put Gumby dolls on a conveyor belt. The clubs in New York at night were creatively vital, full of artists, actors and fashion people – a fun place to be for those seeking a heady escape. It was pretty easy for someone to lose themselves on a regular basis. He continued to drink a lot by night and by day he served coffee to Sting, who regularly came into the restaurant, just off Houston Street.

Downey had several short-lived relationships. 'I like the idea that people want to nurture me, you know?' he told *Movieline*, in 1991.

'That I could probably go into any major shopping centre and find someone who would say the right things or at least rub my feet.' His sister Allyson was more blunt. As a youngster, she recalled him converting her room into a make-out pad while she was away. While in New York, she remembered getting a phone call asking her to bring some orange juice over to his apartment because he thought he had pneumonia. When she got there, 'there's about 30 girls rubbing his feet, feeding him through an eyedropper.'

He was starving and practically penniless. A call to his father for money to feed himself yielded a swift rebuke. Finally, in 1983 he got a gig, performing in cartoonist/playwright Stoo Hample's *Alms For The Middle Class* which opened on 25 February at the Geva Theater in Rochester, NY, where future Oscar winner Philip Seymour Hoffman saw him act. It ran for a little over three weeks, but by that time, he was convinced the big screen was beckoning.

He scored the supporting role of Stewart in *Baby It's You* (1983), a period high school movie helmed by the estimable writer-director John Sayles starring Rosanna Arquette and Vincent Spano. For the young performer, it was a sign others recognised the talent he saw in himself. Unfortunately, when the film was released in March 1983, it didn't go according to plan. He worked on the film for four weeks, only to see almost all his scenes end up on the cutting-room floor. Having told his friends he was a movie star, Downey found himself eating humble pie. 'You don't even see me except in one scene,' he said later. 'You see me in the background until this self-indulgent actress leans forward to try and get more camera time.' His friends laughed at him and jokily renamed the flick *Maybe It's You.*

Humiliated, Downey returned to the theatre. In July 1983, he again trod the boards in the critically reviled musical *American Passion*, a show the *New York Times* called an 'egregious by-product' of the hugely successful *A Chorus Line* and lasted only a single performance. He also starred in Jordan Budde's powerful homosexuality-themed play *Fraternity* at the Colonnades Theatre Lab, about a group of young men forever affected by the time they spent together in a Texas college during the fifties. He was feeling down, sitting in his apartment during the play's run, when the phone rang. It was an agent his father had set him up with, asking if he wanted to read for a family drama called *Firstborn* (1984). Although his obnoxious audition persona hadn't got him very far to date, he stuck with it. Perhaps it was the fact that director Michael Apted (who'd directed *Coal Miner's Daughter* in 1980) was British and he appreciated Downey's ironic sense of humour, but he decided to cast him as Lee, one of the supporting roles alongside stars Teri Garr and Peter Weller. *Fraternity*'s director, Gideon Schein, could see Downey's cinema career might take off and told him never to forget the theatre. But for the young actor, in spite of the debacle of *Baby It's You*, there were dreams of a million-dollar payday, his name above the titles and his friends' validation. First, though, there was that quirky-looking girl in the *Firstborn* cast, the one who'd been in that cheesy TV show. She had, you know, something.

Sarah Jessica Parker could teach him a lot. That's what a nineteen-year-old Downey thought when he saw her sitting across the room, on the set of the film in April 1984. He was immediately drawn to her, but she seemed more put-together than the flighty girls he usually dated, most of whom, he thought, went out with him because he seemed like he was going to be a star, not because of his personality. Much of that was to do with the fact that Sarah too had been working since she was a child, only she had been brought up a bit differently from her would-be beau. Born in Ohio, a little more than a week before Downey, Sarah also came from a broken home, though her father Stephen left the family nest while she was still a toddler. She was raised by her mother and stepfather and, like the Downeys, the Parkers often had to go to bed early when the electricity was cut off. Despite no particular background in show business, Sarah gravitated towards the arts, gaining a scholarship to a music college in Cincinnati when she was eight and honing her dance skills. She began to pick up theatre and television roles, her family eventually relocating to New York in order to help her career, where she became queen of advert voice-overs. Her big break came when she understudied the lead role in *Annie* before taking it over, playing the perky orphan on Broadway on and off for two years. When she was sixteen she got an offer to star in CBS's *Square Pegs* and travelled to Los Angeles with her mother for filming. The show only lasted one season, but attracted some buzz, Sarah getting particularly good notices for her performance as Patty, a brainy girl desperately trying to fit in at high school. The heat from the show led to a supporting part in the movie *Footloose*, where she met – and broke up with – her first serious boyfriend Chris (brother of Sean) Penn.

Sarah had grown up with something of a different work ethic from Downey and, like her *Square Pegs* character, was more buttoned-up than the average teenager. Growing up in theatres and on sets, she had spent more time with adults than people her own age and despite her fling with Penn was fairly naive about relationships and boys. Meeting Robert in 1984 was no different from several romantic scenarios she later faced as Carrie Bradshaw in *Sex and the City*. 'Opposites attract', 'Falling for the bad boy', 'He's different when he's just with me', 'I can fix him' – all of them could be applied to her attraction to this punky, funny boy she saw in front of her wearing glasses decorated with Superman stickers. He probably came along at the right time, when she was ready for a risk, while Downey appreciated her perky personality and positive outlook on life, far removed from the cynicism he was used to. 'I always got the feeling they adored each other,' remembers Alan Metter, who directed them in *Girls Just Want to Have Fun* in 1985.

Although they were young and seemingly very different, they soon became involved, Sarah making the first move by asking Downey to meet her after she finished the off-Broadway play she was performing in by night. He did. They moved in with each other two weeks later. They would share a cab to the set of *Firstborn* but, worried that people would see them as too impetuous, Sarah would get out a hundred yards before they reached their destination. In the evening, they would hang out at home. Downey Sr loved the effect the young woman was having on his son, but Sarah put off telling her mother, thinking she wouldn't approve of the flamboyant young man her daughter had fallen in love with – when she did finally tell her, her mother's main worry was that the couple were moving forward at a velocity that could only spell disaster. Proving her naivety, Sarah did not initially realise quite how profound her new boyfriend's drink and drug exploits were. It never occurred to her to partake as well, and soon their relationship was a strange mix of domesticity and Downey's hell-raising lifestyle. He would wake up with a raging hangover and they'd go and buy furniture. Their finances were picking up, and they had houses in New York and Los Angeles, though they spent more time in the former. 'I can't make him toe the line,' said Sarah to *Vanity Fair* in 1990, 'but I can sure make him smile.'

While she may not have been able to curtail his appetites, she made him focus more closely on all aspects of his career, a word he shied away from. She appreciated the fact he appeared to need her and was unfailingly loyal, despite often spending weeks or months apart during filming. Ever since her father had left, she had had issues with trust. Downey grew to enjoy the languid pace of the relationship, as opposed to the shorter, more intense couplings he was used to. They were dubbed a hot new couple by the tabloids and he introduced her to some of his industry friends. They were literally growing up together.

Downey gave Sarah a confidence in public she had previously been lacking. 'He helped me a lot going out,' she said. 'Being courageous, not wanting to throw up all night.' She, on the other hand, helped him open a proper bank account and gave him a glimpse of a 'normal' home life. She was, as he admitted, 'the best thing that's ever happened to me'.

Interviewers who met the couple in those early days noted a refreshing immaturity about them too. Unlike a lot of modern young stars, who are groomed and styled and media-trained from the moment they hit puberty, Downey and Sarah revelled in their youth and the enjoyment earning good money could yield. Their two-storey carriage house in LA's Beachwood Canyon had previously belonged to both John Lennon and Bette Davis, but by the time the young stars had finished with it, the bedroom was pink, stuffed animals dotted the rooms and their neighbours had got used to being occasionally pelted with water balloons. Sarah wore a diamond ring on her wedding finger, though the couple made only hypothetical plans to marry. They joked they wanted a Jewish wedding with flamenco dancers and came up with possible baby names. Though Robert continued to drink and take drugs – a spectre that hung over their relationship like a pot cloud – he had found his soul mate. Or so he thought.

Hollywood

'Live from New York, it's a tired young man!' (1988)

Six weeks after he met Sarah Jessica Parker, and still a teenager, Downey nailed another audition and got his first Hollywood-set movie. *Tuff Turf* (1985), a high school flick starring a neophyte James Spader, was shooting in Los Angeles. Head over heels in love, it was hard for Sarah to see him go, but they both agreed it ridiculous, given the brevity of their courtship, that he turn it down. Downey loved it. He hit it off with Spader, who encouraged his bad behaviour, staying at the legendary Chateau Marmont Hotel where they partied like there was no tomorrow. 'I couldn't believe I was flying first class,' said Downey. 'I came out here and was under Jimmy Spader's wing and he said, "Don't stay in the Sportsman's Lodge, Bobby, it's a dump, the elevators smell of urine. Come stay at the Chateau and get some hookers and blow, it's going to be great." I was like, "Fuck, man, this guy knows what he's doing."'

The film itself is a dud, an awesomely eighties mess with moody outsider Spader facing off against some gang-bangers for the love of a good woman. The dull plot culminates in Downey coming into a warehouse at the end with two big dogs and getting shot in the leg. Looking very young, a little pasty and with wonky, pre-stardom teeth, he inevitably gives flashes of his charisma, even when tackling some poor dialogue. He gives it his best shot, speaking many of his lines like he's making them up in the moment, demonstrating some of his musical talent with an awesome display on the drums for one of the on-screen bands (often the movie comes across like you've stumbled across ninety minutes of old-school MTV) and even trying to shoehorn in a catchphrase. Sadly, 'state of the arts' never caught on.

Downey loved being back in Los Angeles, especially with the added kudos now he was a bona fide working actor. He fitted right in. His career was on the up and up. Next was television, playing Bruno Mussolini to George C. Scott's Benito in NBC's prestige mini-series *Mussolini: The Untold Story (1985)*. A seven-hour epic, Downey only lasts just over two hours before Bruno is killed in a plane crash. But he more than holds his own against Oscar-winner Scott and Gabriel Byrne, who plays his brother. More quirky than sexy in *Tuff Turf*, *Mussolini . . .* is the first time he looks like a handsome young actor. A man quintessentially of his time (Scarlett Johansson is another actor who suffers from this latterly), he looks a bit at odds with the pre-war setting, despite fine costume and set design. But playing the 'party' son, there was more than a little of art imitating life, especially when Scott – a famous boozer – says to him, 'Don't follow in my footsteps.' There are plenty of elements of the character that reflected, or were to reflect, his real life, including his impulsive and spontaneous attitude to love. But more than anything, these early films see him establishing his style. Playing Bruno Mussolini required him to cut down on his natural swagger and sense of humour, but there's a definite impression he is feeling his way into his approach to on-camera acting. If nothing else, these early forays proved invaluable training grounds, particularly for an unschooled, more instinctive performer like Downey.

Was he a member of the Brat Pack? Probably not, despite knowing the Sheen/Estevez clan. He wasn't part of the seminal teen movies of that period (however hard he might argue, no, *Tuff Turf* doesn't count) and he was in the only John Hughes eighties failure, *Weird Science* (1985), in which two nerds create a woman using their computer. Sarah Jessica was waiting in the car while he auditioned for Hughes in his office and watching, while fiddling with the stereo, was Hughes's male muse Anthony Michael Hall, one of *The Breakfast Club* and the star of *Weird Science*. Downey had a good feeling walking back to his vehicle, reckoning Hall had responded to his reading. He was right. Hughes cast him as Ian the bully, one of Hall's on-screen tormentors who eventually gets his comeuppance, loses his girlfriend and has to wear a bra on his head. The film was a big deal, but Downey didn't enjoy it, even though he made a lifelong friend in Hall. And he was almost fired after defacating in British model co-star Kelly LeBrock's trailer. Producer Joel Silver was livid, accusing Downey of the 'crime', knowing that he had threatened to mount some kind of bowel movement-related protest if he felt he wasn't being treated right. Downey carefully managed to feign innocence, but demonstrated again via his actions his self-belief, even if its manifestation was over the top.

It was at this time that Lorne Michaels, the legendary producer and founder of *Saturday Night Live*, decided to return to the show after a five-year personal hiatus. It was late summer 1985 and the classic late-night comedy broadcast was coming off a hugely successful season in which NBC's Dick Ebersol had brought in Billy Crystal, Martin Short and Christopher Guest (*This Is Spinal Tap*) among others in order to boost the ratings. It had worked. The cast, which had been reeling from the comedown of Eddie Murphy's triumphant regime there, had re-established *SNL* in the nation's consciousness and Michaels felt it was right to return.

But he wanted his *own* cast – he felt while the experiment had been successful, Crystal, Guest and co. were already well-known comics and *SNL* was about launching new ones, like it had done with John Belushi and Chevy Chase during the seventies. Above all, he was consumed by the idea of youth and set about trying to find up-and-coming talents who fitted the profile. Seventeen-year-old Anthony Michael Hall was just the ticket. Already a movie star, he hadn't really tested himself comedically, and Michaels targeted him relentlessly. Hall was a huge fan of the programme and readily agreed, negotiating himself a luxurious contract and stipulating one other requirement – Downey should also be on the show. Michaels wasn't prepared to recruit anyone unseen, so Downey was duly called in for an audition and did an uproarious impression of a drunk Iranian he had seen in a Beverly Hills nightclub. Speaking in faltering English and swinging his T-shirt over his head, he made the NBC brass laugh and was promptly hired, alongside actors like Jon Lovitz and Randy Quaid.

Life on *Saturday Night Live* has always been abnormally chaotic. All-night writing sessions, partying in the offices – the revolutionary attitude initiated by Aykroyd and co. in 1975 was still going strong ten years later as the eleventh series got under way. Downey vamped it up with characters including Jimmy Chance and Rudy Randolph III, as well as contributing a number of cutting impressions, notably George Michael (replete with a perfect English accent), Paul Simon and, for the first show of the year, Sean Penn. Madonna was hosting and the cast were doing a sketch about her wedding. Afterwards, Downey met Sean: 'He shook my hand a bit too hard,' he related. 'I just kissed her!' The Madge episode went down badly and immediately the cast started coming in for criticism, even though it was more to do with the quality of the sketches. The writers complained that with such a young group of actors, it was impossible either to write multi-generational skits or, more importantly, to tackle the political issues crucial to the *SNL* canon by lampooning the current elected officials. Whoever was right, Downey was having a blast. He and Hall were hitting the New York clubs like a pair of troubadours, capitalising on the latter's Brat Packer status. He loved the rush of the weekly format, telling *Rolling Stone* 'Live TV is the ultimate medium. Two hundred of your best friends in the audience, five cameras in your face, not enough time to get it together and 30 million people watching.' Downey and Hall had Belushi and Aykroyd's old office, into which bunk beds with NFL sheets were delivered at Hall's jokey behest, where they enjoyed themselves watching midget wrestling on TV.

One of the writers remembers him 'wandering the halls with untied basketball sneakers, in a time before untied sneakers had become an urban or suburban statement. He and Anthony Michael Hall scuffled through the offices once or twice in my short time there like entitled teenagers, looking less than wholly alert, keeping to themselves and making me self-conscious about trying to fit in at the grand old age of 36.' Having annoyed Sean Penn in his first show, things turned especially sour for Downey when former cast member Chevy Chase came back to host the second episode of the season. 'We were all so excited because, to us, Chevy was like a god. This was someone returning who'd been one of the original people and was this legendary figure,' said cast-mate Terry Sweeney in the book *Live From New York*. 'And when he got there, he was a monster. I mean, he insulted everybody. He said to [Robert], "Didn't your father used to be a successful director? Whatever happened to him? Boy, he sure died, you know, he sure went to hell." Downey turned ashen.'

He was beginning to become famous. He would head uptown with Hall to visit friends where people would point him out like some kind of big shot. One girl who met him at a house party around then remembers, 'I was in a friend of a friend's house.

That's when I met him. It was like, "Oh, another groupie," I could see it in his eyes. So I left. He looked like a little punk kid to me!' It must have been difficult for Downey to stay awake that year. On top of shooting the show in New York, he was traversing the country to make *Back to School* (1986), a ribald college comedy starring cult stand-up Rodney Dangerfield. Once again, he played the cocky best friend, this time to proto-nerd Keith Gordon, a quiet type whose rich, gobby father (Dangerfield) joins him at university. Written by Harold Ramis (*Caddyshack*) and directed by Alan Metter, it's hardly the subtlest comedy in the world, mainly thanks to Dangerfield's bug-eyed schtick, but it has its charms. Downey – looking more eighties than ever with an Adam Ant kerchief, Ray-Bans and dyed blue hair – looks like he realises he is still paying his dues and seems to kind of wander into scenes at opportune moments, improvise some lines with an amused smirk on his face and leave. Due, as ever, to his charm, it works very well. Casting the role, director Metter looked at a number of actors, including *Short Circuit*'s Fisher Stevens, but when scheduling conflicts arose, he remembered back to a young man he had met on the previous film he directed called *Girls Just Want To Have Fun*. A romcom starring Sarah Jessica Parker, Metter had been struck by her ebullient boyfriend who often visited the set during breaks in the filming of *Weird Science* in a nearby studio.

'He would come down and hang out with Sarah Jessica,' says Metter, a deep-voiced, funny man, now retired and living in Florida. 'Apparently they were fighting in her trailer, so she would come on the set to do some happy scene in tears with her mascara running. I remember saying to Downey, "Don't come down here, you're ruining my movie! Stop making her unhappy! She's playing a happy girl in this movie." That's how I got him to do a cameo. I said, "You're going to have to do me a cameo, you're such a pain in the ass." So he got under the table. Nobody notices that!'

One thing the couple did enjoy doing together was baby-sitting Metter's son, and they were good at it – friendly, down to earth and kind. 'I remember him and Sarah Jessica came over on a couple of Saturdays to my house and my son at the time was twelve,' laughs the director. 'They would take him out around LA. Go shopping on Melrose. Of course, he loved it. He thought they were cool, he didn't care they were movie actors. He had two cool baby-sitters.'

By this point, Downey had been acting professionally for three years, with parts on mainstream television and in studio movies. But while Metter remembers a young man with obvious ability and a forceful personality, he was, he unhappily admits, also disappointed with much of his performance. What's amazing here is Downey prided himself on his ability to ad-lib, his belief (perhaps initially misguided) that he knew how to make the script and the character better with his own words.

'We had a good script, written by Harold Ramis,' says Metter. 'Robert was most comfortable when he was improvising. When we got into the written dialogue, he tended to stiffen up a little bit. I found he was frustrating to work with as a director because I saw his best performances in the blocking and rehearsals and by the time I rolled the camera, he was kind of just going through the motions. I actually started rolling the camera early. For me, I would much rather have a great performance modestly lit, than a poor performance perfectly lit. But I was constantly duelling with my DOP [director of photography] about rolling the camera on Downey early.'

But did Downey know he wasn't up to snuff? 'I told him that,' recalls Metter. 'Once a director says that to an actor, the actor's probably going to hate him forever.' And how did Downey react? 'He shrugged. What could he say? He never argued that the stuff you're getting is better than the rehearsals, because he knew it too.'

Metter sighs when asked whether he feels partly responsible. 'I knew improvising was his strength and basically, I let him do anything he wanted,' he says. 'As long as the story point was conveyed in the scene, as far as dialogue he was free to change anything. [But] I always walked away feeling like I didn't get it. That's the worst part of directing. What you want is "I caught magic". But the performances I filmed were never as exciting as stuff I saw in rehearsal. I can hear myself telling him many times on that movie to do it like he did in rehearsal, but we never seemed to get back to it. And that sort of wore me down, so that my memory of working with him – and don't forget I wasn't working with the great Robert Downey, I was working with Robert Downey the actor – it was always a little disappointing.'

The director's favourite scene, however, did involve some inspired Downey improvisation. 'There's a scene where Downey comes into the room and tells Rodney [that] Dean Martin wants to see him right away,' he reveals. 'I wanted Downey to come running in the room and run up to Rodney and tell him. There was a couch between him and Rodney and Downey was going "move the couch" and I'm going "No, get around the couch". It's more fun to watch an actor struggling with something than having an easy time. So Downey comes in and vaults over the couch and lands on his feet and comes right up to Rodney, chin to chin, and delivers the line. And it's in the film. It was one of the great moments in the movie. There's an example of a day when I drove home and thought "That was great".'

Although Downey was frequently exasperating his director, everyone on set loved him. Keith Gordon became a friend (the pair would collaborate again on 2003's *The Singing Detective*) and Dangerfield was fond of him, as well as recognising him as a bit of a wild child. 'I brought Downey over to the apartment [Rodney] was renting on the beach in Santa Monica,' recalls

Metter. 'Downey showed up with Anthony Michael Hall. So Michael and Robert are meeting Rodney and they're in awe of him. You could tell they were as nervous as hell. And Rodney says, "You're not scared of me, are you? Because I'm from the gutter," and that made them laugh and relax.'

But the combination of travelling cross-country and all-night parties did finally catch up with Downey, the start of a trend that later would threaten his career and call his professionalism into question. With hundreds of crew costing thousands of dollars a day, the last thing producers want to see is nothing happening. But when your actor's missing and people are sitting around getting more and more irritated by the lack of action, there's not much you can do – other than get your own back.

'We were supposed to be filming a scene that featured him and he didn't show up on the set,' remembers Metter. 'We had his friends and his father and the police and everybody looking for him, while my eighty-man crew were sitting around reading newspapers. I had my camera operator sitting on the dolly with the *LA Times* open and we were paying him. [Robert] finally showed up in the afternoon and he had been up all night. We were filming in a little dorm room and Downey fell asleep on one of the beds. So I had the grips get gaffer tape and, like in *Gulliver's Travels*, they used a hundred or so strips of tape and we taped him to the floor. He woke up and couldn't move. That was my payback.'

Metter didn't see the young star taking drugs during the production, but he had his suspicions. 'I suspect that sometimes he was working stoned,' he says. 'That makes the actor what I call brittle, a little clench-jawed.

'In the editing room, I manicured his performances,' he adds. 'I can honestly say his best work in *Back to School* is on the screen. I really dug deep. I'm not saying he stunk in the movie, he didn't, but it's possible he didn't have the skills he had later. Or maybe he learned a lesson on my picture? I doubt he'd admit that.'

Creatively, *Saturday Night Live* was a bit of a bust. At the end of the series, baseball star Billy Martin, who was co-hosting the final show, was 'sacked' by Lorne Michaels and set his dressing room on fire in retaliation. In a controversial move, Michaels only actively saved Jon Lovitz, leaving the audience to ponder which cast members would 'survive' the off-season cull. As it turned out, only Lovitz and two other performers were re-hired the following year. 'Robert was one of the people [Lorne] really wanted [after his audition] and it wasn't a terrible idea, but it wasn't a good idea either, in retrospect,' showbiz manager Bernie Brillstein told authors Tom Shales and James Andrew Miller. 'It just didn't work. And there were a few problems among the cast; I mean alcohol and drugs and whatever. It wasn't good. But Lorne was still young then, 39 or 40, and he was trying something different.'

But Downey's star was not dented. Indeed, another quirky outsider, a writer/director with a documentarian's spirit and the right Hollywood connections, had spotted the young actor among the many wigs and accents and wanted to turn him into a leading man.

Leading Man

'It really disturbed me. Even now, it's hard for me
to see the film.' (1987)

James Toback liked Robert Downey Jr. The writer/director – who
scored a critical hit with Harvey Keitel-starring *Fingers* (1978) –
was looking for someone to play a version of himself in *The
Pick-Up Artist* (1987), the story of a slick womaniser who falls for
Molly Ringwald. When Toback signed him up, Downey was
ecstatic. It was his first lead role after years of playing the sidekick.
Once again he was convinced that *finally* he was getting his big
break. His time in the trenches had been fun and occasionally
gruelling. Now it was time for the world to see what he could
really do. Unfortunately, the world didn't want to see a sleazy
lothario lech onto their beloved Ringwald, even if Downey did
infuse his character, Jack Jericho, with every ounce of charm he
had. Toback was best friends with Warren Beatty and the pair
regularly went out trawling for women. Toback, though believing
himself to be sexy and cool, patently benefited from basking in
his movie-star pal's glow. What's more, many critics believed
Toback didn't have the subtlety of touch to lend Jack the pathos
needed to make audiences want to see him happy, branding
Jericho a sexual-predator-in-waiting. Roger Ebert in the *Chicago
Sun-Times* called it 'an appallingly silly movie, from its juvenile

comic overture to its dreadfully sincere conclusion'. The *Washington Post*, however, was full of praise for Downey's performance. '[He] makes a tremendous contribution here,' it wrote. 'Downey, who worked for one season on *Saturday Night Live*, has just the right emotional weight for the role of Jack and the right touch of goofy boyishness to soften his aggressiveness.'

Certainly the role provided an outlet for the actor's natural quick-fire, slightly glib conversational style, even if he believed his chat-up abilities never measured up. 'It's never worked for me,' he told *The Frederick News*. 'I just don't feel comfortable in the situation of walking up to someone and saying, "How's about you and me?" Seeing through all the layers of that kind of thing repels me.' However, disregarding the womanising aspect, much of the character does ring true. In real life, Downey also has that magnetic ability to make you feel like the most important person in the room at any one moment, dazzling you with a flurry of clever wordplay that often when read back, or reminisced about, appears to mean very little.

Producer and friend Chris Hanley, who worked with him later on 1997's *Two Girls and a Guy*, sums it up. 'It's a bit like Warhol, the words don't mean anything,' he suggests. 'You have to look into the being that's standing in front of you. You watch the movement of the eyes, the shoulders. If you typed it out, you wouldn't get it. Because he's an actor, you've got to experience him on that level. The reason he's a good actor is because he uses every facet. He doesn't rely on words alone to project himself.' Downey does lend Jack a naivety that turns him into more of a boy doing anything he can to find love, rather than someone lying and manipulating to get laid. But his efforts can't obscure what is ostensibly a rudimentary romantic comedy-drama that tells us nothing about the nature of male/female relationships, or even the psychology of promiscuity. Instead it's a waste of a great cast, which includes Harvey Keitel and a dipsomaniacal Dennis Hopper, who give this slight, trite 75-minuter a veneer of kudos it doesn't deserve.

Downey and Sarah were spending more and more time in Hollywood as their careers took off. Their house in Beachwood Canyon was a hive of activity, full of young performers all either breaking, or about to break, into the big time. They officially shared with Billy Zane and an actor called Tom O'Brien. Then Kiefer Sutherland started showing up, since he and Billy had just done a TV movie together called *The Brotherhood of Justice*. Downey and Kiefer became fast friends – they both came from film-making families after all – and it wasn't long before they were partying hard together. 'He was so talented, witty and intelligent – a great buddy,' said Kiefer. 'He knew the dangers, but he took the risks all the time.' Sutherland admitted they took it to the limit, though doesn't reveal specific drug-taking. Downey is not so shy about that period. He later said there was drinking, cocaine and sometimes magic mushrooms but, then, he was a young, successful, monied man. He revelled in the music and the style, marvelling at the way the men's and women's clothing departments in shops often couldn't be told apart. He was in love. He was . . . indestructible.

There's a moment in the film *Less Than Zero* (1987) when the character of Julian Wells comes crashing through the doorway of an apartment. His eyes are wide and vacant, he's pouring with sweat, he looks like he's about to have a heart attack. The scene is terrifying, moving, honest and incredibly effective. It is, perhaps, the greatest overdose committed to film. Bret Easton Ellis's eponymous book was published in 1985, when the author was only 21. It quickly became a smash hit, both as a journal of the age and a warning to the decadence of the eighties. As in Ellis's subsequent novels there are no heroes, only shades of grey. Essentially, it's the story of Clay – a rich, disaffected, self-absorbed college freshman who returns home to Los Angeles for Christmas to wallow among the equally shallow, coke-fuelled, hateful crowd he left behind. There is sex, drugs and rock and roll, a nihilistic vision of youth with no real sense of catharsis. Hardly the building blocks of a successful film, especially in an era when the multiplexes preferred Stallone and Schwarzenegger blowing people away with an Uzi. But it was a bestseller and producers believed that, with a few little tweaks and an awesome sound-track, they could have something special.

They approached Brit director Marek Kanievska (*Another Country*) to direct it and Harley Peyton wrote the script, completely revising the story to make Clay a more sympathetic character and the message of the film decidedly anti-drug. The plot became a more simplistic tale of three best friends forced to grow up when one of their number falls off the rails. Jami Gertz signed on as Blair, Clay's on/off girlfriend, and auditions started for the lynchpin role of Julian, the third leg of the tripod, whose plunge into addiction and debt is the catalyst for the film. To Downey's mind, he *was* Julian. He wore the same clothes, breathed the same air, he had snorted the same drugs, only not to the same extent. Kanievska originally met the star while researching the film in the nightclubs of New York. 'There are certain personalities you remember because they have an incredible intensity about them,' he said to the authors of *Brat Pack Confidential*. 'They're the centre of attraction, they have incredible charm and they're very seductive. They're also incredibly bright and know how to make everyone feel like a million dollars. I met Robert out and about and thought "That's the character for me". And that's the reason I cast him.'

Once he started building the character, it was as if Downey didn't know where he stopped and Julian began. Several actors had baulked at testing for Julian, partly because he gets so in debt to drug dealer Rip (James Spader), he is forced to perform sexual acts on men, a story point actually dealt with subtly in the finished film. Downey didn't care. 'You can't be paranoid about what people think,' he said. Though he wasn't gay, Downey had no qualms about stoking the fire of gossip, or simply letting people believe what they wanted to believe. He admitted some people thought he was also attracted to men, saying several considered him 'an eccentric bisexual'. He caused uproar at *Less Than Zero* production meetings by challenging people's homophobic prejudices and eagerly saying, 'I'll suck cock for base money,' to play the part convincingly.

Reading reviews and interviews after the film was released at the end of 1987, it's interesting to see how much he distances himself from the character. He went so far as to tell one interviewer flatout, 'I didn't do drugs.' He spoke to others, talking about the fact it disturbed him and that while he believed the movie to be 'frighteningly real', drug-taking was something in his past. 'I've made the decision to be straight,' he explained to writer Bob Strauss at the time. 'It was just like a great big "No" I heard in my head, a sign flashing "Stop!" Even in my off time now, I don't like to go and get drunk. I don't enjoy being drunk.' As it turned out, this wasn't true. Throughout filming, he had been partying hard. It got to the point where his co-star Gertz worried for his safety. 'You had the feeling, "Is what happens to Julian going to happen to Robert?"' she said.

Downey observed that he had to be able to let go in order to produce a good performance. He had been doing drugs for years anyway and here he was finally playing a drug-addled character – his commitment to putting something spectacular on film tied in with his off-screen persona. 'It's the closest I've ever come to leaving a part of myself up there on screen,' he said. 'I consider myself very lucky to have gone through that period with a career and a working respiratory system.'

It is mainly thanks to Downey that the finished film is a fascinating and affecting study of addiction. Critics and Ellis fans have maligned it for straying from the original text, but anyone who has read the book (and it's a problem some more recent Ellis adaptations have also faced) will know that putting his story on screen unadulterated wouldn't have worked as mainstream drama. As it is, the actors manage to turn Ellis's disinterested, aloof teenagers into real people with identifiable problems. Even if you're angry at Julian, there's humanity there, thanks to Downey's performance. He brings a potent mix of arrogance and vulnerability to his portrayal. It was by far his most authentic piece of acting to date. Given what happened later in his life and the revelations of his real-life drug-taking, there are moments of terrible prescience, which audiences in 1987 wouldn't have been aware of. 'I'd just really like to wake up and know where the hell I am for once,' says Julian at one point. 'It'd be a nice change of pace for me.'

What's phenomenal, given the bleak ending, is how the film didn't shock him in some small way into knocking his off-screen exploits on the head. 'Julian's been doing that since he was ten,' says Clay, talking about his coke intake. Sadly, when Julian ignores Clay and Blair's offers of help, it's hard not to get taken out of the story, just for a moment. When you see the desperation in his eyes as he begs Clay for money, or tricks a little girl into letting him steal jewellery, there's a tiny part of you that wonders whether that's the same face Downey pulled to his friends and family when they suggested he get clean. Then there's that breakdown scene. How many times had he really gone through that? When Julian faces his father and entreats him to let him back in the family house, are we seeing a version of truth played out in front of our eyes?

His *Back to School* director Alan Metter pointedly says, 'When I watched him in *Less Than Zero*, it kind of made me sad. I felt like that movie was played from experience. He was expressing the pain of a lonely childhood.' Certainly, Julian is a rich kid whose parents have substituted lashings of money for quality time together. He has more of a relationship with his uncle than he does with his father, who has already given up on him. While the Downeys never had much money – mayonnaise sandwiches were an occasional dinner option – absenteeism on Downey Sr's behalf did play a part in his son's childhood.

Downey gave some inkling that Julian's dilemmas were filtered through his own family traumas. 'Something happened to my psyche or spirituality while I was filming,' he said to *Mademoiselle* in 1988. 'I mean, you start digging into your duffle bag that's filled with all your repressed ideas. Maybe there's a family crisis, but you think, "I've got to put this to the back of my head because I've got other things to think about." Until finally there's this pile of dirty, mismatched socks at the bottom. I started to mentally pick them out and fluff and fold them.'

The critics were generally cruel to *Less Than Zero*, which incidentally was the first time Downey added the suffix 'Jr' to his screen name. Because both he and his father were now members of the Screen Actors Guild, they couldn't have exactly the same moniker on a set of credits. Junior decided he should be the one to change because 'I didn't want Dad to think I thought I was so important that he should have to change his name.' The *Washington Post* said the film was 'noodle-headed and faint-hearted, a shallow swipe at a serious problem'. *Variety* dubbed it 'specious and shallow'. But, as with the rest of his filmography, Downey's acting stood out as one of the few positives. In the

Chicago Sun-Times, Roger Ebert said he was 'so real, so subtle and so observant that it's scary'. Meanwhile, the *Austin Chronicle* called it a 'rip-roaring performance' and the *New York Times* wrote, 'Mr Downey gives a performance that is desperately moving, with the kind of emotion that comes as a real surprise in these surroundings.' The film again was not a success, but for once Downey felt like he had achieved the goals he set out from an acting point of view. For the first time, he also got a sense of how his work impacted on others. In Georgia, a woman walked up to him, shaking with nerves. He was polite but abrupt, then she told him that because of his performance in *Less Than Zero*, two of her friends went into rehab. It left Downey with a satisfied glow.

He was in Georgia to shoot *1969* (1988), a Vietnam-era coming-of-age drama with his friend Kiefer Sutherland and a young Winona Ryder. Like everyone he seemed to work with, Winona gravitated towards Downey and they became friends. Later, when her advisors were telling her not to do *Heathers*, saying it would ruin her career, even though she was desperate to sign up, he was one of the few people to encourage her. The film went on to be a cult classic and a breakthrough role for the young actress. She always appreciated that advice. For the serious young actress, Downey's carefree attitude was invaluable. 'Robert is the only young actor I know who really helped me keep a sense of humour about everything,' she said. 'He reminds me to laugh at what I do, to remember it's all a mirage.' *1969* was written and directed by Ernest Thompson, best known for *On Golden Pond* – it received decent notices, but failed to generate much interest.

Meanwhile, Downey also starred as a porn star called Wolf Dangler for his father in *Rented Lips* (1988). He loved working for his dad again, who called him by his character name on set during the day. But while he was having fun and working constantly, he wasn't capitalising on the buzz *Less Than Zero* had afforded him. Back at home, his drugging and boozing continued.

Hollywood has always been a party town, but at the end of the eighties, it was like the last days of Gomorrah: jam night on Mondays at The China Club, where celebrities got up onstage with the house band to play covers; Tuesday at The Roxbury, one of Downey's favourites, where Big Tony preserved the sanctity of the VIP section; Bar One on Wednesdays, where people were seen openly doing drugs at the tables – unsurprising, considering it was owned by one of the alumni of New York's famously decadent Studio 54. Thursdays meant Stringfellows and the weekend was mega-club Vertigo downtown, or Stallone's place Black & Bloo. 'There was a lot of carnage,' says John Young, a clubster who worked in several of the hottest spots. 'Robert was right in the mix of it all.' Ecstasy was big at the time and people would munch pills all night, then go and get crack or coke at six in the morning and stay up the rest of the day. 'There used to be a spot off Sunset where all these Mexican guys hung out,' says Young. 'You'd drive up there and they'd rush your car.' Drug dealer Rayce Newman recalled meeting Downey around this time. 'I ran into him on and off at parties and clubs,' he says in his exposé *The Hollywood Connection*. 'We shared a line here, smoked some rock there, you know, the usual things people in Hollywood do when they get together.'

Downey was feeling creative too. He realised one way to attain some kind of longevity in the business was to generate his own material, a lesson learned in part from his father. So he spent five months writing a script with Anthony Michael Hall called 'Seth and McGuigan', about two guys in a rehab centre, which as yet hasn't come to fruition. Sarah Jessica Parker was becoming increasingly worried about his substance abuse. She began to feel more like his mother than his girlfriend. 'I believed I was the person holding him together,' she said to *Ananova* in 2006, and she was probably right. 'In every good and bad way I enabled him to get up in the morning and show up for work. If he did not, I was there to cover for him, find him, clean him up and get him to the set or theatre. The machinations of all that are the worst. You are not even in a romantic relationship any more. It is like a parent-child thing.'

He was still besotted. He said she began to look more and more like a 'wife' every day, like a together woman wearing jodhpurs and a sweatshirt. It wasn't exactly what she was hoping for.

They moved house, to a pink stucco pad that had been built by one of Cecil B. De Mille's set designers for Charlie Chaplin. A short walk from the Sunset Strip, it had a red piano in the front room. She tried to keep his mind occupied by getting him involved in politics. She had grown up within a family of activists and though the Downeys had been anti-establishment, they had never been ones for genuine polemicism. The couple got involved in a voter-registration drive during the 1988 presidential campaign, hooking up with other celebrities like Judd Nelson, who became a close friend, in trying to build up political consciousness amongst the young. Downey was interested in learning about the issues, but felt uncomfortable trumpeting them to the press. 'I just want to be an active citizen,' he told interviewer Len Sherman. 'To get these kids out there. I don't care what gets them there, I really don't care if they're there to see me or whatever, but they're going to hear words and they're going to make up their own choices anyway.' Some of the more high-brow publications didn't take well to these young actors talking about their views, polluting (to their mind) the political message with a simplistic celebrity one. *Spy* magazine wrote an article bashing them with the headline: 'The Importance Of Looking Earnest: We're Serious, You're Serious, Everybody's Serious – Especially Judd Nelson'.

In fact, Downey treated the subject very carefully and urbanely, with a dash of sweet naivety, focusing on issues close to his heart like the environment and voter registration, reading voraciously around the topics and never trying to come across as anything other than a keen young man who felt that he could lend his fame to create awareness. 'I think it really comes down to whether you wholeheartedly know what you said and felt was true,' he commented. 'To me, it's really about becoming informed.'

Between February and the end of summer 1988, Downey got involved in two roles that required him to enter new ground. *True Believer* (1989) saw him playing Roger Baron, a callow and idealistic attorney who convinces cynical civil-rights campaigner James Woods to take on the case of a wrongly imprisoned Korean man. Meanwhile, *Chances Are* (1989) was a comedy also starring Cybill Shepherd and Ryan O'Neal, with Downey as a young man who finds out he is the reincarnated soul of Shepherd's dead husband, who sets out to win her back more than twenty years later.

'We needed the male lead,' remembers Mike Lobell, *Chances Are*'s producer. 'We read a lot of actors. Robert didn't mean anything in those days and there were rumours he was difficult, but he was great with us and really wanted to do it. We put a lot of pressure on the [production company] to hire him and they finally agreed.' The story was a tricky balancing act. Through a series of coincidences – or fate, as the movie would have you believe – Downey's character Alex Finch finds himself in the house of Cybill Shepherd, more than two decades after she lost her perfect husband in a tragic accident. She has never got over him, much to the chagrin of O'Neal, who has always loved her. The situation is made even more difficult by Shepherd's (and thus

Alex's previous incarnation's) daughter, played by Mary Stuart Masterson, who fancies Alex and is constantly trying to bed him. This *Back To The Future*-esque plot twist didn't really work and Shepherd herself admitted she would have preferred the reincarnation storyline to be dropped in favour of a straightforward older-woman–younger-man romance, a situation she had encountered more than once in her own love life. For Downey, it was the first time he got to play a non-sleazy straight-up romantic lead, which would potentially open up his Hollywood options. He also got to indulge his slapstick side, skills that would serve him particularly well a couple of years later on *Chaplin*. Above all, though, he was unsatisfied with how his career was progressing and realised he needed to be in a mainstream hit. Playing a fishnet-wearing woodsman in his dad's indies wasn't the ticket to fame and fortune.

Chances Are had a lot going for it. Shepherd was hot thanks to the TV show *Moonlighting*, Masterson was considered one of the brightest young actresses around (she probably took some roles Sarah Jessica Parker would have loved to get her hands on) and the director was Emile Ardolino, coming off the back of *Dirty Dancing*. Downey's ambition rang true to Mike Lobell. 'I don't think he'd ever been in a successful movie. He'd done a lot of offbeat things,' he says. 'I think he really needed the work, to be honest with you. He didn't do it for the money, because no one got paid an awful lot of money.'

Unfortunately, his off-screen exploits, like *Back to School* before it, threatened to ruin things before they had begun when he failed to show up for the first day of rehearsal. 'He was very late,' remembers Lobell. 'We had to fetch him, meaning me. I fetched him, he came and he was fine. He apologised to everybody sheepishly and from then on, he was fine.' Shepherd noted Downey had been found asleep in bed, and the producers understood they needed to make sure he didn't compromise their movie. 'I hired Nicky Corello to come and train him,' says Lobell. 'He took really good care of Robert. Took him to the gym twice a day, made sure he ate properly and that he was in good shape. It was a strenuous role.'

As ever, Downey is effective in the movie, playing his most guileless character yet. But the marketing department didn't know how to promote it and, despite the preview screenings getting positive buzz, it was dead on arrival in cinemas. 'It's disappointing, it should have been a really big hit,' says Lobell, noting the distributors blamed it on the lack of movie-star names in the cast. What saddened the producer the most at the time was Downey turning down a promising script his partner Andrew Bergman had written. 'In the last week or two of shooting *Chances Are*, I got the final draft of *The Freshman*,' says Lobell. 'He had come down a couple of times [to the set] and saw how good Robert was, so I said, "Let's give him the script, he'd be perfect for it." He kept the script for a couple of weeks and then on the last day of shooting he told me he didn't want to do it. I think he made a big mistake.'

The Freshman ultimately turned out to be a decent-sized critical and commercial hit, starring Marlon Brando in his first on-screen role for more than ten years. The part Downey refused was played by none other than Matthew Broderick, who years later would marry Downey's girlfriend Sarah Jessica Parker. It wasn't the first time Downey's box-office radar would waver, with him turning down a bunch of films that went on to be hits. 'He turned them all down for mixed reasons,' adds Lobell. 'You never knew where his head was at, what shape he was in. He fluctuated over the years.'

True Believer was a strange choice of movie, mainly because his character barely does anything in it. Dressed in dapper end-of-eighties threads, brandishing a big quiff and wearing large tortoiseshell glasses – an outfit that makes him a dead ringer for his friend Judd Nelson – he gamely plays second fiddle to James Woods as Eddie Dodd, who harrumphs and spits his way through a straightforward but entertaining crusading-lawyer pic. It's strange, because every time you think he's going to get a chance to act a memorable scene, Woods shows up at the last minute and upstages him. It's as if he's happy to settle into the background. Even when he jumps up in court and vehemently objects to a ruling, the camera is focused on a close-up of his co-star. Downey enjoyed making the film, though, even if his sartorial savvy should have stretched to telling the hair department to get rid of Woods' embarrassing ponytail. He learned a lot from his fellow actor, who gave him the nickname Binky because of his preppy style and said Downey wore more silk than it took to land all the troops in Normandy.

'I cast Downey because he's got this current going on that's fascinating to watch,' said the film's director Joseph Ruben, though it's difficult to spot this quality when he's merely rifling through police reports looking for a piece of exculpatory evidence. What Woods did do was sharpen his instincts, hone his concentration. This came to a head one day when, as Downey explains, '[Woods] got this weird look and cocked his head a little bit to the side and he just reached over and fucking cracked me right in the middle of the take.' Incredibly, Downey didn't get angry, realising Woods had spotted something in him that needed a re-adjustment. 'He was missing the magic that I knew he was capable of,' said Woods in the *Chicago Sun-Times*. 'I hate to see anybody that brilliant not be really up to the mark, you know what I mean? I just woke him up for a second.'

For his part, Downey was impressed and willing to learn, even if it took unusual methods. 'I would appreciate it if he did it for me,' added Woods. 'I can't really remember if anybody has ever done anything like that to me.' Face-slappings aside, the two got on famously and while the film occasionally veers into TV-movie territory, Woods' scenery-chewing and a neat twist make it watchable.

There are two ironic moments in the film, one where Downey's character berates Dodd for using legalese to plead out drug dealers, and another when ex-hippie Dodd blows pot smoke in his protégé's face, much to Baron's annoyance. That wouldn't have been Downey's reaction. He was never discreet about his partying in the way many of his peers were. He'd go out wearing an Oscar Wilde ensemble, complete with spats, and offend someone, only managing to avoid a fight by using his charm or because someone else was there to smooth over the cracks. '[It's] really hard not to like me,' he said once, 'because whatever's not likeable isn't really out for guests.'

There were some legendary evenings. His then manager Loree Rodkin remembered a night when Downey offended a famously diminutive actor by criticising his height in front of the assembled throng. It got to the point where a fight was beckoning, so in order to avoid trouble, Downey went out to the limo outside but somehow, during the melee, hit himself in the head causing a wound that required stitches. He went to the hospital and got fixed up, only to return to the party at four in the morning. His friend Josh Richman was still there, pouring a bottle of gin over someone, and Downey wandered in wearing a blood-stained shirt. Inevitably, they wanted to carry on the party. Rodkin told them it was time to go home.

Richman has said that even though they had some extremes, the best times with Downey he remembers are when they just drove around, talking. Downey tried for the most part to keep it from Parker. He had become friends with *Less Than Zero*'s author Bret Easton Ellis, who was around the same age. But though he wrote about the drug-afflicted youth of Los Angeles, even Ellis was surprised at the lengths Downey would go to for his partying. While he was filming *True Believer*, they were out in New York with friends club-hopping and ended up in Downey's hotel room at dawn. The phone rang, and it was Sarah asking to speak to him, but Downey handed the phone to Ellis and told him to say her boyfriend was talking to one of the film's producers and that the author was just waiting to take him out for an early lunch. All the while, Downey was sitting in the room in his underwear, freebasing cocaine.

He knew he had a drug problem, though he has suggested he was dealing with a more holistic problem – a spiritual crisis – which manifested itself through drug-taking. He always talked about needing mentors in his life, people to look up to. Often he found them on movie sets – James Woods, James Toback and so on – but the people he was supposed to look up to, his parents, were too wild; while they loved him, they had never provided him with the guidance he needed to keep him on the rails. 'I don't think I ever wanted to die,' he revealed in a 1991 *Movieline* interview. 'I think what I meant was I wanted to change and couldn't think of a way to do it that was more direct.' Outwardly, he was projecting an air of defiance and asceticism, telling people he was free of his vices and that one of the primary misconceptions people had about him was that they would see him wandering out of a Palm Springs hotel room looking high.

In reality, things weren't so great. His substance use was getting so bad that he voluntarily checked himself into a 28-day rehabilitation programme at the Sierra Tucson facility in Arizona. Sarah felt like she couldn't cope and eventually it was Loree Rodkin who convinced him to take himself away to the 160-acre ranch nestled in the shadow of the Santa Catalina Mountains. When he got out, he fired her. But he emerged clean and set about trying to separate himself from his old life, which he admitted had him waking up in university dorm rooms with people he couldn't remember meeting. 'The eighties for me was a period about abusive behaviour and drugs,' he said. 'You start to realise you're not dealing with your life. You're living it, but you're not dealing with anything.' He admitted that the desire to party continued to be strong and it was like he was trying to have a conversation with an older version of himself, convincing him that he needed to think about the future, as well as the here and now.

He took to writing poetry, performing it in front of other celebrities and admirers at the weekly theme night Poetry In Motion, which began at the Hollywood club Helena's and then moved to Café Largo. There, wearing a black turtleneck and sitting among Judd Nelson, Ally Sheedy and Alec Baldwin, he showed off compositions like his update of Edgar Allan Poe's 'The Tell-Tale Heart'.

He chopped up the body like a gourmet magnifico
And put those pieces under the floorboard very specifico.

His absurd sense of humour also came into play with a poem riffing on *Gorillas in the Mist*, which he re-dubbed 'Gorillas on My Dick' and a short story about a virgin called Nancy, featuring bizarre metaphors and similes. He started painting, writing a screenplay, trying to get over his so-called 'grandpa' phobia of dancing in public and enjoying time at home with Sarah and their Persian cats Mr Smith and Scout. His girlfriend admitted that without rehab, she would have left. But Downey spoke of being at ground zero, a new plateau, grateful for the fact he had people who confronted him about his problems. He didn't lie about his past or his pleasant experiences with narcotics, avoiding the usual progression of a rehab-ee who turns into a vehement opponent of their chosen poison, instead admitting he had had some of his most telling life experiences while under the influence. He stayed strong, despite attending Hollywood parties where everyone else was off their heads. This was the *new* Downey. Still, he said, 'Part of me really likes that bacchanalian vibration supplied by drugs.'

When he met Mel Gibson about playing a role in the megastar's new film, *Air America* (1990), Downey was in the middle of detoxing. He was a bit intimidated by Gibson, who he had never seen around, and was self-conscious because his skin looked bad. He met the actor's family, whose kids didn't understand the concept of tact, blurting out that he looked like he had measles. 'We both laughed,' said Downey, 'and I knew things between us were going to be OK.' *Air America* was a big deal. A studio film directed by Roger Spottiswoode, it was adapted from the book by Christopher Robbins and told of the covert and corrupt civilian-manned American air force that operated in Laos during the Vietnam War. Downey was keen to work with Gibson and secure a big payday, especially since he was now clean and sober. He hadn't worked for a year because of his personal issues (though his official studio biography said he 'took a year off') and he was keen to start acting again. He was turned down for the lead in *Edward Scissorhands*, but was still only 25, in the nascent stages of his career, and a Mel Gibson film was as close to a sure-fire blockbuster as you were likely to get. Gibson had originally been asked to play the role of Billy Covington, a LA weather-chopper pilot, who gets fired and is drafted into the illicit Far East company Air America. But the actor wanted to play the mentor role of Gene Ryack and, with his agents out talking up their client, Downey got the gig. Standing in for Laos, the film was shot in

Thailand's Golden Triangle, an area with a frontier vibe and morals to match. Drugs, whores and more were readily available, but instead Downey found himself as the guy looking after everyone else's keys. For once, said a crew member, 'Downey was a typical Hollywood actor, out jogging at dawn every morning and in bed early most evenings.' He got most of his kicks playing with Thai fireworks with the crew.

He found the country depressing. A weekend trip to Bangkok was cut short when he was offered child prostitutes on the street, leading him to rush back to the set. But Downey found the process of making a blockbuster boring and felt stifled by the content of the film. 'I'm used to being the weirdest guy in the room and now I'm not even in the running,' says Billy, and one can see the actor's genuine detachment as he says it. It's as if he is realising as he's speaking his lines that the movie is not what he was hoping for or expecting. 'It's just so tedious,' he said of the experience in a 1991 interview with *The Face*. 'It's acting, but all the acting comes from just bearing it, getting through all the technical shit as opposed to interacting with someone, taking some chances, making some huge mistake – doing anything except jumping out of airplanes.'

He certainly looks the part – movie-star handsome, fresh-faced, no quirks. But his character is passive. There's no cockiness, no spring in his step, even though Billy is supposed to be self-confident and brave. Even Gibson's Gene Ryack is left out in the cold, not given any good buddy banter and there's a certain meekness that dulls the movie's personality. It's particularly frustrating given the subject, which is perfect territory for a black action comedy. That seems to be what Spottiswoode is going for, but it's neither exciting enough nor funny enough to win either battle. The whole company appears unsure of the tone, though given the political and cinematic climate of the time, it's very possible that studio interference may have had to do with the project falling between two stools.

What is amusing is Downey's involvement in yet another anti-drug film, though this time it was slightly less ironic when he blew up a makeshift heroin factory. And he does lend some skittish charm when spewing lines like: 'The politics of Saturday night – I can relate to that.' Or: 'Down on the ground's where I tend to fuck up.' But while he got on with Gibson, whose laid-back attitude to acting echoed his own, *Air America* turned out to be a disappointment. He whinged about the famous 'one for you, one for them' mentality which is a mantra in Hollywood, referring to having to follow a personal, intimate film with something more high profile and commercial in order to keep you in the public eye. He tried not to be cynical, a trait he all too happily slipped into, but it was difficult, especially after seeing the finished product. 'I'm not going to be doing a big action movie again for a long time,' he said.

Air America stalled at the box office, only grossing a little over $30 million in the US. Critics attacked the film and, for once, Downey was involved. 'It is impossible to identify with Gibson's cynical, selfish loner whose lucrative sideline is gun-running,' wrote *Time Out*. 'That leaves the uncharismatic, ineffectual Downey holding the conscience ticket – as the wide-eyed new boy whose efforts to expose such nefarious activities cause the faeces to hit the propeller – and a huge hole in the middle of the picture.' *Rolling Stone* was no kinder, saying, 'There aren't any ironies in the depressingly predictable screenplay . . . the film remains stuck in a farcical groove, with Downey playing green kid to Gibson's grizzled vet.' Downey couldn't believe it. Here was a studio picture with Mel Gibson and it was a failure. He had ditched the drugs and booze, was working with a clear head and had picked wrong again. Nevertheless, some writer did single him out for praise. 'This is a magnetic young actor, regardless of the material,' said the *Washington Post*. 'It's fun just watching him think things through on-screen.' Buoyed by this, he promised himself: 'From now on, it's all for me.'

Sobriety didn't last long. Things had been going well with Sarah for two years after Downey checked into Sierra Tucson and they continued to grow together. But, by 1991, despite managing to stay drug-free in Thailand and beyond, the demons soon returned once he got back into the swing of LA life. He tried to stay on the rails, eating out at celebrity haunt The Hollywood Canteen three or four times a week, pulling his Porsche 911 up outside while the restaurant was preparing to open and politely asking if they'd let him in for an early breakfast of Belgian waffles, strawberries and cream with his friends.

'Robert was never arrogant,' remembers John Young, who worked at the joint. 'He didn't push his celebrity. If the chef wasn't in, he'd leave. He was such a gentle, charming guy, I was always taken aback by that.' Sometimes he took his dad in. They talked a lot about wanting to be a serious actor and not wanting to get stuck in a rut like the Brat Pack. 'It's hard to imagine the demons he was fighting at the time,' adds Young.

Part of the problem was those so-called friends. Some, like Judd Nelson and Winona Ryder, did genuinely look out for him. Others were close to him, but their own party lifestyle only added fuel to the fire. Then there were the people who hooked into anyone famous they could get their hands on and quickly identified what it took to keep them in the entourage. Downey seemed to have a lot of them around. He was always a people person, it was a quality he'd inherited from his father. He liked observing them, finding out about them. "Robert's like James Joyce," says producer and friend, Chris Hanley. 'He can start talking to a cab driver or a dock worker . . . he's like that. I'd be going out for a jog at six-thirty [when I lived next door to him] and there'd be some weird person going 'Robert! Robert!' He would befriend sundry characters, just because he would get interested in them.'

He also knew drug dealers, people who trawled the posh nightclubs selling coke, pills or worse. Rayce Newman was one of them, a man dubbed 'The Hollywood Connection' because of his skills hooking famous folk up with their favourite illegal substance. Downey had got used to buzzing on the door of his apartment on Burton Way in Beverly Hills, even though LA dealers often made home deliveries. It was more difficult for Downey – Sarah was at home. He popped round to Newman's one evening, walking in chewing a straw. By this point he had started smoking cocaine, a far more potent way to ingest the drug that had previously led him to collapse while at Rob Lowe's house. He had just bought his Porsche and was enjoying driving it around. Newman was on his way out to see 2 Live Crew at mega-club Vertigo downtown, but Downey asked him if he could do a couple of lines first. Newman went into the bedroom, retrieved a mirror covered in a pile of coke and proffered it to his client. Without even bothering to divide the white powder into the trademark lines, Downey took a hundred-dollar bill from his pocket, rolled it up, thrust it into the pile and started hoovering it up his nose. By the time they reached Vertigo in the new car, the band had already finished.

Just before starting *Soapdish*, Downey found time to work with his father again on *Too Much Sun* (1990), a film co-written by Downey Sr's new girlfriend Laura Ernst. It told the story of a billionaire who dies and promises $250 million in his will to his kids if either of them can produce an heir within a year of his passing. The only problem is they are both gay. Co-starring Karate Kid Ralph Macchio and Eric Idle, Downey played a con man and also wrote and performed the title song. He enjoyed working on his father's films, but Downey Sr – though happy in love again with Ernst – had lost his pizzazz. *Rolling Stone* summed it up by saying the director had 'become what every true satirist fears most: outdated'.

Downey Jr tried more mainstream farce in *Soapdish* (1991), also starring Sally Field, Whoopi Goldberg and Kevin Kline. 'He was drinking cranberry juice and everything was completely fine,' says Cathy Moriarty, who played the target of his sexual longing in the film, which is set backstage on a daytime soap opera. 'We worked very well together. I let him do what he wanted to do and for some reason we meshed well.' Playing David Barnes – a producer who schemes with one of his supporting actresses to bump up her profile in exchange for sleeping with her – he held his own among a parade of heavyweight co-stars. The part was originally written for a 50-year-old actor, but director Michael Hoffman had cast him some years before in a dramedy called *Back East* which was never made and wanted to work with him again. He suggested it be rewritten for Downey. 'The studio at the time was a little bit like "really?"' says Hoffman. But he convinced the producers to look at what Downey could do. They agreed with Hoffman and cast him. Even though the actor knew little about the daytime world, he admitted getting his break there was something he considered before he had found success in movies. 'I thought if I could only get on a soap opera, everything would come together,' he said to the *Logansport Pharos Tribune* in 1991. 'I could work in New York, get an apartment, wouldn't have to work in restaurants.'

Soapdish grossed just $36 million at the box office, despite Downey's high hopes. 'I remember when we went to the premiere,' recalls Moriarty. 'He said, "I'd like to rock the world with this movie."' It wasn't to be.

Unfortunately, Sarah Jessica Parker had finally had enough. In 1991, she broke up with Downey after seven tumultuous years together and moved back to New York. They were both devastated, but Parker felt they were past the point of no return. Drugs weren't something that had ever been a part of her world and suddenly an addict had been thrown into it. She had done her best to help him through it – it had even worked a couple of times – but she couldn't fully right the ship. She had run through the gamut of emotions, from sympathy and understanding to resentment and anger and ultimately resignation. 'He's one of those tortured souls,' she said in a 1996 *Redbook* Interview. 'You feel so impotent. You're always wondering and waiting for a call from someone saying, "We went to his trailer to get him and he's dead." I felt so sad and by the end I felt exhausted.' Downey was gutted, but he had already started gearing up for *Chaplin* (1992) when it happened and the misery piled on the stress. 'I was in love with Sarah Jessica and love clearly was not enough,' he said. After the inevitable romantic fallout during which Sarah had a high-profile fling with John F. Kennedy Jr, the pair managed to reconnect as friends and started to write occasional letters to each other, or have intense five-minute conversations on the phone. Downey even wished her well with her new beau Matthew Broderick.

For Downey, it was the end of an era. But just around the corner was a strange man with baggy trousers and a moustache who would change his life.

Becoming Charlie

'I'd never done anything that I came to care about so much.'

(1993)

When Richard Attenborough announced in 1991 he was making a movie about the life of Charlie Chaplin, every young British actor immediately rang their agents and begged for an audition. The part had it all. It was a biopic, which are notoriously awards-friendly. The subject was an iconic celebrity – the writer, producer, director and star of some of the most well-loved films in history. Plus he was a great lover and had enough ups and downs, quirks and foibles to challenge the most adept RADA-trained thesp. It was, as they say, a star-making role.

So imagine everyone's surprise when Sir Dickie announced Charlie was to be played by a young American who had been floating around the fringes of Hollywood for a few years quietly making his name, but never quite breaking through. Suffice it to say, Attenborough came in for some stick in the press, who believed Chaplin should have been played by a Brit. Initially, the director agreed. 'Obviously, I would have preferred an English actor to have played a character who was born and bred in the East End of London as Charlie was,' he said. 'But I couldn't find one.' RSC veteran Antony Sher was just one of the people who had been mentioned as a possible candidate by Attenborough himself. Having made his decision, however, he was convinced. 'If you bring in a star, someone with other connotations, you start with a disadvantage,' countered the director. '[Downey] will be a world figure as an actor within a month of the film opening . . . He's an extraordinary boy.'

When he got the role, Downey was in something of a crisis. *Air America* had failed to take off at the box office, plus he was in the process of breaking up with Sarah Jessica Parker, his substance abuse was spiralling out of control again. He was eager to throw himself into something not only that he could actually be proud of, but that would take his mind off his problems at home.

In 1991, Attenborough and his longtime collaborator Diana Hawkins were finally able to announce their intentions to make their long-gestating project. Hawkins had had the idea four years previously to make a biopic of Charlie Chaplin, but despite Attenborough's Oscar for *Gandhi*, money was hard to come by. They had convinced Universal to take a punt on the film and now set about the near-impossible task of finding someone to fill Charlie's shoes. 'I believed it would be sacrilege to attempt to mimic any of Chaplin's great movie performances, so we had to find an actor who truly could be like the man himself,' said Attenborough. 'Another requirement was to find an actor with Charlie's amazing agility who could not only pull off the stunts Charlie used to do, but could also replicate his distinctive stance. If you ever saw Charlie out of character he walked and stood very much like a marionette. Finally, we needed an actor who had a fine ear for accents. Anyone can walk along twiddling a cane but it takes a man of real talent to capture Charlie's changing Cockney accent, which had a peculiarly pedantic edge to it.' Kenneth Branagh was interested in the role. Dustin Hoffman, Billy Crystal and Robin Williams were all names that came up. Attenborough and Hawkins were at a meeting with Marti Baum, their agent at

CAA (Creative Artists Agency) in Los Angeles, when they got their first taste of Downey, who was brought down to meet them by his own agent Bryan Lourd, whose office was upstairs. 'This mad character came in with black boot-polished hair all sticking up,' said the director. 'He said: "I am the one actor, Mr Attenborough, to play Charlie Chaplin. One day you'll come back to me. Goodbye, I'm very glad to have met you."'

Unaware of Downey's previous work, they listened to him courteously, marvelling at his worn clothes, two-day stubble and earring. 'I can't say I was totally convinced at that point,' admitted Attenborough. They continued their search, as well as beginning to build sets north of Los Angeles and in the UK's Shepperton Studios. Various names came up, but their ability to play the part had to be balanced against their box-office potential. It was a situation Attenborough didn't much like. He prided himself on his ability to cast. Whomever got the opportunity to take on this legendary figure had to be able to convey genius. Dickie was a huge Chaplin fan, had been brought up with his work, and the film had the backing of the Chaplin family, most notably his widow Oona (who died in September 1991) who continued to live in Vevey, Switzerland and who had granted the rights to her late husband's autobiography. Indeed, when Downey visited the director's house, he was amused to discover his cabinet and beds had been designed using the same white wood as Chaplin had chosen for his interiors. Casting presented further problems because the original version of the script – by Bryan Forbes and William Boyd – required Chaplin to be portrayed as a teenager. That cut out a lot of potential stars who wouldn't have been able to pull off the section of him as a young man. Eventually, they whittled the list down to seven actors – four American (one of whom was rumoured to be Jim Carrey) and three British – who they felt could do the role, but also please the backers. 'And sort of as an afterthought, we said, "Oh, you know that boy we met, we better give him a chance, let him come in",' said Diana Hawkins. 'I remember him being a little bit concerned about the audition for *Chaplin* because he knew it was a big undertaking,' says Cathy Moriarty. 'Plus he'd have to beat out all these people.'

Though slapstick wasn't a skill he had shown a lot on screen, Downey did have some empathy with Charlie. After all, he lived in a house that used to be owned by him. But he and his friend Billy Zane also spent a lot of time making each other laugh by doing pratfalls in their living room and, as Billy remembered, emulating 'our heroes Buster Keaton and Charlie Chaplin'. Downey was desperate to impress and spent six hours with a coach, practising for the screen test. 'He was the last one to test,' said Hawkins. 'He came in looking like Chaplin. He'd researched some old photographs, had his hair waved like Chaplin wore his when he was a young man. He had an impeccable English accent, his lines came across wonderfully and we said, "Thank you very much." He said: "I wonder if you'd let me go on a bit longer? I've got a little bit of comedy business to show you." He'd brought a stepladder with him and he did this routine where he came in with a stepladder as the Tramp, tried to put it up, got caught up in it, got his hand caught, his head caught. He went up the steps, it collapsed – and he finished on this amazing pratfall where he landed like a cat completely on his feet and we just knew, from a two or three-minute routine, the whole crew knew that this boy had to play Charlie Chaplin.'

Attenborough was to comment: 'He provided the fire in the belly and the turmoil behind the eyes. Robert had the ability to convey that driving, unqualified determination to achieve what he set out to achieve.'

However, convincing the studio was trickier. The stories about his extracurricular activities were an open secret in the industry, but the British director assured the worried executives everything would be all right. Furthermore, Downey had never been in a successful movie. Hoffman, Crystal and the like were movie stars, Downey was not. But Attenborough was adamant and unflinching. Downey was over the moon – and petrified. '*Chaplin* was the culmination of an opportunity – and the biggest humiliation I've ever experienced,' he said. 'It was like winning the lottery, then going to prison. I realised that nothing that had worked for me before was going to work here. I'd watch one of Charlie's films, but by the end of it, I was wildly depressed, because I realised that what he'd done in this twenty-minute short was more expressive and funnier than everything I've thought of doing my whole life.' He dived into the research, working with a dialect coach, learning how to play the violin and tennis left-handed and, most importantly, how to pull off the physical comedy Chaplin was famous for. But Universal were stalling. They began by offering Downey a puny salary, telling Attenborough the young actor desperately needed the role and would do it for nothing. The director was fuming and, as with Ben Kingsley in *Gandhi* before it, told the studio to either sign the contract or back out. Unfortunately, they called his bluff and put the film in turnaround. 'Even if this movie had never gone ahead, knowing that if it had been done it would have been done with me would have been reward enough,' recalled Downey.

Frantic, the producers looked around for other financiers and found Mario Kassar, a man best known for action films like *Terminator 2*. He watched and loved Downey's screen test and was keen to make the movie, although there were some provisos. He wanted the film to include the latter part of Chaplin's life in Switzerland, which would mean Downey having to age from a teenager to an octogenarian over the course of a two-hour film. The actual transformation using state-of-the-art make-up would take seven hours. When the director called 'Cut' in the middle of the afternoon after seeing his leading man could take no more, Downey would grab at the latex, tearing it off in strips.

Attenborough's team had reservations but, desperate to make the film, they acquiesced, bringing in Oscar-winning writer William Goldman to write the extra scenes. With the money now in place, Downey could bury himself in the Little Tramp's life. And how he did. 'Eighteen months of research brought forth an avalanche of information,' he said. In *In Entirely Up To You, Darling*, Attenborough's autobiography, Hawkins said of his devotion to the part, 'Robert, convinced of his spiritual affinity with Chaplin, went on to approach the task of reincarnating him for the film with a dedication which, at time, bordered on fanaticism.' He went to the Museum of the Moving Image in London, where he convinced the staff to let him try on one of Chaplin's actual Little Tramp suits and boots. The latter fit him perfectly, plunging him even further into the character. He also found a cigar stub in one of the pockets, a memento he treasured.

The money-wrangling gave him more time to perfect his performance – and to obsess. He worked with a movement coach to perfect Chaplin's posture and walk, constantly watched the star's films and spent hours with Attenborough's cockney chauffeur Bill Gadsdon to perfect his accent. He printed out digital photos of specific expressions so he could mimic them. Diana Hawkins recalled one bizarre night when he invited her and Attenborough over to his house in the Hollywood Hills for dinner. Even though there were only three of them eating, there were four place settings. Hawkins wondered who the third guest would be, only to be greeted by a tailor's dummy, dressed as the Little Tramp. 'I was like a pregnant woman going through a particularly difficult labour and Sir Richard was the dedicated midwife,' said Downey. 'I felt he would never ask me to do things he couldn't help me through, he would go through every moment with me. I would ring him up in the middle of the night because I couldn't sleep for worrying about some small detail of Charlie's life and he never seemed to mind. He might suggest that it could wait until morning but he never minded being called.'

Filming finally got under way towards the end of 1991. Attenborough had already formed a close, paternal bond with his leading man and wore a brown cowboy hat – a present from Downey – throughout most of the shoot. He made it easier for his star to hold his accent by filming almost chronologically. When Downey visited the parts of London Chaplin came from for research with his dialect coach Andrew Jack, he kept his cockney patter up the whole time. He did the same during the making of the film. The actor would listen to Debussy, thinking the composer's music contained some kind of geometric rhythms that would help him zone into his performance. At night, he would change it to Tom Petty in a bid to forget about the pressure he felt under. Doing all the stunts in the film meant there were several bruises, though he wore them as a badge of honour.

Charlie's actress daughter Geraldine, who played her own grandmother Hannah in the film, couldn't believe how well Downey captured the essence of her father. She had first seen him in action when Attenborough took her to a small theatre in Los Angeles to look at footage of Downey he had already shot. When the fifteen-minute reel was over, there was a long silence. Attenborough was worried he had blown it. Instead, she turned around to him and said, 'I have to tell you, I had never, ever dreamed that anybody could convince me that they were Daddy. But that young man *was* Daddy!' Later, after watching him further, she was moved to add, 'It was as if my father came down from heaven and inhabited and possessed him for the length of the movie. It was just so shocking . . . he's heartbreaking and he has my father's sense of melancholy. The first time I met him as the Little Tramp I hugged him and he hugged me and there I was with my father as a young man in my arms. We had quite a Freudian moment there.'

When the production went to film in Switzerland, Downey got a chance to visit Chaplin's home Manoir de Ban, a mansion overlooking Lake Geneva. During their Swiss sojourn, the actor would walk into the kitchen of the house where they were shooting where some of Chaplin's real-life children and grand-children sat, looking strangely at this man looking uncannily like their dead father, since he would be wearing the old-age make-up. While they were there, one of the legend's former maids gave Downey a wing collar Charlie had worn as the Tramp. Downey admitted he took it and kept it in a safe. Wearing the latex mask, his assistant would feed him tortellini one at a time, hold a cigarette or a straw up to his mouth, then grin when the star miraculously recovered the use of his hands to play away at the on-set piano. Attenborough, convinced they were getting lightning in a bottle, was proud of the way he had stood up for Downey. Downey's performance is all the more remarkable given his mental state during filming. He was suffering from depression as a result of his break-up from Sarah Jessica Parker and also struggling under the weight of expectation of playing such an iconic and potentially career-defining role. The film's associate producer Diana Hawkins remembered the star being driven onto the set most mornings bleary-eyed, having heard he was drinking a bottle of vodka every night just to get to sleep, as well as scoring drugs from an alley dealer any chance he got. Downey's behaviour was brought to the attention of director Richard Attenborough, who said he wouldn't intervene while he was getting such an incredible performance, not out of some sadistic apathy, but rather because he felt it was up to the actor how he lived his life.

He did try to curtail some of the excess, organising it so that Downey effectively had to walk through his director's bedroom to get out of the hotel where they were staying. But Downey was used to giving people the slip, especially after seven years with Sarah Jessica Parker. What's more, this wasn't the first time he had spent his downtime from shooting getting drunk and high. Far from being angry with Attenborough for allowing him to cut loose, as we have already heard, Downey subsequently acknowledged the director for being his 'midwife' during the *Chaplin* shoot. And, as Hawkins recalled, Downey was always on time and once on set was never anything less than professional and generous. It's also worth noting Attenborough kept in touch with the star later while he was in prison.

Ultimately, *Chaplin* was a seminal experience for the 27-year-old actor and rates as one of the highest points in his acting canon. Diana Hawkins remembered with fondness a moment from the end of filming – a glimpse of the man with the capacity to cause joy and frustration in equal measure. Asked to interrupt a European holiday to re-record some dialogue as the aged Chaplin, Downey arrived late and angry at a German recording studio. He glanced down at his pages of dialogue and then threw away the script. Attenborough asked him to provide a sound level and, in his gruff old-man voice, Downey barked: 'If you're happy and you know it, clap your hands!' He then proceeded to speak every line word-perfect, without once looking at his text, before jumping into a waiting car and being whisked away into the night. Everyone in the studio looked at each other in amazement, before Attenborough finally said, 'Would you believe it? The little bugger can act, sing, dance, play the piano, compose like an angel – and he's got a photographic memory!'

Downey believed that the film had changed the way he looked at his career. It gave him a sense of his cinematic lineage and shocked him into scrutinising the choices he had made thus far. Movies like *Air America* and *Chances Are* seemed like flippant decisions, made even when he knew he was getting into something he didn't want to. He resolved to act more on gut instinct and rely on his intuition to tell him whether he was doing a part for a good reason or simply to maintain his lifestyle.

He was petrified about the film coming out, scared that people would see him as a fraud, an imposter. 'Having the chance to play someone like Chaplin was to experience everything from feeling honoured, to waking up sweating, convinced I was an absolute sham,' he said. 'I went through a whole host of emotions in taking this role, from humility and frustration to feeling like I've really found myself. It has sent me off in all different directions – I feel reborn.' He couldn't get Chaplin out of his head, continuing to watch Charlie's films at night long after shooting wrapped, even though his friends told him to move on. By the time the premiere came around, he was telling reporters he was once again clean and sober. 'God, it was so nice experiencing that night after [the *Chaplin* gala screening] without the need for a drink,' he said to the *Salina Journal* in 1993. 'And also it was nice to remember the address of the place I was going afterward.'

The film, which also starred Kevin Kline, Dan Aykroyd, James Woods and Diane Lane, cost $35 million and received mixed reviews when it made its debut in the UK on 18 December 1992, before premiering in America a week later. Some appreciated the languid pacing, fine production design and recreation of period detail, as well as the flashback structure, which sees Anthony Hopkins playing a fictional biographer travelling to the dying Chaplin's home to quiz him on the vaguer parts of his life story. Others, like critic Roger Ebert in the *Chicago Sun-Times*, wanted to see more about Chaplin the film-maker, rather than Attenborough's focus on the star's personal life. '[*Chaplin*] was not that interested in revealing the secrets of the various marriages, romances and scandals which figured in his life, but that is a lack that Richard Attenborough is willing to compensate for,' Ebert writes. 'This is a disappointing, misguided movie that has all of the parts in place to be a much better one.' Peter Travers' review in *Rolling Stone* was just as scathing, though he seems to believe there wasn't enough of the icon's so-called 'dark side'. 'All the nuances Robert Downey Jr invests in playing Charlie Chaplin, the clown prince of the silent screen, are blunted by a skim job of a script and inert direction from that Madame Tussaud of film biographers, Richard Attenborough,' he wrote. The film does have its moments. When Downey gets a chance to perform Chaplin's slapstick early on in the piece it's phenomenal, especially his youthful vaudeville sketches and the impromptu audition for Mack Sennett. Then again later when they begin dealing with more adult and compelling topics like his paternity suit, his nemesis J. Edgar Hoover and the furore over his decision to make *The Great Dictator*, which allude to a complex, contrary character. But Attenborough seems so worried about offending anyone (apart from obvious baddies like Hoover) that no one ever gets truly examined, in the way a good biopic should. Great cinematic classics like *Modern Times* come and go without any sense of its impact. Chaplin goes from drunken impersonator to millionaire in the blink of an eye. Only when he ignores wife Paulette Goddard (Lane) and she dumps him in anguish does the viewer get any idea about how the movies took over his life and how hard he had to work at it.

The film's co-writer William Goldman summed up many people's frustrations. 'I think ultimately the reason the film did not work is that it is so hard to cover that span of years,' he told author Andy Dougan in *Actor's Director: Richard Attenborough Behind The Camera*. 'It just is. I had read the book [Chaplin's autobiography] and my impulse would have been simply to tell the story of the childhood . . . I would [have] tried to end the movie at the moment where Chaplin discovers the Little Tramp but that is not the movie that Dickie wanted to do.'

Nevertheless, in spite of the tepid reaction to the film as a whole, Downey's lead performance, in which he imbues the character with pathos, steel, wit, ambition and genuine comedic verve, was singled out for praise. Even Travers, who patently hated the movie, was moved by the actor's gifts. 'Everything you see Robert Downey Jr do in it – the way Chaplin moves, how he behaved as a mime – you could put it in a time capsule and use it to teach people about acting,' he remarked. Similarly, Roger Ebert wrote: 'Robert Downey Jr succeeds almost uncannily in playing Chaplin; the physical resemblance is convincing, but better is the way Downey captures Chaplin's spirit, even in costume as the Tramp.' The actor is particularly interesting when slathered in latex, wistfully reminiscing on the past and expressing sadness and fear through his eyes alone. When Chaplin talks about smiling through emotional pain, there's a brief glimpse into the soul of the actor himself.

Attenborough was right – Downey had become a world figure as an actor, a fact made flesh when he won a BAFTA Best Actor Award three months after the film opened, beating Daniel Day-Lewis for *Last of the Mohicans*, Stephen Rea for *The Crying Game* and Tim Robbins for *The Player*. The film scored nominations for Best Make-Up, as well as Best Costume and Production Design. He was also nominated for an Oscar, but lost to sentimental choice Al Pacino for *Scent of a Woman*. He briefly thought he would win the Academy Award, figuring another youngster Marisa Tomei had for her performance in *My Cousin Vinny* and because he bore a passing resemblance to the previous year's winner, Daniel Day-Lewis. But standing backstage waiting to present the award for Best Sound, he spotted the table where all the trophies were sitting. He noted how many there were, how this prestigious award was actually given to more people than he realised. He resolved not to think of it as such a big deal. When Pacino's name was called, he dutifully paid his respects, but even the cameraman filming him in his seat joked that the gesture was one of the better pieces of acting he had seen that year. He was disappointed, but genuinely honoured to have been nominated, even if he thought he had been snubbed for *Less Than Zero*. Nonetheless, he had finally been recognised by his peers in a public setting. It was an Oscar nomination, an actor's dream. The only way now was up.

Marriage and Fatherhood

'It's time to do something a little more courageous than just make faces for cash and chicken.' (2005)

Love strikes fast in Hollywood. If you're Robert Downey Jr, it can take just 42 days. Seven years without an engagement in sight with Sarah Jessica Parker and 42 days was all it took to get Deborah Falconer to say 'I do'. He even got a big black woman to conduct a house-blessing to clear out the spectre of his ex. Falconer was a girl-about-town – a model, actress, aspiring singer/songwriter. Mostly, though, she was a nightclub hostess, working at BC on the Strip. 'Debbie was lovely, very sweet,' says John Young, who worked with her there. 'She was always quite personable. She was tall and lovely looking – one of those people who have that confidence about them.' She was certainly beautiful: big pouty lips, long brown hair, svelte figure. A stunner to be sure, but not aloof.

She was born in Sacramento; her parents divorced when she was two and as a child she travelled back and forth between her mother and her father, who was a lounge singer. Occasionally she would get up on stage at a club called The Palomino Room and sing with him. She dropped out of college and headed to LA, where her beauty and height quickly secured her some modelling gigs, as well as a couple of acting roles in Oliver Stone's *The Doors* and *Pyrates*, alongside Kevin Bacon. She didn't enjoy it; music was always her first love and she wasn't sure if she was any good in front of the camera.

Falconer had briefly dated his friend Josh Richman and Downey knew her vaguely from the circuit, but had always been with Sarah. One night, he was out on a date at an art gallery with another girl when he saw her crying over a break-up. He invited her to join them and immediately realised she was the one he wanted to be with. A short while later, she called him up at home and asked if he wanted to meet. And so it began. It was a tumultuous time. During their first date, some of Downey's friends and family staged an intervention in a bid to get him off drugs again. 'They were all looking at me like I was the devil's child,' she said, though she later found it funny. Humour played a big part in their relationship – known for her raconteurial skill, she appreciated and matched his biting humour and was up for anything. As a friend remembers: 'She can do Robert better than Robert.' After six weeks, they drove quietly to Northern California and got married in her mother's backyard in Walnut Creek on 29 May 1992. Their best friends didn't know about it until they read it in the papers. 'Basically, I got married fast because I don't think many people ever get a chance in life to do what they want when they want,' Downey told *GQ*. 'I took the opportunity not to be one of those guys who, three years later, goes "God, I fucked up, she was the one, she had it all and I was so selfish".'

Although diabetic, she was also into drugs, but the pair initially tried going on the wagon together – sorting out the house, staying in, dressing up in Chaplin outfits that Downey managed to blag from the shoot. At five-foot-nine, Deborah was the same size as him and fitted into the clothes perfectly. The lessons learned from his parents were ones he was able to apply to his new marriage. His dad would always go away, then wander back to the family home and expect everything to be all right. Downey realised that was not enough and sought to do the opposite. He tried to shrug off the past. He dug a hole in the backyard and buried his outfits from *Less Than Zero* in a symbolic ceremony. Far from being freaked out, Falconer brought him some lunch and let him get on with it.

But sobriety didn't last, not when there was so much fun to be had and they had each found the perfect person to have it with. They loved doing crazy things, like taking part in Jean-Paul Gaultier's West Coast fashion show where Downey wore a striped sailor's shirt, morning coat and leggings, all of which was part of the dress Deborah was wearing as she walked down the catwalk beside him. He liked challenging people's expectations – some of the audience that night thought it was a bad career move, especially when he pirouetted and walked back down the catwalk, waggling his bottom as hard as he could. Downey didn't care. He thought about giving it all up, just hanging out with his wife, letting her do the acting, being her assistant. But the artist in him wouldn't let that idea dwell for long. Indeed, in 1993 he released three movies – the supernatural romcom *Heart and Souls*, political documentary *The Last Party* and Robert Altman's classic *Short Cuts*.

It's always difficult coming back after a celebrated role. Do you plough straight back in and capitalise on your new buzz, or wait patiently until the next award-friendly part comes along? Downey did a bit of both, going mainstream with *Heart and Souls* and Oscar-bait for Altman. As for *The Last Party*, he shot it in 1992, during the presidential campaign. Hope was high, Clinton was playing the saxophone, promising change, spurring the youth of America to cast off their apathy and make him their leader. Downey's friend Josh Richman was keen to make a film about the Democratic Convention and teamed up with another twentysomething LA gadabout Donovan Leitch to produce it. Needing money, Richman had the idea of asking his movie-star friend to front it. He agreed and before long they were making a full-length feature documentary, co-directed by Mark Benjamin and Marc Levin and covering both conventions as well as the hot-button issues of the campaign like drugs and abortion. Downey had indulged in politics before, but mostly it seemed to impress Sarah Jessica Parker or friends like Judd Nelson. This suited the film-makers who, Levin said, 'picked a pop star who admitted he didn't know much about the system'.

A fully immersive journey, it's one of the few – and remarkably lesser seen, despite being on YouTube – chances to see the star at his most candid and often most vulnerable. He's also sincere and a good host who encourages people to talk, though his attention wanes as the razzmatazz of the conventions takes over. In fact, the purely political sections of the movie are the least interesting, touching on AIDS awareness and the bias of the liberal media without getting to the nitty-gritty of the issues. But it's when the film-makers concentrate on Downey's private life (with political activism acting as a pseudo-reason for doing so) that the documentary is at its most revealing. There are two meetings with his father that shed some light on their relationship. In the latter, we also meet Laura Ernst, by now Downey Sr's second wife, who is in a wheelchair suffering from amyotrophic lateral sclerosis (ALS) and whom Downey Jr touchingly calls 'my other mother'. The first, however, is early in the film. 'Why did you make me ugly and shiny?' berates Downey jokingly to his dad. 'I have zits and I'm shiny and I'm not happy.' It's at the last remark that a tension hits the room, as his father decides how to answer. They obviously have a closeness – there's a lot of hugging and kissing – but there's a strange energy whenever they're together. Straight afterwards, Downey Sr admits, 'I'm just happy he's here,' and after revealing there were many times he thought that might not be the case, Junior does an expert job of stopping further prying by telling the off-camera interviewer it's none of his business. The film ends with the father telling his son, 'I'm glad I know more about you than you know about me.'

Downey's also honest about his attitude to women and his parents' divorce in two diary-style segments. With the latter, he looks uncomfortable as he remembers how his father and Elsie were always thought of as the couple who would never split. This leads onto the former, which is particularly insightful considering he had only recently got married, when he says, 'Somewhere along the line I became really intimidated by the idea of a real trust and closeness.' Falconer makes several appearances, as Downey on the voice-over spouts lines like 'with intimacy comes responsibility' and talks about marriage being an 'ideal state' for excitement and creativity.

But the most startling sections are those in which he acts very oddly, though it's difficult to tell whether it's at the urging of the documentary-makers, or under his own steam. He runs through a park in a pair of red Y-fronts before sitting with his knees crossed in some kind of mock protest against boredom. And in one of the more potent scenes, he engages in a hearty argument against capitalism with a group of Wall Street traders before swimming fully clothed in an ornamental water feature (recalling his high school/mall-banning incident). Then, in the nuttiest bit of the film, he bounces around on all fours like a frog, though he's keen to make sure the audience realises it's supposed to be a goat. This 'goat boy' is an alter ego he uses to explain his more extreme tendencies, saying he wasn't brought up to believe in delayed gratification. It comes across as bizarre and show-offy. But when a random young onlooker tells him to have more self-respect after seeing his semi-naked antics and they end up discussing the hell of parental separation, you see Downey's humanity shine through. 'There's a lot of imperfections going on in my life,' he says. 'But I'm trying to be comfortable with them.'

Short Cuts was a different fish, an ensemble film based on intertwining Raymond Carver stories that fit firmly into the Altman canon among classics like *Nashville* and *M*A*S*H*. Despite being one of the hottest stars in the movie, he happily plays second fiddle to a revolving cast that includes Matthew Modine, Julianne Moore, Tim Robbins and Andie MacDowell. He is Bill, a prosthetic make-up artist who spends most of his time on-screen (which isn't much) jabbering away to his wife Lili Taylor or his friends Chris Penn and Jennifer Jason Leigh. Deborah Falconer also shows up near the end as a 'sexy girl' he tries to chat up with Penn, leading to one of the film's brutal denouements amid the chaos of a Los Angeles earthquake. No doubt he thought the film would look good on his CV, and an Altman set is renowned as an exciting place to be, but it was an interesting choice for an actor straight after an Oscar nomination. *Short Cuts* was reviewed well, being called 'cool, complex and funny' by *Empire* magazine and '[Altman's] most complex and full-bodied human comedy since *Nashville*' by *Variety*. Although the cast was highly praised, it was the director who won most of the plaudits.

The two-day facial growth, shorts-and-vest combo, reefer-smoking and potty mouth were left firmly behind for *Heart and Souls*, which is a far more adept attempt to profit commercially from his *Chaplin*-earned kudos. Ostensibly a straightforward studio romcom, closer viewing unearths a far shrewder decision on the actor's part. The film begins with the death of four disparate (yet likeable) characters played by Charles Grodin, Tom Sizemore, Alfre Woodard and Kyra Sedgwick in a bus crash. Nearby, Thomas Reilly is born in a car and the four dead souls are whooshed into him as a quartet of guardian angels he can see and hear. After a while, they decide to stop talking to him and let him get on with his life. Cut to 30 years later and Thomas (played by Downey) is a self-absorbed yuppie who has forgotten these angels until they find out they have to use him to fulfil their destinies so they can get to heaven. The extra acting challenge comes in the form of the souls' ability to take over Thomas's body, meaning Downey has to *play* all four characters as well as his own. Taking a cue from his time on *Chaplin* when he dived so deep into the role it sometimes seemed like he wouldn't come out the other side, he originally planned to set up video cameras around the set to record Sizemore, Woodard, Grodin and Sedgwick's movements, which he would then interpret before the requisite scenes. But whether it was *Chaplin* fatigue, or simply the belief *Heart and Souls* wasn't quite worthy of such excesses, he chose not to do it. 'I observed them closely, then trusted my instincts,' he said. 'I thought there should be something spontaneous, rather than studied, about this performance.' Director Ron Underwood didn't care how he did it, as long as he was able to pull it off. 'We had to have someone with very great personal charm, who would make you root for this guy even when he's pretty abrasive toward the beginning,' he said to the *Syracuse Herald*, just after the film was released, 'but who also had the acting ability to pull the character changes off. There was no one else around, of the right age, who could have done it except Robert Downey Jr. I honestly don't know if the film could have been made without him.' The film received decent reviews and, as ever, Downey scored highly with the critics, who at the time appeared to be the only ones other than the film-makers themselves who believed he should be a huge box-office star. 'Downey shows an explosive talent for physical comedy,' wrote *Rolling Stone*, after calling the film 'a magical fantasy'. '[It's put to use] most memorably at a business meeting when a feminine spirit moves him and at a B. B. King concert when a shy Grodin uses him to sing a national anthem. The scene is a show-stopper, highlighting a potently acted, buoyantly funny film that trades on emotion without making you gag on it.'

They're right. Downey gives a lovely, warm performance – and looks fantastically handsome in a perfectly cut suit – even if he often seems more like a supporting player to his ghostly partners than a leading man, not even appearing until half an hour in. The fivesome have a natural chemistry and while there's some sentimentality, it's balanced out by its sweetness and pace. But what really makes the movie are the moments his body is taken over, though as he commented, 'It was tricky, because I had to suggest each of the other characters without mimicking them, which would have belittled the whole thing.' Utilising some of the comedic movement skills he used as the Little Tramp, his possessions scenes are laugh-out-loud funny, as well as acrobatic and frenetic to watch. As Thomas has to explain to a disbelieving onlooker: 'I'm not drunk. I'm not on drugs.'

Downey showed up to the premiere of *Heart and Souls* with his wife, who was by this time on the brink of giving birth. Falconer had fallen pregnant at the beginning of December 1992 and the couple were ecstatic about the impending birth of their first child. She had cleaned up again and now they waited anxiously for the big moment. On 7 September 1993, Falconer gave birth to a son, whom they named Indio. Anthony Michael Hall was asked to be his godfather. As for any couple, parenting came as a shock, especially for a pair who were used to the flexible and nightlife-based existence of a well-paid movie star. Nonetheless, they threw themselves into it. They moved to a new home just north of Los Angeles and tried to sell the Chaplin house. It became one of their sober periods, as they raised their son and concentrated on keeping him out of the public eye.

Downey was still working hard. Director Oliver Stone had toyed with casting real-life tabloid reporter Geraldo Rivera in his new media satire *Natural Born Killers* (1994), but eventually decided he wanted a proper actor. He was looking for someone to play Wayne Gale, the relentless gutter hack and host of 'American Maniacs', who idolises (mostly for ratings and glory) serial killers Mickey and Mallory Knox in Quentin Tarantino's gory, buzz-worthy script. Stone had wanted to work with Downey for some time and was an Oscar-winner himself, so when he called and asked the actor to play the part, Downey eagerly accepted. He grew a beard and let his hair get longer, as well as asking the producers if there was someone he could hang out with to get a feel for the character. The king of tabloid TV at the time was journalist Steve Dunleavy, an Australian ex-pat in New York, whose writing for the *New York Post* and hard-hitting exposé reports on the syndicated series *A Current Affair* had lent him a certain notoriety. Producer Don Murphy arranged for Downey to hang out with Dunleavy to get a feel for his methods. 'To my disappointment, I don't know whether it was to his disappointment, when he went with me and a crew on an interview, it was a really tame interview,' remembers the Australian. 'Rather than going with me to South America to do the drugs wars!' Instead, the pair visited heavyweight boxer Riddick Bowe. 'If he was looking for blazing guns, that certainly wasn't it,' says Dunleavy.

'He was interested in the subject, I don't think he was interested in me,' he adds. 'He was very intense, didn't ask any probing questions. He did sit in on our editorial meetings. He was very quiet, he wasn't the least bit bored and you got the impression he was soaking up every word that was said.' Unfortunately for Dunleavy, who is himself a keen boozer, there were no heavy nights. 'It was just a couple of gentle beers, we were in Virginia I think,' he recalls. 'Nothing over the top. I was a bit disappointed myself – I wanted to get one on!'

Still, the journalist must have made more of an impact than he thought. By the time he returned to the *Natural Born Killers* set, Wayne Gale had an Australian accent. 'I've been out of Australia for 50 years, so the accent has mellowed a bit,' laughs Dunleavy. 'But I'll tell you this, his accent stunned me. I thought it was terrific.' Downey loved his new voice, seeing it as a way into the character. He'd sometimes keep it after work, pitching up to a restaurant and talking in booming Aussie. It always signalled the start of a funny routine.

Life on an Oliver Stone film is not an easy ride. He pumped loud, industrial rock music through speakers onto the set to ratchet up the energy and when everyone got overheated in the New Mexico locations, he refused to let them use fans. As for the weekends, Downey described them as 'basically pagan Rome 26AD'. He loved having the opportunity to go to such extremes, especially because it was all in the name of radical comedy. 'He was forever throwing lavish dinners, where he'd invite everyone from the day players to the sound guys,' said producer Jane Hamsher in her memoir *Killer Instinct*. 'He really just wanted everyone to be happy and had a genuine desire to be loved . . . I'll say that there is no doubt that Robert loves to party, but I never saw him out of control or in such bad shape that he couldn't do his job. As he told me one time, "I'm a 50/50 man – if I can feel great 50 per cent of the time, I'm willing to feel like shit for the other 50".'

To those who have seen *Natural Born Killers*, the shoot probably sounds about as chaotic as the end product. It's a hyperbolic, scattergun affair that works on some levels and is frighteningly facile and idiotic on others. It was the cause of much consternation in the more conservative press, who used it as an excuse to write about the dangers of movie violence. But in fact it's far too silly to be used as an example of anything and mostly comes across like a rather patronising vision by an ageing man (the director was in his late forties at the time) of what 'youth' film-making should look like. Stone is undoubtedly a fine film-maker and there are some effective sequences, like a twisted family sitcom parody and a genuinely oppressive prison riot shot in a real jail (The Roundhouse at the Stateville Correctional Center, Illinois, where the minimum term is two life sentences). But much of the efficacy is lost in the mish-mash of subliminal frames, overacting and handheld camerawork. Downey committed to the carnage, even though the environment was like 'purgatory on a per diem', or 'psychological warfare'. But even he had his limits. While he and fellow actors Woody Harrelson, Juliette Lewis and Arliss Howard were escaping through the bowels of the prison during the finale, he realised the sewage pipes were dripping. 'That means we're walking through criminal shit,' he said. 'Seventy-eight per cent of these guys are HIV positive. And the others, it's their shit!' He decided his work for the day was over.

If it had been another film, Downey could well have been Oscar-nominated for his portrayal of Wayne Gale, but such was the reaction to *Natural Born Killers*, it was never going to happen. 'There was a fuss in the States about [the film],' he said. 'It pushes some weird buttons, you know, and I don't necessarily endorse the film. It's pretty violent, but it's less violent than films you see on aeroplanes sometimes. I don't really get it. The news programmes fed off each other, just like Wayne did in the film. It's just as Wayne would have wanted it. I was already on my next movie when the controversy blew up, but it was weird just the same.' He had a more philosophical view on the hullabaloo. 'On Main Street in Santa Monica, there's this statue,' he said. 'It's of this ballerina's body with a clown's head and people freak out about it. You never know what's going to freak people out.'

Gale provides the only genuine laughs in the movie (most of them not related to his eighties rock-band hairdo), pillorying a voracious media, lampooning people's obsession with fame even when it comes in the form of a murderer, and spouting lines like: 'I'm doing a benefit tonight for Homeless Transsexual Veterans.'

Dunleavy isn't annoyed about his filmic 'alter ego'. 'I don't give two tucks of a Turkish tit!' he says. 'My mates never mention it. And the average punter doesn't even know.' So Downey didn't go too far? 'No. Hollywood isn't the Vatican. Movies are designed to be over the top. I've seen cop movies and gangster movies where I've seen the people involved. Of course it's over the top.'

After talking of stopping to think about creative choices and extending himself with films like *The Last Party*, it's disappointing that *Only You* (1994) was one of the first he made soon afterwards. The pedigree was there – Marisa Tomei in a lead role having won an Oscar for *My Cousin Vinny* and director Norman Jewison, best known for *In the Heat of the Night*, but more recently for acclaimed romances like *Moonstruck*. Set in Italy, it's about a young woman called Faith (Tomei) who was given, so she believes, the name of the man she is destined to marry by a gypsy fortune-teller when she was a little girl. Days before her wedding to a good-guy podiatrist, she is thrust into a journey for true love when she accidentally talks to 'Damon Bradley' on the phone, following him to Rome and Positano. There, she meets Peter

Wright (Downey) and, through a series of mistaken identities, destiny attempts to prevail. It was Downey's highest-paying job ever – two-and-a-quarter million dollars for seven weeks' work – but its mercenary nature shines through. He admitted as much: 'With *Only You*, it was like "Oh. I'm broke again. What, Italy? Wow, that'll get me out of debt, seven weeks, no accent, pair of chinos." It was great.' In fact, the film dampens all his best qualities. For the first time, his role could have been played by any number of other actors, provided they didn't mind wearing cavernous trousers and had an Italian phrasebook. Tomei is a talented actress, but has always suited more edgy material. Her character here is irritating and has a dubious attitude to marriage from the start. On the first day of rehearsals, Jewison leaned over to Downey and whispered, 'This guy's light.' Downey's portrayal of Peter apparently still had some Wayne Gale in him. The film would have been more watchable had they left that darkness in. *Only You* paid the rent (and got him an Italian stamp in his passport), but it didn't push him creatively. And when he wasn't being challenged at work, it meant more free time for his brain. Which meant one thing . . .

Getting a Taste for It

'I've always been the type of fellow to put all my eggs in one basket and then promptly take a dump in the basket.' (2003)

Fatherhood wasn't changing Robert Downey Jr as much as everyone hoped it would, at least not in those early stages. There's no doubt he doted on his son and revelled in his new role as much as he could, but that didn't seem to be putting a stop to some of his other more self-destructive tendencies. The Downeys were living just north of Malibu in a two-storey glass-and-wood house backing onto the coast. A reflecting pool separated the main residence from a guest house, which the couple had converted into a music studio. The walls were decorated with large paintings in the style of the old masters and a baby grand piano sat alongside an antique chaise longue. The curtains in their bedroom – which they often shared with cats and two dogs – were Indian saris and the master bathroom housed a huge Roman bath made of marble. Photos of Indio were dotted throughout the house, a reminder of Downey's new life.

He told anyone who would listen he had calmed down; he

worried that people didn't see him as a family man, started getting angry at people who broke the speed limit when he was ferrying Indio around and was concentrating on being more selfless. He was keen to make sure his son didn't have the laissez-faire upbringing he went through – indeed his own father appreciated the effect his grandchild was having.

Unfortunately, all the goodwill in the world won't necessarily stop an addict. 'He was high as a kite,' says a young woman who was working at a Malibu gift shop in the summer of 1994 when she got a visit from the star and his son. 'It was one of those posh shops that sells things to people who have everything,' she continues. 'Celebrities came in all the time and I was rarely put off by any of them. But one day, Robert came in with his son. Three things became immediately clear – he loved his son more than anything in the world, he was high and he was really nice. He sort of drifted around the shop picking up the most random purchases which me and my assistant just kept throwing into bags while watching his son carefully to be sure he didn't bump into anything or drop him, which he didn't. About 40 minutes later, with about a thousand dollars' worth of stuff, we handed him his bags and he left. It was only ten minutes later we both realised that neither of us had charged him for anything! To be honest, I don't think he realised he did it, I think he was just so high it all sort of went over his head.'

Downey was convinced he wasn't dropping the ball with his son and he was definitely putting in the time, but he was about to step into uncharted territory. He had started with marijuana, graduated to cocaine before he reached Lincoln Junior High and since then had indulged in a variety of drugs, including mushrooms, speed and good old-fashioned booze. But he had always avoided heroin, saying he would never touch crack or smack. Until now. The reasons he tried it are murky and some of the stories around his beginnings with it are outlandish. One tale suggests an A-list actor turned him on to it. Whatever the case, it signalled a new era in his behaviour. He wasn't injecting, only smoking it like he had done with cocaine. He developed what he called his 'lizard brain', which was the ability to go from a hotel room in any major city where he was working and return within 45 minutes carrying heroin. Often he would be recognised, but that would generally help with the buying process. He had always been a big spender, whether it was on designer clothes or a sports car. Having just bought the house and with an extra body to provide for, he was running through his account like never before, especially because account management (despite Sarah Jessica's best efforts) was never high on his list of priorities. The drugs and booze cost, too. And with a dwindling bank balance and a celebrity lifestyle to accommodate, there was nothing to do but sign up for as much work as possible.

Home for the Holidays (1995) was another ensemble film, a farcical festive drama about a kooky family in Baltimore. It was directed by Jodie Foster and starred Holly Hunter as an art restorer who returns home for Thanksgiving only for much hilarity and soul-searching to ensue. Downey is Tommy Larson, Hunter's gay brother who likes to stir trouble. In the original draft of the script, he wasn't gay, but as the story developed Tommy's homosexuality was introduced as a reason why he is so unrelentingly obnoxious. Foster's idea was that though his family appear to accept him (and the surprise news he has 'married' his lover), it hasn't been an easy road. Rather than deal with that, Tommy concentrates on trying to make everyone laugh. Watching the film with no prior knowledge, audiences probably wouldn't spot the fact it was the first movie on which Downey smoked black-tar heroin throughout the shoot. It's also the first time he admits to being high on set, spending the downtime in his trailer working on various complicated projects that seemed pertinent seen when through the prism of a Class A drug user.

Though he considers it one of his most relaxed performances, his acting actually tends towards the opposite end of the emotional scale. It's a showy role, over the top and self-consciously quirky, though much of that is to do with the film, which tries to tread a fine balance between slapstick humour and emotive posturing. In many ways, he is the soul of the piece. Looking less kempt than he has before, with collar-length hair and a pasty complexion, he also displays an increasingly slim physique. Stuart Kleinman was *Home for the Holidays*' executive producer. He remembers a young man struggling with family problems, but always generating something exciting on set. 'I was obviously concerned as a producer, but only because you're always concerned when actors are having personal problems,' he says. 'He had problems with his wife, but he didn't ever create problems for us as producers.' In fact, the film-makers joked about giving him a co-writing credit such were his improvisational contributions to the script.

'Downey's a different beast,' said Foster. 'He can't say the same thing twice.' She noted how he would get bored and would let him create dialogue simply to make it fun for him.

'Jodie grew up in Hollywood,' says Kleinman. 'She's more comfortable working from a pure script.' Certainly, Foster believes improvising can be a dangerously arrogant and negative approach, but admitted Downey was the only one who could pull it off. 'He has an amazing brain,' she said. 'There are a few other scenes you can't believe come out of his sick little mind at the time.'

Making the film echoed *Less Than Zero*, where he could go out all night doing illicit substances, then come in and deliver. In his mind, there was no accountability. As long as he was showing up and doing what he was asked – to his usual self-imposed high standards, of course – that was all that mattered. The problem is, acting was easy for him. Jodie Foster could see things were potentially about to get a lot worse. She thought he was one step from being out of control, from falling off the bar stool. She wrote him a letter begging him to seek help, telling him he may have got away with it on *Home for the Holidays* but he wouldn't again. Downey just laughed and carried on with what he was doing. While Kleinman doesn't say he witnessed drug-taking or addict-like behaviour, he admits he knew the star was going out a lot. 'I knew that and I scolded him a few times and I scolded the people he was going out with,' he says. 'But the going out is not the issue, the issue is whether you show up. You have issues like insurance and schedules and budgets.'

Downey made a couple of close friendships on the film, most notably with his on-screen mother, played by Anne Bancroft. '[They] fell immediately into their roles,' says Kleinman. 'Their relationship was almost like the mother and son in the movie.' When Downey goofed around, Bancroft took him to task, giving him a real sense of maternal discipline. After the shoot, the film-makers took him aside and had a conversation about his bad habits. He appeared to be well aware of what was going on and the problems he faced. 'He loved his wife, he loved his kid and whatever was going on was probably affecting that,' says Kleinman. More suited to television viewing – *Empire* magazine called it 'likeable in that cosy, wet Sunday afternoon, family sort of way' – *Home for the Holidays* didn't make much of an impact at the box office when it came out at the end of 1995. Critics noted the episodic nature, some saying the comedy was too forced or prosaic. But *Variety* picked up on Downey's efforts, saying he 'shines – his multi-nuanced portrayal of a gay man is notably unstereotypical'.

The home problems Kleinman talks of must have related to Downey's newfound love of heroin. Falconer said later that drugs were the demise of their marriage and, as with Parker before her, they were the cause of many arguments during her relationship with her husband. She watched Indio, aware that despite his lack of years he was inadvertently witnessing his father's indiscretions, even if it didn't appear to directly affect him.

Life chez Downey was still exciting, though. They would visit their friend Billy Zane, where Downey would battle Tom Cruise at ping-pong while the wives nattered away in the next room. Even though he turned 30 in April 1995 he was still indulging his youthful pursuits. One day, when Cruise beat him, Downey tried to jump the net and congratulate him, resulting in a broken table-tennis table. 'He sent me a better table than the one he broke,' said Zane. Downey was matter of fact about it: 'I jumped the net because I still like breaking things.'

The heavy weight of drug abuse was beginning to take its toll when *Restoration* finally made its bow in limited US cinemas at the tail-end of 1995, just in time for Oscar consideration. Journalists attending the press junket in London were struck by Robert's kooky demeanour, which appeared narcotically induced. Its release had been delayed by eighteen months thanks to story concerns and re-shoots – so long, in fact, that Downey had had the time to play a supporting role in a film version of *Richard III* (1995) starring Ian McKellen, an actor he befriended on the initial *Restoration* shoot in England during 1994. The latter movie was directed by his *Soapdish* helmer Michael Hoffman, adapted from a novel by Rose Tremain. It tells the story of Robert Merivel, a doctor during the reign of Charles II (Sam Neill) who longs for the good life in the king's court and achieves it after accidentally saving one of His Majesty's royal dogs. A period of debauchery follows until he makes a deal with the monarch and is married off to one of Charles's mistresses, on the proviso she is the one person he can't fall in love with. Inevitably, he makes a pass at her and falls out of favour. He returns to work with his Quaker friend John Pearce, played by David Thewlis, at a mental institution where he meets and impregnates an Irish cuckold (Meg Ryan). When she dies in childbirth, he pledges to help cure London of the plague and inevitably gets caught up in the Great Fire of 1666 before everything is resolved.

This almost *Zelig*-like period tale looks fantastic and in fact won two Oscars for Art Direction and Costume Design. It's not hard to see why – all the money is up on the screen, even though Hoffman says a lot was done with not very much, banking on the audience seeing two big CGI scenes of London and buying the rest of the cinematic world. Working again with his *Chaplin* dialect coach Andrew Jack, Downey pulls off a masterly English accent, even joking that people thought he was now actually a British actor. 'Sometimes I'd feel self-conscious about [the voice],' he said. 'But more often than not I was too hot, sweaty and tired to worry too much about it.'

On screen, he looks suitably foppish in flowing curls and breeches, though his enjoyment at making *Heart and Souls* because he had only one costume was in opposite effect here as he dealt with the heavy, embroidered finery. 'With the hours I was working and the costumes and everything else, it got to a point where I said, 'You let me know when you're three minutes away and I'll throw those rags on',' he said. 'We got it down to a science in the end.' He also had to do some serious walking practice in the buckled high heels worn by men of the seventeenth century. 'There was this whole thing about these special shoes that they were going to make me,' he said. 'They traced the outline of my foot, sent it to Italy and it came back, but come the day of the shoot, they gave me these size sevens. It was like I was running up and down these hallways with some leftover shoes from *Dangerous Liaisons*. I wondered why they bothered sending my foot outline to Italy if that's all I got. And besides, I take a nine.'

Early buzz on the film suggested it wasn't liked by preview audiences and Downey worried the film company were pandering to the poor test scores, spoiling the original intention to make a bawdy romp. The end result does have some craziness in it – Downey having sex with a whore and running round a palace wearing only a feather to protect his modesty among it – but the rest is resolutely PG material, focusing more on the dour aspects of the era like illness and poverty, as well as suggesting Merivel's involvement in early examples of psychiatry.

'A lot of the movie was fun, a lot of it was gruelling,' said Downey, who was challenged by his director to be more honest than ever before and worry less about being entertaining. 'It was a much more down and dirty experience than Robert was necessarily used to,' says Hoffman. 'But he embraces it. I always think the testament is what does the crew think of the actor? The crew just adored him.' Speaking about Mike Leigh graduate Thewlis as well as himself, Downey said, 'I think for two guys who are sometimes most comfortable being spontaneous and loose, without the constrictions of a film like *Restoration*, it was a challenge.' He continued as before to improvise, occasionally to the annoyance of Michael Hoffman, who told him to focus on saying the lines in the script better, rather than trying to write new ones. Downey argued the actor knew his character the best and any performer with a talent for writing should be encouraged to rewrite where he deems it necessary.

Ian McKellen, playing Merivel's doting manservant Will, was struck by his co-star's talent and attitude, especially among other

British actors like Hugh Grant and Polly Walker. 'Some of the English actors who should have done better assumed an artificial archness as they aimed for the subtleties of the Caroline period,' he wrote on his website. 'Robert meanwhile improvised hilariously for the camera, accent and stylishness never faltering.' One time, McKellen challenged him to do something unexpected on-screen. The scene – which never made it into the final cut – saw Downey fake-vomiting into a carved wooden box while carrying a pineapple. McKellen wondered: 'My stifled guffaw must have ruined the take.'

Downey appreciated having such a celebrated thespian around and Hoffman acknowledges that sometimes it's tough for American actors to come and shoot something in Britain with English actors, because there is a sense that they are all theatre-trained, 'real' actors. 'Ian was so gracious and so warm in terms of helping Robert get over that.' Said Downey: 'I didn't mind Ian playing my servant, I don't mind being catered for by a real knight. I just remember being down in Dorset with Ian and he was giving me a copy of *Coriolanus* and spontaneously launched into a monologue from it and I literally felt the energy change in the room.'

Downey continued, '[He] said it would help get the film financed if I took the role in *Richard III*. What am I going to say to that? We became pretty big friends during *Restoration* and it was great to come back to England because I hadn't been back here for, oh, hours. I hadn't studied Shakespeare before doing *Richard III*. I didn't know anything about it. I won't be starting, I'm not particularly interested.'

Restoration is the kind of film now that would probably be a Sunday-night mini-series co-production between the BBC and HBO rather than a feature. But it gave Downey the chance to be centre stage again, carrying the film's fortunes on his back despite

A-list support from a dubiously accented Meg Ryan and a pre-megastardom Hugh Grant, as well as Neill and Thewlis. 'It did put pressure on me,' said Downey. 'I want to be a character actor and play some supporting roles for a change. But sometimes you don't pay attention to the pressure because you want to get the job done. Every once in a while you wake up screaming, "Mommy, save me!"'

A lot of the time on set was spent practising the baroque oboe, which Merivel plays only a couple of times during the movie. Such was Downey's real-life musical bent that he felt compelled to make it as real as possible. 'It wasn't only obsession that made me do it,' he insisted, admitting when he saw the finished film he could have pretended just as well. 'It just irks me when I'm watching someone play the piano in a film, for instance, and it's clear they're just miming to a piece of music. I didn't get very far with the oboe, it's such an incredibly difficult instrument and I was simultaneously pompous and naive to think I could get anywhere with it.' Suggestions he kept it up were met with a wry laugh. 'Oh yeah!' he said, before adding, 'I wanted to snap that thing over my knee at the wrap party.' What he did respond to were themes that could well have applied to his real life. 'I just loved that you could see the character who, in the book as well, is so honest about his shortcomings, about how human and indulgent and pathetic he is sometimes,' he said. 'Also he has a great interest in things spiritual and in mankind. A fascination and a curiosity with medicine and science.'

Merivel enjoys a party, a trait he shares with his portrayer, at least according to someone who happened to be staying at the same five-star resort in Evershot, Dorset, during the making of the film. 'He was occupying the suite below ours,' remembers the holiday guest. 'The whole crew were there, including Hugh Grant and Liz Hurley, but Downey showed up at three a.m. on a Harley-

Davidson and then put the stereo on, forcing us to wake the owner and complain. The noise did stop shortly after that!'

'The things that happen in this film almost mythologically are things that happen in life,' Downey believed. 'Loss and fear, avoiding responsibility, wanting the accolades for something without necessarily going through the hard work to get them, thinking that one way of life is preferable to another and not thinking about what's in front of you that needs doing.' You would have to be blind not to see the real-life parallels. After Merivel is banished from court, he beseeches the king to reconsider, reminding him how His Majesty loved Merivel's foolishness. 'No,' says Charles, 'I liked you for your skill.' As Merivel stands in front of him in desperate silence, the king warns him how that skill has fallen by the wayside, leaving only a fool.

By the time *Restoration* was released across America, Downey was facing some serious personal demons – and avoiding responsibility. At home, Falconer put little baskets with rolled-up towels and soaps in every bathroom in their house to make it seem like a hotel. He loved it. Ironically, while he was spiralling out of control personally, he demanded more and more order at home. He spent so much time in hotels shooting his movies, it seemed normal for him. But also it was because living in a hotel meant never having to put down real roots, catering to his lizard-brain mentality.

When he went to promote the movie at the Berlin Film Festival in February 1996, he became even more erratic. A publicist working on the campaign recalls, 'He agreed to do a normal full interview schedule and then suddenly refused to do it unless Miramax flew in his friend. The friend arrived and was a much older man whose first comment to us was how lax customs were at Berlin Airport. It transpired he was Downey's dealer. Oliver Stone was there for *Nixon* and both films were released in

Germany by the same distributor, so there was a joint dinner for them. During it, both men kept disappearing to the toilets at the same time.'

Downey was there with his wife and another female friend and arrived late to the official screening. Being Germany, they didn't bother waiting for the talent to arrive. 'Afterwards, Miramax arranged a dinner at the extremely swanky Schlosshotel just outside Berlin,' continues the publicist. 'It was really posh. Downey rocked up in jeans, T-shirt and a leather jacket high as a kite and when he walked into the main dining room he screeched out (in song), "Everybody dance now!" at the top of his voice. The next day he cancelled most, if not all, of his interviews.'

Finally, his excesses were starting to impinge on his career in a demonstrable way. The press, who were aware of his Dionysian tendencies but had mostly just been told about it by the man himself, were seeing him high before their own eyes. He was taking the hardest drugs possible and in quantity. It was about to get a lot worse.

Addiction

'It's like I've got a shotgun in my mouth, and my finger's on the trigger and I like the taste of gun metal.' (1999)

In April 1996, Deborah walked out, taking Indio with her. Not long after, actor Sean Penn turned up unannounced on the doorstep in a final desperate attempt to help his friend tackle his problems. Downey cowered inside his home, refusing to answer. In fact, he looked round for a way out – no one would want to face the wrath of Sean Penn.

It wasn't the first time Penn had tried to do something about Downey's addiction. Aware that his friend was threatening to ruin his career with his drug-taking, he had warned him about losing his reputation as a great actor to one of a party boy. Downey's response had been to go and buy drugs. He was back within 45 minutes.

But now was the time for something more radical. Downey was asleep when Penn arrived with a couple of other guys (one is rumoured to be Dennis Quaid) and proceeded to bust down their friend's door. They grabbed Downey and, before he knew it, he was on a private jet back to Sierra Tucson, the rehab facility he had visited a few years previously. They welcomed him back and the dizzying speed with which he had been 'kidnapped' meant he went along with it for the first couple of days. But three days later, reality set in – as did the desire to escape. The centre had taken all his ID and credit cards, so he grabbed a water bottle – he was in the desert, after all – and left. It required all his storytelling skills to get back into town. He flagged down a car, told them he had spent the night with a prostitute and she had stolen all his money, but he needed to get back to his son's bar mitzvah. The driver took pity on him and gave him a lift, while Downey woke up his accountant in New York and asked him to book a flight back to Los Angeles. He got an economy ticket and made his way to the airport where the staff recognised him and bumped him up to first class, where the booze was free and plentiful. By the time he touched down in Los Angeles he was drunk.

Downey did fret about what Penn would think, but now the future Oscar winner, like many before him, gave up trying. He had enough on his plate and had done his best. If Downey wasn't going to listen, there was nothing he could do to change his mind. 'He wasn't convinced he was dying,' says Dr Drew Pinsky, a celebrity addiction expert who knows Downey. 'An addict has to believe they're dying before they get sober. Very few severe addicts have a straight road to recovery.'

Downey hadn't been working too hard after the drawn-out shoot for *Restoration* and before moving on to the quickly shot *Home for the Holidays*, he had managed to cram in an easy-paying gig, reuniting him on screen with his *Only You* co-star and real-life mate Billy Zane. His friend Elie Samaha, who owned one of his favourite clubs, The Roxbury, had offered him half-a-million dollars for two weeks' work on a movie shooting in South Africa called *Danger Zone* (1996). Kiefer Sutherland had been considered for the role but, according to director Allan Eastman, Downey was the obvious choice for the MacGuffin character Jim Scott – a CIA agent whose cavalier actions screw up the tiny country of East Zambezi and disrupt the easy life of Zane's

A five-year-old Downey on the set of his first film *Pound*, which was directed by his father. The star remembers being cast because it was cheaper than a babysitter.

Downey Jr, in 1978 (aged 13) at the Stagedoor Manor theatre camp in upstate new York.

The poster for Robert Downey Sr's 1966 film *Chafed Elbows*. Elsie Downey played all the female roles.

The young star alongside Sarah Jessica Parker in a shot from *Firstborn* (1984), on which they met.

Grinning at the Democratic convention in 1992, political documentary *The Last Party* (1993) was actually more of an insight into the actor's personal demons.

Downey Jr with Sarah Jessica Parker at *L.A. Story* premiere in London, shortly before they broke up.

Happier times with his father in 1995.

Downey Jr has been behind bars three times, culminating in nearly eighteen months at the California Substance Abuse Treatment Facility at Corcoran. He drew pictures, wrote letters and led the inmate Christmas choral group.

PALM SPRINGS
POLICE DEPARTMENT
MUGSHOT PROFILE

NAME:	DOWNEY ROBERT J
AKA:	
CASE NUMBER:	00-3300043
CII:	A11290504
MNI#:	
BOOKING #:	00-004687
PHOTO#:	40007068
PHOTO DATE/TIME:	11 / 26 / 00 00:55
DATE OF BIRTH:	███
AGE AT ARREST:	35
SOCIAL SECURITY #:	███
DL STATE:	CALIFORNIA
DL NUMBER:	███
ADDRESS:	██ ███ BLV -
CITY:	LOS A
STATE:	CALIFORNIA

PHYSICAL DESCRIPTION

SEX:	MALE
RACE:	WHITE
HEIGHT:	5'09"
WEIGHT:	165
HAIR:	BROWN
FACIAL HAIR:	NONE
EYES:	BROWN
GLASSES:	NO

TATTOOS

L-ARM:
R-ARM:
NECK:
CHEST:
BACK:

CHARGES

#1:	11350 HS
#2:	11377 HS
#3:	11550 HS
#4:	
#5:	

40007068 Printed 11/26/00

Downey Jr's mugshot profile following his arrest at the Merv Griffin Resort in Palm Springs for possession of cocaine and diazepam and being under the influence of a controlled substance. He told police who searched his room 'I'm not a movie star. I'm a guy with a drug problem.'

Supporters protest the actor's incarceration at the premiere of Downey Jr's film *Black And White* on 4 April, 2000 in New York. Sister Allyson also showed up.

The star on the set of *Home For The Holidays* (1995) with actress Holly Hunter who played his sister. He took heroin for the first time just before filming.

In the first throes of love with first wife Deborah, Downey Jr struts his stuff on the catwalk with her at a Jean-Paul Gaultier catwalk show in 1992.

Sean Penn was rumoured to have been not entirely happy when Downey Jr impersonated him on *Saturday Night Live*. Despite having a great time, the actor only lasted one season on the seminal sketch show. Pictured here with Madonna and actor Randy Quaid.

A heavily pregnant Deborah Falconer accompanies her husband to to the *Hearts and Souls* premiere in August 1993.

Sister Allyson Downey suffered her own personal problems. 'If she was in trouble...he would make sure it was taken care of,' says a friend.

'Captain' Rick Morgan. 'It was a nice little payday for [Robert] and there was a chance for him to come to South Africa, hang out with Billy and do this nice little turn,' says Eastman.

It was April 1995 – winter in South Africa. Eastman knew Downey and Zane were partying hard, though didn't think hard drugs were involved. 'There is definitely a bad-boy streak in him,' says Eastman. 'South Africa's full of great restaurants and clubs and those boys definitely took advantage of it.' Sometimes a little too much. Downey's role required him to be part of two big action scenes – one later in the film when his character has dropped off the map and one near the beginning, which is the catalyst for the plot. 'The battle scene that starts the film was about a week into Robert's shoot,' remembers Eastman. 'It was a gigantic set-up, with helicopters and lots of stunt people. That particular morning, Billy and Robert showed up late on the set. They were late being picked up and they'd been up late the night before. And I was quite simmering because they were a good hour late. They kind of walked in and I was like a stern schoolteacher, like, "Who do you think you are?!"' Eastman stuck them on their marks and shouted 'Action'. 'Their first reaction on that day was [to] everything blowing up around them. They were contrite schoolboys and worked very hard.'

If he didn't get a chance to sleep in, Downey often found some novel ways to catch up after a big night out, like he had on previous sets. To set up his character arriving in Africa, Eastman did a series of shots of him being driven cross-country in the back of a car. 'We'd arrive and Robert would be asleep in the back seat of the BMW, in wardrobe and make-up,' says the director. 'I'd walk over and tap on the window and he'd shake himself like a dog, run the scales, slap his face a few times, walk on set and he'd be absolutely perfect. We'd get a couple of takes and then he'd go back to the BMW and go right back to sleep!'

Despite this, Eastman enjoyed working with the actor. 'I've worked with Oscar-winners and there's absolutely no doubt Robert's the best I've worked with,' he says. 'And that's because you have such an inventive process working with him. I was always fascinated to see what he would do. There are a lot of famous actors who are only the characters they play. That's one of their tragic flaws. They have to become something so they can be something. But Robert isn't like that at all. It's great just to talk to him about anything between set-ups. Robert *is* someone. Robert is all the characters he plays, but he's also Robert. And he's a very impressive individual.'

It was the first time the actor had got to play with guns. 'He was really excited to do that,' says Eastman, 'to be an action hero. Fire the machine guns and get blown up and all that. We talked a lot about politics and the spy and espionage world. I was telling him about the history of Africa. We talked about US politics in the context of world imperialism and he was very interested in that.'

Downey didn't really need to know about African history to play Jim Scott, though he does essay a vast amount of the exposition in the film, which is a straightforward B-action pic. Sporting a Southern accent – chosen after doing some background reading on the CIA and finding out that a lot of them come from Texas – he disappears for a vast portion of the film, an annoying fact considering the alternative is watching Billy Zane. Initially a kind of loveable rogue, he becomes something of a Marlon Brando/*Apocalypse Now* figure, living anonymously in a tribal village with an appalling ponytail and an African tribeswoman for a wife. Allan Eastman figured he appreciated the incognito part. 'I freaked him out one time shooting a scene in the village, when there were a lot of extras and press around,' he says. 'Robert was going through that endless cycle of crew members and cast members having their picture taken with him. I said, "That's weird. There must be five or ten thousand people with your picture on their wall with your arm around their shoulders as if they're your friend." He flinched at that.'

Luckily, Eastman managed to catch him before he really went off the rails, although he has his own ideas why it happened. 'I always thought some of Robert's problems with drugs was because he was bored, you know?' he says. 'He's so smart and alive. Normal reality can be a little boring for him. I think [going deep as an actor] comes very easily to him. Maybe a little too easily. He can go there anytime and be anyone. Maybe that's why he gets into trouble? When he wasn't having the opportunity to do that? I ran into him a few times [afterwards]. I have a vague memory that I talked to him and said, "You got to be real careful where you go. The more you get into it, the more dangerous it becomes."'

Mere months after making the film, Downey was taking heroin. But it's also important to note his alcohol intake was still epic. 'I felt like a parent to him, I wanted to look after him and protect him,' says Eastman. 'I ran into him in LA [a while later] and he was pretty fucked-up. It always seemed to be fuelled by drink too. He was drinking a lot. I laughed so much watching *Iron Man*, because I know he's lived that. His relationship with bartenders . . .'

As well as playing protector, Sean Penn was sharing the screen (though not actual scenes) with Downey during his dark period in mid-1996. Once again, Downey was helping out his father in Downey Sr's new movie *Hugo Pool* (1997). It starred Alyssa Milano as a beautiful young pool cleaner during one hectic day in her working life, dealing with her deadbeat dad (Malcolm McDowell), gambling addict mum (Cathy Moriarty) and falling in love with a man (Patrick Dempsey) suffering from ALS, better known as Lou Gehrig's disease. The movie was co-written by Laura Ernst Downey, who had finally died in 1994, aged just 36, after battling the same disease herself for several years. *Hugo Pool* is dedicated to her memory.

'It's nice to watch father and son work together, but I think it was difficult circumstances at the time,' says Cathy Moriarty, who is and was a longtime friend of the Downey family. She had participated in several staged readings of the script during the previous two-and-a-half years in a bid to find financing, which had finally come through. 'I think the admiration for [his] father was beautiful and the concern of the father for his son was kind of hurtful to watch.' Like his previous work, *Hugo Pool* is a mannered film, though this time Downey Sr had A-list stars to work with. Junior's performance as Franz is tough to watch for many reasons. He is being deliberately outlandish, sporting a muddled accent that sticks in his mouth and making bizarre creative decisions like bouncing out of a scene, rather than simply walking. But he's also supernaturally skinny to the point of emaciation, white and sweaty. There's even a bit of a twitch. It doesn't seem like a man playing a crazy character. It feels like a crazy man playing a character, though how much of that is only considered in hindsight is difficult to pinpoint. Either way, floral-shirted foreigner Franz is funny and one can see some of the other cast members (notably Dempsey, who's supposed to remain almost motionless throughout) struggling with the giggles on occasion. 'Sometimes we had to do retakes, because no one could hold in their laughter,' says Moriarty. 'We'd be peeing in our pants. The take on that character was absolutely brilliant.' Not everyone agreed. When it was released, the *Los Angeles Times* said it put on public display 'one of the worst performances he or any major star has recorded on film. It would be better for all concerned if the movie were being shown only in Downey's cell. Being forced to watch himself playing Franz Mazur, a punch-drunk, homicidal, tongue-tied Dutch film director, in this woebegone farce would be tough love indeed . . . his manic, presumably improvised performance here is the sort of thing that rocked the Downey household. But given the actor's off-camera adventures, it's hard not to regard it as the work of someone who's not thinking straight.' *Variety* was kinder to the film as a whole, adding, 'It's also not surprising that the most idiosyncratic performance belongs to helmer's son, Downey Jr, a brilliant actor who has a tendency to overact and here has a field day with his over-the-top European accent and mannerisms.'

Moriarty is more forgiving. 'No matter where he is in his head, he pulls it out of the hat every time,' she says, adding that Downey lived in her guest house during the shoot and would come to eat in her pizza restaurant with his old man. 'When it was Junior's scenes, whether you were working that day or not, everybody came to see what he could do.'

For all involved, it was a labour of love. Nobody got paid very much and Dempsey had known Ernst before her death. 'It was definitely an emotional film to make,' says Moriarty. 'The devastation it caused to all the people around her who loved her so much. But [Downey] looks for the humour in a very hurtful situation.' Although everyone liked to sit around listening to Downey playing music and singing in the evenings, the idea of further interventions didn't appear to come up. 'Everybody has a time in their life when they're not going to listen to anybody,' says Moriarty. 'Some people need help, but you can't get help unless you want to. Looking at him and knowing him so well, I always knew he'd conquer and beat it. It was just getting him to do it quicker!

'I think his brilliance is probably too overwhelming for him,' she adds. 'On *Hugo Pool*, I guess he had a little slip.'

By the time *Hugo Pool* was finishing up filming, Downey had other problems to deal with. It was 23 June 1996 – a Sunday – and Downey was driving his Ford pickup along the Pacific Coast Highway near Malibu. It's a 50mph zone and a police car spotted him edging up towards 70mph. He had been cited for speeding three times since 1994 and had failed to appear in court for his last ticket, so the patrolmen pulled him over. According to Los Angeles County Sheriff's Deputy Gabe Ramirez, when the cops arrived at the side of his car to examine his licence and registration 'they observed that Downey appeared to be under the influence of a controlled substance and placed him under arrest'. They searched the car and found rock and powder cocaine, quantities of black-tar heroin and a concealed – unloaded – .357 calibre Magnum handgun. They whisked Downey to Lost Hills sheriff's station and booked him on suspicion of carrying a concealed weapon, possession of a controlled substance and driving under the influence. He posted $10,000 bail and was let out at 7 p.m. that night, with an edict to appear in court to answer the charges on 26 July.

Where he went after that is impossible to say. Home wasn't home anymore, not since Falconer had left with Indio. He had taken to living in five-star hotels around Los Angeles, like The Argyle on Sunset Strip and Shutters On The Beach in Santa Monica. Deborah had had enough. She knew her husband needed help, but with a young son to think about it, she wasn't taking any chances. She has said drugs never got in the way of his parenting specifically, but a friend at the time admitted Downey's behaviour was simply too manic. 'He would come over like a bag lady,' they told *Entertainment Weekly*. 'He comes over with some kind of bag, throws everything on the floor, starts searching, frenzied and panting. You should see what he has in his bags. Like toys, like his kid's toys. It's scary to watch him.'

Weirdly, on top of any tabloid pictures from the time, audiences also have a film record of his state at that moment. That's because as well as *Hugo Pool*, Downey was shooting a supporting role in Mike Figgis's relationship drama *One Night Stand* (1997), a part he had met with the director about some weeks before his arrest. It's amazing he got the job at all. The pair met at Kate Mantilini's, a swish restaurant on Wilshire Boulevard in Beverly Hills. Figgis had heard about Downey's reputation, but even he wasn't prepared for what showed up. The star was two hours late and barefoot. He was high and carried a small man-purse, which had a gun sticking out of it. Figgis was shocked. His first impression was that there was no way he could cast Downey in anything. But as he got talking to him, he started to think perhaps making a movie would give him some kind of purpose. He asked the actor why he was carrying a gun. Downey replied that he didn't want to leave it in his car. Figgis was intrigued.

They spoke for an hour and Downey was pleased how the helmer chose to talk to him as though he was normal – addicted but normal – rather than as a charity case. The lead character in the film is Max, a married man who has an affair that spirals out of control. 'So you want me to play Max?' he asked Figgis. The director looked back at him. The star usually weighed 170 pounds, but was down to 138. He was slick with sweat, wide-eyed, his skin almost translucent.

'No,' replied Figgis, 'I think you should play Charlie.' Charlie is the catalyst for the happenings in the film, an old friend of Max who the latter reconnects with when he learns Charlie's ill. The character has AIDS. The reply came as a big shock to Downey. In his mind, he was still the dashing leading man of *Only You* and *Chaplin*. He retired to the bathroom to do a line of coke and while he was there he looked in the mirror. For the first time, he really saw himself. And took the role.

Once they started filming, Figgis decided Downey's behaviour wasn't going to be swayed by what anybody said. He did give his performer a dressing-down, but by this point the addict was immune. Nevertheless, he showed up for work every day and on time, finishing well within schedule. He also produced some devastating work. Someone dying of AIDS is an easy tearjerker in many ways, but Downey imbues the role with not just his body and words, but with a spirit. The movie showcases one of his best attributes as an actor – the ability to *fill* the role completely. It's not just that his real-life experiences are similar to his characters (after all, he's not dying of an incurable disease), it's that his real life *envelops* the character.

Max was eventually played by Wesley Snipes, while Kyle MacLachlan is Charlie's brother. Downey has little to do with the central conceit of the film – that of marital infidelity – but his slow death is crucial to the plot. There are several key scenes, though it's sometimes difficult to know whether it's because the audience knows what it knows now that makes them even more poignant. When we first meet him it's at a pavement café, catching up with Max. He looks young, almost like a little boy. As he gets progressively sicker, so is he more and more effective. When the orderlies deal with him in his hospital bed, it harks back to the overdose scene in *Less Than Zero* when Jami Gertz and Andrew McCarthy take care of him. His friends putting him to bed, taking off his clothes, carrying him barely moving to the bathroom. His funeral scene, where he's eulogised by a tearful MacLachlan, is especially moving. A huge black-and-white picture of Downey in character dominates the frame. MacLachlan talks about a life lost too early. Mourners weep. Sadly, as they filmed the moment, the thought rife in Hollywood was that this could really happen at any time.

You don't have to be an addict to get caught with drugs in your car. You don't have to be one to have a gun, particularly not in

Los Angeles. But what Downey did on 16 July 1996 was a turning point. It was the moment a young man in trouble became a young man with serious narcotic and emotional issues. He passed it off as a harmless mistake. If he had tried to get into the Curtis house rather than his own on Broad Beach Road in Malibu using his keys, then realised his miscalculation and left, that would have been a mistake. But that's not what happened. Bill and Lisa Curtis lived down the street from Downey, in a house overlooking the ocean. They had three young kids: Daniel, Jenny and Chelsea, then aged eleven, eight and six respectively. On the night in question Bill wasn't home, but his wife was putting their daughters to bed. She went into Daniel's room and saw a lump in the bed. 'She thought it was Daniel playing a trick on her,' said Jenny in an interview with *Entertainment Weekly*. From time to time, Lisa left the front door open, whether to enjoy the evening breeze, or in this case, because she had burnt the family's chicken dinner. She investigated the clump, which turned out not to be her son, but Downey, stripped down to his T-shirt and boxer shorts covered in a quilt. 'We were scared,' said Chelsea. 'We didn't know him.' Lisa called the police, who showed up with the paramedics. 'He seems to have passed out in my child's bed,' she told the 911 operator. 'We kind of shook him and he would moan and kind of talk but he seems to just go right back to sleep.'

The paramedics gave him an injection of Narcan, which woke him up. Then they led him away. 'The policeman came back and said that [Downey] would say he was sorry,' said Jenny. He was initially cited for being under the influence of a controlled substance and trespassing, though the Curtis family ultimately chose not to press the latter charge. He was taken to Santa Monica Hospital Center and treated, then transferred to the jail ward at Los Angeles County/University of Southern California (USC) Medical Center. The incident was a shock for the Curtis clan. 'They don't feel as secure knowing that someone can walk in and climb into bed,' said Lisa.

Entertainment journalist Ken Baker was one of the first people on the scene after hearing about the arrest, later dubbed the 'Goldilocks' incident, around eight or nine the following morning. He was fairly new to the job and the city, having started working at *People* magazine just two months before. Standing at the end of her driveway, he interviewed Lisa Curtis. 'I remember getting this bizarre tale from this woman and thinking, does this happen all the time, this celebrity meltdown where they're so messed up?' he says. 'And the answer is no. It doesn't happen all the time and the closest I've seen to this level of mania was the whole Britney Spears debacle more than ten years later.' Downey later said his driver simply dropped him off at the wrong house. Not an excuse, says Baker. 'I was trying to figure out how he could mistake that house for his house,' he says. 'No matter how hard I tried I couldn't come up with anything legitimate. Did they have the same garage door? No. Were they next-door neighbours? No! The fact is, I believe he had to actually hop a fence into the house. He took his pants off and laid in bed. At that point, you have to be so epically messed-up . . . He had just become a menace in Malibu.'

The day after it happened, Downey left lock-up with a white T-shirt draped over his head and a cigarette in his mouth. He wasn't really thinking much about what he had done other than the fact he had left his bag in the Curtis home. His drugs were in the bag and he wanted them back. His substance abuse had been an open secret within the industry for years. But now, thanks to two arrests, he and his problems were public property.

On 18 July, a judge remanded him to the Exodus Recovery Center in Marina Del Rey to clean up. He was escorted by two large security guards, but Downey already had a plan. 'I'm going to have no trouble getting out of here,' he told them. He knew what doing that would result in. After his first arrest, his lawyer had told him he couldn't make any more mistakes. But two days later, on the morning of Saturday 20 July, he managed to escape. He had been given a Valium and allowed to drink coffee, which made him relaxed and alert. There were three or four policemen hanging around making sure no one got out and he asked someone to get him more coffee while he took a shower. The bathroom had one open window, which Downey crawled through. He wandered into a nearby yacht shop wearing a Hawaiian shirt, slippers and his hospital trousers and asked them to call him a taxi. The sales assistant recognised him and ordered him a cab, which Downey took to a friend's house in Malibu. Four hours later, guards tracked him down and bundled him back to rehab.

Because he had violated a court order, he was taken to prison. It was a bigger shock than he anticipated. At first he was loud and brash, talking himself up. He soon realised it was better to keep his mouth shut.

On 22 July he was back in court, handcuffed and wearing a yellow jumpsuit, standing before Judge Lawrence Mira. His lawyer Charles English entered a plea of not guilty on two felony and three misdemeanour charges stemming from his June arrest. 'I remember being in the courtroom for the arraignment,' says Ken Baker. 'I remember one of the deputies telling me he was in the back, bouncing off the walls. My understanding was that he was going through such severe withdrawals from whatever drugs that he was in bad shape.

'He looked horrible,' he continues. 'I was in one of the front rows, there were maybe five rows max. He was kind of a young guy, 31, but he looked 51. He looked like hell. And when you see someone who's a charming actor with all this talent in this jumpsuit at the bottom, it was just really poignant.'

At the end of each hearing, Downey was taken back to his single-person cell in the county jail, looking depressed and confused. His mum had flown in from Pittsburgh and Downey Sr sat next to her in the back row of the courtroom, alongside Deborah Falconer, who had come to show her support. Debbie understandably found it hard to take. On more than one occasion she went to the toilet to cry, but mostly tried to look stoic for her husband. Todd Bridges, a.k.a. Willis from *Diff'rent Strokes*, and Dennis Quaid also showed up.

The Hollywood community had started to rally. After all, you can only do so much for the environment and animals – a human charity case is far more interesting. Downey had been visited in prison by Bob Timmins, a former addict and self-styled addiction-intervention specialist. He said he had been called by more than six actors keen to help. But phone calls were all that materialised. Sean Penn had put his money where his mouth was before, breaking down some doors. Others weren't quite so ready to take time out from their hectic yoga schedules, but wanted to be able to tell their friends they had done their bit. Downey's closest friend at the time was his business partner, Joe Bilella. The pair had set up a production company called Herd Of Turtles and it was Joe who was acting as the star's liaison between prison and the outside world. 'He was literally the guy who'd go into jail and bring him stuff and get things done outside, make sure his house was taken care of,' says Baker. It was important Downey had positive influences. 'I think there were drug people around him, but I never met them,' adds Baker. 'Joe was a businessman and cared about him and was trying to keep the business together – he didn't want to give up on him.'

Seeing Downey's parents in the courtroom, Baker dug into the actor's background. He was the first reporter to break wide open the story about Robert Downey Sr giving his son drugs as a child.

'I spoke to Robert Sr and he was very, very angry,' says the journalist. 'In my job, I'm used to people getting mad at me. But at the time, I was pretty new to the business and this guy was really laying into me. I felt horrible about it. He was begging us not to run it. My impression was that this was a guy whose son had hit rock bottom and the father felt horrible about it, but was having to come to grips with his contribution to it. It was very hurtful to him that this got out.'

On 29 July Downey came back to court, where Judge Mira, Charles English and LA County prosecutor Ellen Aragon came to the decision to admit Downey to a full-time, fully supervised private rehab facility. Aragon called him 'a danger to himself and the community'. It marked the first time the star had opened his mouth in court. Asked by the judge whether he understood how serious his predicament was, Downey replied, 'Yes, I do.' He was taken to a secret rehab where he filled his room with fan mail, books, pictures of Indio and a letter from his wife, all brought by Joe Bilella. Downey wanted to get better, and participated in the group activities and private therapy.

His legal problems weren't over, though. He still had to face the 23 June charges, as well as the aftermath of 16 July. But for now, he was safe. 'When you talked to people around town, it was just about how talented he is,' says Ken Baker. 'Everyone saying, "I hope he can get it together, because he's so talented." There were people working very hard to help him be able to come back when he was ready. It became clear this wasn't something that happened right away. He had major issues with drugs that he needed to reconcile, he had major problems legally that needed to be worked out. His personal life was a mess.'

The journalist remembers it as an amazing time. 'I'd just moved out to Los Angeles and here was this crazy story. It was tragic and fascinating. He's a brilliant guy and always was. People around the office were like, "How could this happen?" It was an intriguing story – and an ugly one.'

Downey was back in court in September, when he pleaded 'no contest' to the charges from when the police had pulled him over. In November he was sentenced to three more months at a live-in treatment facility, random periodic drug tests and three years' probation. 'If you've ever had the chance here to deal with this problem and maintain your sobriety, this is the chance,' said Judge Mira. 'I wish you good luck. You've made a good start.' The actor had stayed clean so far. He was rewarded with a furlough from rehab in mid-November when he returned to Studio 8H in Rockefeller Center to host *Saturday Night Live*. He was one of the first celebrities to use the sketch show as an opportunity to show everyone he was OK and to make fun of his problems. Of course, it was the first time he had appeared on the programme since being a cast member ten years previously. This season, it wasn't being called 'Saturday Night Dead'. A new crop of talent were populating the team, including Will Ferrell, Chris Kattan and Molly Shannon, who had created memorable characters like the overexcited cheerleaders and Mary Katherine Gallagher.

Coming on at the start of the show to do the opening monologue was an interesting moment for Downey. The whole world knew about his drug problems and were curious as to what they were about to see. 'I've been invited back as part of their "Distinguished Alumni" series,' said Downey. He then told the audience he had brought some slides of his summer holiday and offered to show them. A series of pictures flashed up: him sleeping on a tiny baby bed, to which he quipped, 'When I stayed at this terrific guest house in Malibu'; a shot of him standing next to a barbecue grill with a policeman; another candid snap of Downey taking a package from a freaky-looking guy in front of a fence, to which Downey said, 'Here's me picking up a little prescription from my pharmacist'; before finishing by joking, 'What would summer be without a hot summer romance?' and showing him in a prison cell with another inmate. The star appeared in several sketches and appeared to fit right back into the chaotic *SNL* routine, playing a seventies detective, a hunk at a party who spends 'seven minutes in heaven' with nerd Mary Katherine Gallagher, and a guy called Ronnie in a sketch about a home shopping network. He had put on weight and didn't look as twitchy. The performance was, by all accounts, a success, especially considering the criticism he had come in for the last time he was a part of the show.

He was out again in early December, when he granted an interview to American television news personality Diane Sawyer. He was a hundred days into his court-ordered rehab and he talked about drugs in the family home, how his blood pressure had dropped to a potentially fatal 60/40 and why he wasn't going to relapse. Again.

First Comeback

'I've always felt like such an outsider in the industry. Because I'm so insane, I guess.' (1999)

Director James Toback was watching the news one night during the hoopla when he caught sight of his friend. He couldn't believe it had got this bad. He knew Downey liked to party, but prison? Handcuffs? His first thought was how to get the star back on top. What could he do? The answer was simple – be the one to give him his first shot as soon as he got out of rehab. Now all he needed was an idea.

At one in the morning on 17 November 1996, Downey was sitting in the club Maxim's in New York City, enjoying an after-party. He was with his mother, worn out and emotional, having just finished his hosting gig on *Saturday Night Live*. His eyes were shut when a familiar voice asked him if he was ready to shoot another film. Knowing it was Toback, he didn't need to open his eyes before saying yes.

'What's the title?' he asked.

'*Two Girls and a Guy*,' replied the writer/director.

Toback had had his idea, flown to Florida and holed himself up in a beachfront cottage to write. It had taken him just four days to produce a feature-length script and he finished it on the day he learned Downey was going to be in New York. Having got his star on board, he now needed to put the rest of the film together. It was going to be cheap, quick and pure. He arranged for his casting director to set up auditions at a hotel in Santa Monica, near to Downey's rehab so he could have some input. Helena Bonham-Carter was one of the names bandied around, but in the end Toback settled on Heather Graham and Natasha Gregson Wagner, the daughter of Natalie Wood. The producers found the TriBeCa loft where the entire story would take place at 79 Leonard Street in New York City.

Downey finally got out of rehab in early 1997, clear and ready to work. He didn't want a repeat of the previous summer, which he admitted 'got worse and worse. Everyone knew everything. And people even knew stuff before I did, because I didn't remember doing any of it.' He was keen to get creative again, to work on the film he had written and wanted to direct called *Dan's Best Friend*, about a dog-walker for the rich and famous.

He was on his own now. Falconer and he had separated amicably, though he was desperate to reconnect with his son and they had worked out an informal custody agreement. He noted how different his life was, how people recognised him not as a famous actor, but as that 'shameful heroin addict'. He particularly enjoyed the evenings, around six-thirty, when he settled down for the night rather than thinking about where he was going to get enough drugs to keep him up for another 24 hours.

Two Girls and a Guy (1997) was about lying. It tells the tale of Blake Allen, a charismatic but self-absorbed actor living in a grand apartment who is seeing two women at the same time, even though they don't realise it. One morning, both of them show up at his place to surprise him when he returns from a business trip. The rest rolls out almost like a theatrical play as the characters come to terms with their duplicity and that of those they love, as well as facing up to their own inadequacies. There's also a crucial subplot about Allen's ill mother, a story strand directly pulled from Toback's own tortured maternal relationship. Both the writer/director and male star came to the project in a state of flux. Shooting in January 1997, the producers paid an extra $30,000 to insure Downey and he had to urinate in a cup at the end of each day to satisfy his drug counsellors. Meanwhile, Toback was a gambling addict and struggling financially. His agent was managing his assets and most nights he would be on the phone to someone who owed him money, arranging to meet to make sure they paid up. They were two chaotic personalities.

'Downey appreciated this untoured Harvard graduate's mind,' says Chris Hanley, who produced the movie. 'Both of them, observing them on set, tended towards self-reproachfulness, based on flawed aspects of their personality, their sense of identity. Which could lead to what people would call an addictive personality. I see it more as a focus of the mind on the self.'

There were a couple of people around making sure Downey was concentrating on the work in hand, especially since he cost the production half their $1.27 million budget. But the actor was in a realm of concentration he hadn't experienced since *Chaplin*. If anything, he disliked having to stop filming at all. 'When we wrapped for the day, or there was a break, Robert would smoke a cigarette,' says Hanley. 'I could tell by the way he smoked it he was losing the focus of the performance and was back on the interior self. I could tell there was something gnawing away at him, just by how he was smoking.'

Downey was free to let himself go when the cameras rolled. Toback gave him more latitude than any director previously, even letting him write whole scenes rather than simply improvising over the script. His trust paid off when it came time to shoot one of the pivotal moments in the movie. Blake is talking to himself in the mirror, giving himself a brutal lecture about his self-destructive desire to ruin everything and everyone he cares about. With all he had been through the previous year, it is perhaps the single most truthful representation of Downey the man, as opposed to Downey the actor, committed to film. 'It's the salient scene in the movie,' says Hanley, who watched as Downey twitched and bulged, so much so that he had to disappear for a few minutes after to collect himself. 'I mean, that really was him – and it was really the character. It was an absolute transparent merger of character and actor, which you can't get in every movie, though you get it more often than not with Robert Downey. I think that's the nature of his obsessive personality disorder as it's been described in the media,' he continues. 'He has the ability to look into himself so deeply it bumps him up to the wall of going outside one's identity, where you're just lost to the abyss . . . and that can be very scary. If you go too deep in the mirror, you need something to palliate the senses and sometimes a cigarette's not enough.'

Downey knew this was his chance to impress again and, luckily for him, he had a friend who was willing to show off all his talents. Like many Downey characters, Blake has a musical bent, singing and playing the piano in his apartment, which was all done live. He also performed a monologue from *Hamlet* that was enough to make you wish the star spent more time on stage. 'The Shakespeare nearly made me faint!' laughs Hanley. 'Not only was it Shakespeare, it was one of the best scenes of Shakespeare ever performed in a motion picture. He wasn't messing around. I certainly felt like he ran me through the gamut of his potential.'

Toback, never one to avoid sexuality if possible, had also written into the script perhaps the most explicit love scene Downey had ever performed. There was no nudity, but more than a suggestion of what is going on when Graham's character Carla pulls Blake into the bedroom for an impromptu liaison while Gregson Wagner's Lou sits sadly outside. It became a problem.

Though there was only hand movement and groans, the ratings board saw fit to penalise the movie and threatened to slap it with a NC-17 certificate, essentially a death sentence, because it disallows promotion and blocks certain distribution avenues.

Toback was furious. After all, you could blow people's heads off any time, yet here was a film for adults, with no nudity, that was being held to account. For his part, Downey did find the experience 'unnerving', but only because he found it tough to watch on-screen sex. 'What went on inside the bedroom between Robert and Heather was as close to mutually spontaneous erotic discovery as anything two actors have performed on screen,' wrote Toback in a 1998 *Premiere* article. 'Only [cinematographer] Barry Markowitz and I were present during the hour, at the end of which both Robert and Heather broke into a joint laughter of relief and release as if to say, "That was fun!"' Indeed, Graham had fallen for Downey during the shoot and was surprised he never asked her out, something she mentioned to him years later. Hanley saw the mounting intimacy thanks to the movie's subject matter, though he didn't know the actual feelings being uncovered. 'There was this growing closeness,' he says, 'where there was a unified direction toward the Downey character emotionally with a sexual underscoring of that tendency.

'Nothing was really cut *out* if that's what you're wondering, although we had to do some intercutting,' he adds about the sex scene. 'Once you make a few cuts in deference to the system, they sometimes let you push it through.' Everyone was happy with the end product and, as Hanley says, 'They certainly have a Robert Downey movie.' It was still early days, but he had started to show he was back to his best. 'There was no issue of running barefoot through the streets of New York during the shoot,' grins Hanley.

It also showed clearly where Downey came truly alive. Once he was on set, any sense of personality disorder evaporated. Being in front of the camera was proving to be the one place he felt truly comfortable. 'What Robert Downey does best and what gives him the most out of life, at least from what I could observe, is as a performer, an entertainer,' says Hanley. 'Someone who can expose deep inner flaws, or enlightening perceptions, a deep self-reflection that you won't find with other people and that he happens to expose in his performances, even the comedic ones. He likes to use what he knows about life to create the characters within the setting of the story. I think almost always he adds to it in ways so it shows more of the writer's vision which could never have been imagined during pre-production. I can't imagine having a better union of performer and writer/director.'

But while the producer saw the actor's skills *on* camera he also befriended the person *off* it, getting a glimpse of the man behind the mask. 'There's a little bit of a smokescreen where he doesn't want the vulnerability of exposing his true nature, especially in some kind of public interaction,' he says. 'But if you look closely enough, it's there. He uses humour to mask his inner self. Everybody has flaws and he's willing to expose them, but there's a caution that's also developed.' Still, he worried whether Downey would be able to maintain the focus once shooting wrapped. 'I think people who fall into that depth of thought, you better watch out,' he says. 'It's not about chemicals.'

Just thirteen days after filming started and a little more than two months since Downey had signed on, the movie was in the can. 'The wrap party was the biggest of all time!' remembers Chris Hanley. 'I don't think Robert turned up, but Leonardo DiCaprio, Winona Ryder, Madonna and Willem Dafoe were all there. After that, we thought the theatrical [release] would just be blast off because your thinking gets misaligned by the party atmosphere. But it did pretty well. It sold well foreign. I can't complain.'

Though it's a deeply flawed film, *Two Girls and a Guy* operates most successfully as a full-length showreel for Downey's abilities. His piano-playing and singing are by turns mocking and exquisite and he manages to rise above the self-indulgent subject matter to deliver a performance of honesty and charm. He's also put on weight, thankfully, and even verges on the doughy, a mighty relief considering his physique just a few months earlier. 'You name me one good actor who doesn't lie,' he says at one point, and it's incredibly easy to spot the metaphors with real life. When's he confronted about his cheating, he is evasive and embarrassed, telling the two women that, though he hid parts of his life from them, he never said anything to either of them he didn't wholeheartedly mean. One doesn't have to be Sherlock Holmes to see the parallels.

Reviewers wavered on the end product. *Slate* said: 'Downey has clearly had a lot of practice trying to explain the unexplainable in 12-step groups and with rehab counselors. He's brilliant at reproducing this psychobabble but not so brilliant at winding up anywhere very interesting.' Meanwhile, the *San Francisco Chronicle* wrote: 'Downey is undeniably magnetic, though at times one gets the feeling he's playing the role as a kind of posthumous tribute to himself. It's eerie.'

The experience was enough to fire Downey up again and he plunged himself back into work. Some friends thought that had as much to do with his enjoying his craft as it did with paying his legal bills and, quite frankly, keeping him off the streets. 'When he's working, he's tested every five minutes,' said one. 'It's when he's not working that there's trouble.'

Downey's friend Joe Bilella was one of the people keeping him on the straight and narrow and he was joined by Earl Hightower, a court-appointed drug counsellor. The pair were around him like bees on honey. Immediately after *Two Girls and a Guy* Downey met director Robert Altman, who asked him to appear in a John

Grisham story called *The Gingerbread Man* (1998) that he was shooting in Savannah, Georgia. Kenneth Branagh was attached and he had already had a great experience with Altman on *Short Cuts*. He didn't even read the script before accepting, playing a boozy Southern private investigator who does leg-work for Branagh's anti-hero.

Then came an offer to do *U.S. Marshals* (1998). A sequel to the smash-hit cinematic version of TV show *The Fugitive*, the follow-up focused on a different chase, as Sam Gerard (Tommy Lee Jones) and his team try to track down Mark Sheridan (Wesley Snipes) with the assistance of Special Agent John Royce, the character played by Downey. He had enjoyed playing with guns on the set of *Danger Zone* and was keen to involve himself in a big studio franchise. His quirky film choices also meant he was missing out on mainstream parts that were more family-orientated. Indio was getting older. He couldn't watch *Two Girls and a Guy* for a long time, but a fun action film? Unfortunately, Downey's experience making the movie from April until September 1997 only served to reinforce his feeling that a career is vastly done on gut instinct, not chasing what you *think* you should be doing. He was miserable on location in Chicago, even though his son (now aged nearly four) came to visit. Downey, disappointed he had to run around with a revolver rather than spend time with his offspring, bought an 80-dollar lizard to keep the kid happy. Which it did, until it went into seizures one morning and required a vet.

The film-makers were happy with his performance – even though in the final cut you can see he's phoning it in – but the actor wasn't enjoying himself. He had to get an X-ray after Snipes accidentally punched him during a scene and frequently endured 100-degree heat in the un-airconditioned airplane hangar that housed the set. During the shoot he was on message, battling a heavy cold that required him to chug endless sugary coffee and pop chocolate truffles while telling interviewers how he could guard an embassy with all the skills he had acquired and how he couldn't wait to be in a blockbuster. However, he later dubbed it one of the worst action movies of all time, talking about how damaging it had been to his fragile psyche. His assessment of his time making it was brutal. 'I'd rather wake up in jail for a TB test,' he said, 'than have to wake up another morning knowing I'm going to the set of *U.S. Marshals*.'

By this point, the star's probation requirements had changed so if he failed a drugs test during principal photography it didn't count as immediate violation, but meant he could finish his duties before it was brought before the courts. In September 1997, he relapsed and went on a four-day bender, abusing drugs and booze. How much that was to do with the stress and unhappiness of making *U.S. Marshals* is unclear, but it's obvious the creative drought he felt contributed, as it had before, to his decision to use again. In October he was back in front of the judge at Malibu Municipal Court, where the Deputy District Attorney revealed that his drug counsellor had testified about Downey's mistake. The actor was told to report back on 8 December to face the music, but was allowed to finish shooting *In Dreams* (1999), a Neil Jordan film he had signed up for opposite Annette Bening.

It's a startling, bizarre movie for sure. Downey plays a mysterious ginger serial killer called Vivian who's psychically using children's book illustrator Claire Cooper (Bening) to help avenge his own lost childhood that's somehow closely connected with their town, flooded 25 years earlier to create a reservoir. Like some adult version of a Grimm fairytale that Claire has herself adapted, Jordan's often unsettling shocker hovers between fantasy and reality, though Downey's bogeyman role is effectively an extended cameo. You suspect the original intention was that the audience should feel some sympathy for this strange, rather shaggy, man-child, but by the end it's clear that Hollywood has imposed on writer-director Jordan (who shares the screenplay credit with Bruce Robinson) the requirement that Downey's character be downright diabolical. Robinson (*Withnail & I*) hated the end product, though his bile – which was vented in the book *Smoking In Bed: Conversations with Bruce Robinson* – appeared to be reserved for the director and studio, rather than for the actor.

'What the fuck was Robert Downey Jr, a very fine actor, doing dressed as a nurse cutting people's throats? I didn't know what any of that rushing around was about,' he said. 'Out of all the things I've ever been associated with, I hate that film most . . . I think Neil [Jordan] and I should go to the same funeral of this picture and just say goodbye to it gracefully and put a big fucking slab on top of it.'

Jordan, however, was ecstatic with his male lead's performance. '[Vivian] is someone who is not quite grown-up and at the same time is an incredibly dangerous human being,' he said. 'Someone with the cruelty of a child but the make-up of an adult. I had written some lines of dialogue that were nonsensical, and it took a brave actor to make them come to life . . . to make them real. Robert made all those lines work beautifully in the context of the character.'

Downey loved doing it. There were echoes of his own complex upbringing and he admitted he could relate to Vivian's child-ishness. 'Vivian is so sad, so childlike, so misinformed,' he said. 'His childhood is a void, and he is trying to connect with Claire and get her attention. There is a real sense of a dark destiny between them. They are similar in many ways; the difference is that what she does is right, and what he does is very wrong.'

All the while, the spectre of prison was hanging over his head. Jail wasn't mandatory, but Judge Mira had demonstrated his harsh stance before. On 8 December 1997 Downey was back before him. His hair was neatly parted and he wore a suit. It didn't work. He fought back tears as he gave a statement during the hearing, which was broadcast on television. 'I've been addicted to drugs in one form or another since I was eight years old,' he said. 'I have no excuses. I find myself defenceless.' He said how his 1996/7 rehab had worked, adding, 'That's not the situation today. I don't know why, with this . . . fear of you, of death and of not being able to live a life free of drugs, has not been enough.'

Downey's lawyer Michael D. Nasatir also begged for mercy. 'Sitting next to me is a very decent, loving, talented – to the point of genius – human being,' he said. 'It's not like Mr Downey is going to be holding up liquor stores or robbing banks. He's been clean and sober for over fifteen months. Four to five days he slipped. That's all we have here, your Honour, a slip.'

Judge Mira looked at the defendant. He could sentence him to up to three years in prison (the duration of the probation he was given for the June 1996 car bust), or eschew jail altogether and send him back to rehab. 'I am running out of ways to rehabilitate you,' he said. 'I'm going to incarcerate you and I'm going to incarcerate you in a way that's very unpleasant for you.' He then remanded him to the Twin Towers Correctional Facility in downtown Los Angeles to serve 111 days, before finishing off with a stint in a residential rehab. Some observers were shocked. Downey wasn't a violent felon – the only victim was himself. Others sided with the judge, arguing he was the only person who had ever taken decisive and deliberately scary action to shock the addict into understanding what he was doing to himself. 'At the end of the day,' said one friend, 'maybe the judge is the only one who's concerned about his life.' The judge made sure Downey understood, as he was handcuffed and led away. 'You are going to lose your life in this drug-soaked life you have chosen,' he said. 'You're going to jail because you used drugs.'

Twin Towers is an imposing and frightening place. It had opened that year and featured state-of-the-art panoptic security. It wasn't pleasant. Many inmates didn't bother to shower or clean their teeth. Breakfast was generic cereal, lunch a peanut butter and jam sandwich and dinner was noodles. Because it's downtown, it holds a lot of those accused of crimes and waiting for their day in court. As such, it's always very crowded. Though Downey slept in a single cell because of his fame, he lived among the general population, which in his section consisted of 35 men and was known as The Pod. He didn't have many visitors, refusing to see Indio or Deborah, though they chatted on the phone. Rumours about threats of violence meant friends outside were desperately trying to get him in a safer environment where he could be monitored more closely, in case the threats came to fruition.

He did get a chance to get out in February 1998, being transported to a soundstage so he could undergo post-production audio work on *In Dreams*. These work releases – despite the fact he had to personally pay for the time and effort given over to guarding him, as well as having the days added on to the end of his sentence – caused a ruckus in the Sheriff's Department, who believed he was getting preferential treatment. Los Angeles County Sheriff Sherman Block was angry, even though four members of his own staff had been accused of asking Downey to pose for photographs, sign autographs and even joining him to eat at the studio restaurant as his guests during one of the furloughs. Block complained to Judge Mira, while Assistant County Counsel James Owens insisted, 'We feel that, basically, the court should treat Mr Downey as any other inmate and not give him special favours because he can afford to pay for them.' Deputy District Attorney Martin Herscovitz also said enough was enough.

Downey's lawyer Ira Reiner told Mira he had allowed releases related to finishing up necessary film work and the judge agreed. 'I don't view Mr Downey as being treated specially at all,' he said. 'This is not unusual. People think that it is. And it's not unusual treatment for a celebrity.' When the judge ruled Downey could leave a fourth time, the department took it to appeal, claiming Mira acted 'arbitrarily, capriciously and in excess of the court's jurisdiction'. A state appeals panel agreed and the actor was barred from any more work-release days. The four accused sheriff's personnel and a supervisor were put under investigation.

But this was Hollywood. It wasn't the first time Downey's job had come up in prison. Inmates regularly tried to convince him they were worth doing a film about. And once, a high-ranking guard asked Downey if he could read his script about unicorns. Downey found it surreal.

The damage to his face was definitely real. Officially, he suffered a cut nose during an altercation in the prison's work area in February 1998. Unofficially, the threats that had been building came to a head and Downey lost his temper. The fight started OK for him, as he was up against people his own size. The next thing he remembered was waking up in a pool of his own blood. Ira Reiner had a different story. 'I think it's pretty clear what happened,' he said. 'Some inmates were trying to shake him down. It was no form of mutual combat. Downey was lying on his bunk in the dormitory area and one or more inmates came up to him and beat him up pretty bad.' A friend said he suffered two black eyes and was allowed to leave the prison briefly to be treated by a plastic surgeon of his choosing. One source said the star hadn't paid the required protection money. Certainly it seems like a frame-up, especially since when the guards came to deal with it, they found drug paraphernalia near to where he was resting. He was taken to the disciplinary cell, essentially solitary confinement where he was habitually woken at 5am. He was allowed supervised exercise three times a week, otherwise kept alone behind a thick steel door with one tiny window. He couldn't shower or change his clothes for five days and only ate when a pair of hands came through a gap in the door and handed over food at 6.30 a.m., 11 a.m. and 4 p.m. He hung leftover food high up so the rats couldn't get at it. There wasn't much lower he could go.

Finally, shortly after 5:30 p.m. on Tuesday, 31 March 1998, he was released from prison after serving nearly four months of his sentence. He was transported to a residential treatment centre to complete the rest, all 67 days of it. Once again, he was a changed man, sober, clear and ready to go. But he didn't have many more lives left.

From Career Rehab to Prison

'My frequent appearances on *Court TV* have brought me to another level . . .' (2003)

Richard Attenborough had noticed Downey's photographic memory, but it came as a shock to producer Josi Konski when they filmed screwball relationship comedy *Friends & Lovers* in Park City, Utah, not long after Downey got out of his state-mandated rehab on 7 August 1998. 'He was wrapped for the movie and it was just before lunch,' remembers Konski. 'Before he left, we basically convinced him to hang around and shoot an extra scene in the afternoon.' Downey agreed. 'The director and I wrote three pages of cockamamie dialogue of him talking to the lead actress,' Konski continues. 'I called him over and he read it and thought it was funny, so after lunch we set up the camera and he went through it.' As Downey stood on the snowy road, preparing to spout a slew of esoteric sentences, the producer said he would stand off-camera holding up the script so Downey could read the words from it. 'He said, "I don't need to read them, I got it." I said, "You've only read it once, I don't even remember them!" Sure enough, the director shot the scene and he's saying exactly what he had read. And I thought, this man is a genius.'

Downey signed on to *Friends & Lovers* (1999) sitting on the steps outside the William Morris Talent Agency building in Los Angeles. 'I had a meeting [there] and when I came out Robert and Stephen Baldwin were sitting on the steps,' says Konski. 'As a joke I threw a quarter at them and told them to go and get a cup of coffee.' Konski had met Downey Sr several years previously in New York and had become friendly. Junior had been hanging around too. 'He remembered me from way back and we got talking. That's how we made the deal.' Downey agreed to play Hans, a German ski instructor who owed more than a little debt to his character in *Hugo Pool*. The movie is standard indie fare, a treatise on men and women, only crass, idiotic and unenlightening. Stephen Baldwin had also signed on, alongside Clint's daughter Alison Eastwood and Claudia Schiffer. Set in a ski lodge, Downey spends most of the time wearing salopettes and sporting spiky bleached-blond hair. With a ridiculous Teutonic accent (which this time comes across as comic rather than desperate), he – unlike the rest of the film – is genuinely funny.

'A lot of it was not the director, a lot of it was him,' says Konski. 'He really took the role and built it up.' That included an impromptu song sung to Schiffer's character Carla in a bid to seduce her. 'He composed it in about five minutes. On the set. He said, "There's a piano, do you want me to play something?" I told him to knock himself out, so he went and composed that little song for her, sang it and we put it in the movie!'

Friends & Lovers eased him back into work, although he got a taste of the unease his criminal past presented to new employers, something he'd first encountered on the *Two Girls and a Guy* set. 'We had a bonding company and because of his problems, [they] didn't want me to use him in the movie,' says Josi Konski. 'They made me put additional money in reserve for him. I said absolutely, I know he will be dependable – and he presented no problems whatsoever.' Downey had people willing to back him, but it was becoming increasingly apparent it wouldn't be as smooth sailing as before, despite his Oscar nomination and fine acting reputation. Deborah Falconer accompanied him to the film's premiere in August 1998, but his whole life was changing. For starters, he didn't have any money. Flagrant spending and legal bills had cleaned him out. Throughout the nineties, the IRS lodged a variety of tax liens against him, totalling more than one million dollars. He was literally singing for his supper. He set up a bed on the sofa of his assistant Tim Kessler, a friend he met on the Georgia set of *The Gingerbread Man* who had become his major-domo.

Journalist Ken Baker believes a number of his entourage were working for free. His longtime publicist Alan Nierob had stuck with the star throughout his troubles. 'I really felt like [Nierob] cared about Robert,' says Baker. 'I doubt he was even able to pay him.'

Downey concentrated on writing a film script, working for three hours a day at an office in West Hollywood and going to addiction-recovery meetings twice a day. He talked regularly with Falconer and spent as much time as possible with Indio, now five. 'Indio's happy when he can spend continuous time with me,' said Downey to *Movieline* in 1997. 'It shows up in his expressions. If you love someone, he can spit in your face six times a day and you can still laugh. He thinks it's quite funny.' He relished his father–son time more than ever following his sustained spell in jail. He played him The Police, talked to him about what a good role model Sting was, explained the concept of the metaphor and told him funny stories about insects. 'We were in the Jack-In-The-Box drive-thru and I told him he was beautiful,' said Downey. 'Then I said, "Did you know that God made us in his image?" He thought about it and then suddenly shouted, "I knew it!"'

Both he and Falconer concentrated extra hard on their parenting skills. 'He's much more into the games and pretending and I'm more the adult role,' she said. 'Of course sometimes you just don't want to get up in the morning, but Robert is always pretty game.' They even contemplated getting back together some time in the future. 'There'll never be too much water under the bridge,' she admitted in *Detour* magazine. 'You can only know a person for how you know them. I have a sadness that we separated, but the process of evolution is always changing. We separated, but we're still connected.'

James Toback called on him again for the semi-improvisational *Black and White* (1999), asking him to play a documentary-maker called Terry who along with his wife (Brooke Shields) follows a group of rich white kids desperate to emulate their black hip-hop heroes. 'Downey had just gotten out of rehab,' said Toback to *BlackBook*. 'My intuition is that interesting people are more interesting right after they have suffered. It opens them up even further.' As always, Downey decided there should be a twist. '[He] wanted to be gay,' Toback continued, 'explore that side of himself. Every move of Downey's is formally gay, something that is a kind of complex sexual aesthete he was very eager to do.'

Like many of Toback's efforts, *Black and White* tries a little too hard to be cutting-edge, although the episodic style of narrative flow and performances are impressive. The best moment of the movie belongs to Downey, in a taut exchange with Mike Tyson. 'As soon as Downey decided he wanted to be the gay husband of Brooke Shields and he said he wanted to hit on every guy he met in the movie, I said, "Well, why don't you also hit on Mike Tyson?"' said Toback, who was a friend of the boxer, also just out of prison. 'He said, "OK, but what if he kills me?" I said, "Well, I haven't thought about that. I think it's unlikely – no better than a five per cent chance. But at the rate you're going, you're going to end up dying in the parking lot of a motel in Culver City. So what would be better – that, or dying like this?!" Downey cracked up.'

In the scene, a visibly nervous Downey sidles up to Tyson – who didn't know exactly what was going to be said – and mentions a dream he had about him. Then he says it involved the boxer 'holding' him and Tyson explodes, slapping Downey's face and then grabbing him round the throat. It's an electrifying exchange – pure (genuine) rage, followed by the terror in Downey's eyes that Tyson might actually kill him. As the actor himself said: 'A stage slap from Mike Tyson is like a shovel whack from a normally fortified male.'

He then joined Michael Douglas and Tobey Maguire for the screen adaptation of Michael Chabon's acclaimed book *Wonder Boys* (2000). He played Terry Crabtree, a book editor who travels to see his burned-out author friend Grady Tripp to convince him to finish his new novel. Over the course of several chaotic events, he reveals the insecurities beneath his veil of self-confidence as it becomes apparent his livelihood and reputation are disintegrating. Meanwhile, he seduces Maguire's socially awkward student. It's an affectionate, beautifully crafted film that speaks volumes about the human condition through quiet moments and farcical comedy. It also touched on the issue of lost promise and rediscovery, a fact Downey was all too keenly aware of. 'The film has a real poignancy,' he said, 'because you can experience that "wonder boys" phenomenon regardless of what generation you're in. It reminds me of people in the eighties who were living high off the hog in New York and LA. They were at all the clubs and had all the new clothes and so on. Now, ten years later, they're still wearing the same stuff and still trying to ride on the same coat-tails, except that it's just not working any more.' It was one of his warmest performances, despite the character's seeming superficiality. As the transvestite he picks up at the airport and then quickly dumps says: 'Your friend is into collecting weird tricks.' He became good friends with Maguire off set, the actor frequently coming round to Downey's house and talking on the terrace.

It was the same old story, telling interviewers he was ready to turn his life around. He went for a progress report with Judge Mira in December 1998, who commented on his new gym-toned physique and told him to keep up the good work. He was signed up to voice the Devil, in an NBC cartoon comedy series called *God, the Devil and Bob*. He even thought about finally getting out of his assistant's apartment, renting a room at the Standard Hotel on Sunset Boulevard and hiring a modest car to get himself and his son around.

But just as before, it was all a lie. He had been missing court-prescribed drug tests and was using drugs again, a violation of his probation. NBC replaced him with Alan Cumming. He confessed, hoping for leniency, and on 22 June 1999 he was up before his old friend Judge Lawrence Mira wearing a dark suit and tie. Mira couldn't believe what he was seeing. He suspected there were underlying psychological issues that hadn't been identified. 'I feel very strongly here that there is something going on with you I don't understand,' he said. 'I think there are serious psychological issues that we need to address.' He ordered a psychiatric examination and remanded Downey to the rehab unit of the county prison. Used to handcuffs by now, Downey submitted and was led away, pending a hearing to determine the sentence for violating his parole on 5 August.

'I'm going to recover,' Downey said, 'but I'm still finding that difficult.' His publicist Alan Nierob was as open as ever. '[Robert] came to court today with his drug counsellor and admitted he has a continuing drug problem,' he told the *Associated Press*. 'He asked the court for help and guidance.'

'For a young, brilliant and sexy guy like Robert was in the nineties, drugs can begin as an exciting, even exhilarating experience – full of promises of mind expansion, consciousness-raising and of course a lot of fun mentally and physically,' says Downey's *Danger Zone* director Allan Eastman, who battled his own cocaine problem in the early eighties and eventually spent three months in the Caribbean getting clean. 'The problem arises when you begin to use more and more to get back to the state that you used to achieve easily. That's when the abuse sets in, the needs for huge hits of cognac to soften the edges of the cocaine buzz, the moving on to more powerful drugs as the initial thrill of the old ones lessen. In the Hollywood scene, there are too many enablers who will just keep giving drugs to stars in return for getting to hang out with a famous celebrity. Forget *Twilight*, these are the real vampires. Also, it's a truism that in Hollywood, you know 10,000 people but you're lucky if you have three friends, people willing to tell you the truth when you are fucking up. There is so much support for bad behaviour that the abuser can convince himself that the few people who tell him the truth are deluded when their behaviour is endorsed by so many.

Eastman believes that Downey's main problem, paradoxically, lay in his own genius. 'He is so talented and so keyed to invention in the moment when he is working that I think he found "normal" life a little boring, he says. 'He was probably under-whelmed by some of the crappy projects he found himself involved in. He would be looking for something to give him an artificial high until he could get the next real high from his work. The actor George Sanders said in his suicide notes that he was simply "bored" and I think that Robert was in a similar state – a touch bored by life out of work, so the partying just went on and on and inevitably ended up descending into much darker regions.'

Downey went back to the rehab unit of the county jail. He felt it was working, but had to return to court in August to face his destiny. He hired lawyer Peter Knecht to represent him, who in turn brought O. J. Simpson defence attorney Robert Shapiro on board. 'First time I laid eyes on him I picked him up from his rehab,' says Knecht. 'It was strange to see a fellow who was larger than life in his good moments to be in a cell, looking depressed and sitting in that down-and-out environment I saw him in. When I was representing him I would get letters from across the United States wishing him luck and good fortune. I got a letter from an old woman who had taken her son to the movie set of *U.S. Marshals*. She said to me in her letter that he was wearing dark glasses when they met him. Her son was a huge fan and had always wanted to meet him. But when he took off his glasses she said she could tell right away that this young man was under the influence of drugs. She was a Christian and she was shocked, you know she was thinking he needed to be exorcised or something. Her grandson didn't notice, of course. But it just goes to show that there are people out there who can function and get on with their day-to-day job when they are high.'

Knecht picked him up and drove him to court. 'Unfortunately, in those days, rehabs still allowed cigarettes. In my opinion, nicotine is just as bad a drug as any of them. I remember we stopped half a dozen times for him to have a smoke. It was only from Santa Monica to Malibu, which was about five miles. Not only that but he stopped at a coffee shop for his caffeine fix. He was heavily addicted to anything. I felt bad, especially since his temperament and his personality were just so nice. He was always so polite and such a sweet guy. I remember he noticed I had a nice new car and he would say, "Hey, do you mind if I smoke in your car?" And I would say that I'd prefer it if he didn't. So that's why we made all those stops. It was no big deal but he was so polite. He never wanted to offend anyone or tread on anyone's toes. He didn't talk about his addictions to me. He didn't really have any need to do that. The last thing a lawyer wants to do is be a therapist or a rehab counsellor. He would talk sometimes about planning to stay away from it, or at least just not getting caught.'

Judge Mira seemed more sad than angry. 'I don't think we have any alternative,' he said. 'We have used them all.' Downey begged for one last chance, asking Mira to let him carry on with rehab and remain on probation. 'It's been the right programme at the right time for me,' he said. 'I feel whatever decision you make will be the right one . . . but I feel a transition has happened to me.' More than ever, he was aware how dangerous his addiction had become. And as always, he described it eloquently and vividly. 'It's like I've got a shotgun in my mouth, and my finger's on the trigger and I like the taste of gun metal,' he said.

'He was obviously able to rise above it all emotionally, even in the courtroom,' says Knecht, which is ironic considering it wasn't always just the defendants engaged in substance abuse. 'In the old days before metal detectors and searches, attorneys would go into the courthouse and when you visited the bathroom all you could hear was sniffing,' he adds. 'It was no big deal. Everyone was doing it. Guys were able to win jury trials when high on coke. There was nothing he did in my opinion that he did wrong at the time he did it. He started when he was a kid. He was given drugs by family. It became a normal thing to do. Of course, there came a point in time when he realised it was against the law and not everyone did it. But one thing is for sure – when you live in Hollywood and the people in your circle do it, they aren't criminals. They are generally millionaires and people of substance and people of importance.'

Shapiro – who had got O. J. Simpson off – also urged clemency. 'This is a person who is suffering from a disease he can't control,' he said. 'Even the dire threat of jail or prison is not enough of a deterrent.' But Judge Mira wasn't easily swayed by emotional statements. He invoked Downey's three-year probation and sentenced him to the same amount of time in jail, citing the fact that the actor had promised change in seven court-appointed rehab plans and failed to deliver. He credited the star with 201 days for time served and fined him $600, before sending him upstate to the California Substance Abuse Treatment Facility in Corcoran, some 170 miles north of Los Angeles. 'I am shocked and saddened by the sentence,' said Shapiro to the *Associated Press*. 'It is wrong, it does not serve justice. Mr Downey was on the road to recovery.'

'He was the victim of his own crime,' says Peter Knecht. 'He wasn't getting high and robbing 7/11s to get his fix. People that are affluent and live their lives doing drugs live a lifestyle. It isn't a life of crime he was living. In the seventies and eighties, cocaine, LSD, was just a lifestyle. No one really considered it illegal. Sure, if you got caught you got arrested. But most of the stuff he did wasn't to hurt anyone but himself and I think that's important to remember. When he was found in his neighbours' bed, he hadn't done that to hurt anyone. He was simply wasted and got the wrong house. Technically it could have been called burglary. But he didn't steal anything and he didn't enter with the intent to commit a crime, he entered with the intent to go to sleep. He never spoke with me about that. People do stupid things when they are high and I never wanted to rub it in his face. If he had wanted to talk about it I would have chatted. It was an embarrassing situation which I didn't think it was fair to bring up.'

Downey approached incarceration with stoicism, even though he was initially angry that he was put in prison, unsurprisingly sharing the belief among a lot of prison-reform campaigners that non-violent drug addicts shouldn't be jailed. However, as he grew accustomed to the nightmare of being locked up, he began to convince himself there were some positives to be taken out of it. 'It taught me the consequences of continuing a self-destructive path in life,' he said. 'Being in prison is not a lot of laughs. When I was first sentenced I felt it was unfair and unconstitutional. But once I was inside I realised you need to be taken away from your usual lifestyle. You need to have a shock to your value system, your ego, your arrogance.'

In the end, he was sounding like a campaigner himself – for the other side. 'I think that for people like me who have all the opportunities in the world to have a great life but instead choose to destroy themselves, jail is definitely an answer. It's not pleasant, it's not fun. In my case, though, it was probably necessary.'

Indeed, Knecht was surprised at how calmly he dealt with the judge's decision. 'I would be concerned. Everyone should be concerned,' he says. 'It's a dangerous environment. But for some reason Robert didn't show concern. When I visited him he was mostly in the rehab facility, which was a nicer environment, a bit nicer than the main jail. It wasn't as violent. He just took a deep breath and dealt with it. His temperament is unusual. He isn't a whiner, he isn't a complainer. I guess I also knew him when he wasn't high, he was supposed to be in recovery. But even on drugs, I couldn't imagine him being a bad man. It was an interesting experience. I can honestly say that I enjoyed his company.'

He arrived at Corcoran after a brief stop-off at North Kern State Prison in Delano on 25 August 1999. He was given his prison uniform and assigned an inmate number, P50522. He was then placed in Cell 17 of the F-1 Block, a moderate-security section of the facility. He shared a room with four other prisoners: a redneck called Big Al; Timmons, an old-school gangster; Figueroa Slim, a.k.a. Charles Bell; and Sugar Bear, who spent most of his time as a clerk in the prison chapel. Downey took a top bunk and was assigned kitchen duty, where he earned eight cents per hour handing out the meals, or sometimes washing the dishes. He spent a lot of time in drug therapy, constantly under the threat of an impromptu urine test. He stayed clean. He saw his behaviour as the final step in his self-abuse, which was now complete. 'I thought I was capable of enjoying my abusive lifestyle and somehow working things out, which is obviously a huge act of self-delusion,' he said. 'But in a strange way I needed to go so low, to see how bad I could be and get away with it.'

Sean Penn, *Wonder Boys* director Curtis Hanson, Deborah Falconer – who by this time had set up home with a new boyfriend – and Indio all visited him, as did his sister Allyson, who he talked to about his lows, even though they never definitively manifested themselves. She felt he was cautiously optimistic about a legal appeal. At the beginning of his sentence, he seemed to be fine – cracking jokes, marvelling at some of the insanity within the prison walls, making the most of the visitors' ability to buy him extra food from the vending machines. The drug treatment seemed to be working.

He was increasingly aware of his demons. 'If you repress the devil inside you, he will nail you,' he said some years later. 'I don't know why, but I kept letting the devil back in. It's so nuts – I would have a great week, feel good, feel that I'm getting healthy again and then return to my old habits.'

He reconnected with his family, writing poems to mother Elsie and sending a birthday card to his sister for the first time since she could remember. Elsie had been housebound in Pennsylvania thanks to two heart operations and relished the communication. 'I hang on to every word he writes me like it was the law,' she said in *Vanity Fair*. 'I pay close attention to what he's saying.' Allyson called him an idiot savant. Unfortunately, she too was reported to have succumbed to drugs, allegedly battling addiction and an eating disorder for many years, before finally beating it. 'She won!' says her former flatmate. 'She ended up in hospital, I don't know if it was drug-related. When I went to see her, she asked me to get her out and we got out. I don't know exactly what was going on. When she was in trouble, she'd come and live with me. Or she'd go home [to her mother's place]. When she didn't want to live in Connecticut or whatever, my door was always open. She was the type of person who was there for *you*.' Because of her experience, Allyson took the time to counsel addicts herself, spending time at various rehab facilities as an intern. By the end of the nineties, she was living in New York's Soho, running a management company to handle actors and writers. Her friend says she struggled to hold down a relationship. 'She never seemed to have a relationship with someone else for a long period of time,' she says. 'I never really met a boyfriend. She didn't want to deal with them!'

Her brother wrote a lot inside – he had always found prison a creative environment like that – responding to some of the hundreds of letters from fans he received every week and jotting down crazy short stories for his friends. He wrote several letters from prison in red ink on pink paper to members of his fan club, thanking them for helping him through his ordeal. Three of them were to the fan club as a whole, some of them to individuals. The efforts of his global network of supporters – from Australia, Russia, Britain and Sweden among others – contributed to what he called his 'triple latte awakening'. 'There was much going on in trying to help Robert,' says a member of the club. 'We had online petitions to sign, we continuously sent Robert books, gifts, letters of encouragement, talked to his lawyer. Doing our best to help him get out of there and keep his spirits up.'

Downey had had a private revelation on 24 June – the date of his father's birthday, in fact – a feeling that everything was going to be OK while in rehab awaiting sentence. He was still in a positive frame of mind four months later, when he wrote again from Corcoran to wish his fans a happy Thanksgiving and tell them about his case, which he was pleased to report was moving steadily forward. But that mood changed after the Thanksgiving holidays and he was less frequent with his correspondence. He explained how the letters and the gifts that were sent were often the only things keeping him going. He enjoyed getting books from the outside, even if some of them were confiscated (you can only receive books from certain designated sellers in jail). And he began to read *Sleeping Where I Fall*, a memoir by the actor Peter Coyote (*E.T.*), about his life involved in the counter-cultural movement at the end of the sixties and beginning of the seventies, which he found enlightening and instructive.

His friend Josh Richman took some of the art Downey drew using crayons on any piece of paper he could find and sold them on to celebrity pals to help top up the real-world bank balance. He drew personal pictures too – one was a caricature of his friend Moogy Klingman, to which he added the legend: 'St Klingman Of Moogimus'. He made friends with a guy called Mike and two others called Dvorak and Cisco, played racquetball every morning and got given the nickname 'Mo' Downey.

'I invested a lot of time in rebellion, self-destruction and random acts of insanity,' he reflected in 2000 just after leaving prison. 'But I don't think I ever treated anyone badly, not even my ex-girlfriends. I think I grew up feeling like a lot of LA kids – I didn't know what to do with myself except that I knew I wasn't happy with what life was offering around me. I was restless, I didn't have as much attention from my father as I think I needed and I became a typical wild Hollywood teenager. And I continued that reckless behaviour into my adult life. I had a lot of fun, but the fun got out of hand.

'Fear was part of the motivation for engaging in excess,' he continued. 'What's amazing is that no matter how much I try to destroy myself things have had a way of straightening themselves out. Walking the line between creativity and self-destruction scares me.'

He got involved in arts and crafts and led the inmate choral group at Christmas when they sang carols. He was allowed to view small amounts of television, although the shows were decided by democratic vote, so he found himself watching a lot of *Friends*. He listened to Sting CDs and started taking himself more seriously, promising himself he wouldn't be such a goofball in the future.

Thoughts of Indio got him through a lot of the time. He remembered the little boy sitting on his knee, watching his dad cutting up his food for him at the *Black and White* wrap party. He had considered lying to him about his prison sentence, telling him he was going away to be a spy, but Falconer had persuaded him otherwise. It hadn't been easy. Indio asked him if he was bad and he had to convince him he wasn't. Falconer knew Indio had seen his father go away before, but this time was different. As he spat his toothpaste into the cell toilet and waited to hear news of the appeal his legal team filed in late September 1999, he concentrated on his recovery, receiving guidance from television evangelist Tim Storey and having meetings with drug counsellors, all of whom lauded him for his focus and dedication to getting better. He started counselling other addicted inmates and even finally graduated from high school – kind of – when he took the G.E.D., the high school equivalency test, scoring the highest mark of anyone ever at the prison.

But as time wore on, things got tougher. Another inmate called Reginald Harris reported that Downey had been targeted by a Mexican gang for snitching on two of their members and had almost been knifed while coming out of the shower. He added that the star had been beaten up twice – once by a new cellmate called Water Buffalo who took offence to his walking around naked and another time by a disgruntled prisoner who beat him so badly Downey ended up taking a painkilling pill that sent him into convulsions. Downey said people had overactive imaginations, though when he was visited in May 2000, his hair had begun to grey and he had a cut next to his nose. He was tired, he was depressed . . . he was ready to leave. He had another close call when a racquetball opponent got a little bit over-physical on the court, trying to goad him into a fight. He walked away from it and his friend Mike managed to talk the other guy down. After Mike was transferred to another prison, he was threatened again, but defused the situation by staying mentally strong and refusing to lose his temper.

Three of his films came out while he was inside. *Wonder Boys* was released to great acclaim, the BBC's website writing: 'Witty, intelligent and sophisticated, this is a Hollywood rarity. A film with the courage to do what it wants, safe in the knowledge that its characters are strong, funny, and interesting enough to suck the audience in.' Meanwhile, *Auto Motives* (2000), a short about cars, co-starring James Cameron and *The West Wing*'s Allison Janney and directed by Sopranos actress Lorraine Bracco, was shown at the Comedy Arts Festival. It wasn't one of his finest hours, though according to people who worked on it, it had been shot while he was at rock bottom and he hadn't been the typical cool guy he usually was.

At the opening of *Black and White* at Union Square in New York on 4 April 2000, a group of friends organised a demonstration to protest against Downey's prison sentence. About twenty people descended on the cinema and the police barricaded them in across the street from the theatre. They made flyers and held up banners attached to fifteen-foot poles, chanting 'Rehab not jail for Robert Downey Jr!' and 'Free Robert!' Some of the demonstrators did interviews with the press and they handed out self-made leaflets. 'We became activists of sorts,' explains one of the key personnel in the event's organisation, 'struggling for Robert's release and to have the laws changed in California for drug offenders. We wrote lots of letters to Congress members and various US politicians.' Downey's sister Allyson flew in from Pennsylvania to help out and work the media. Web pages were set up called 'Support Robert Downey Jr' and 'Free Robert Downey Jr'. Anthony Michael Hall wrote an open letter to his best friend's fans telling them how inspired he was by their energy and persistence.

Elsewhere, his team of lawyers were working hard on making the protestors' demands happen. Thanks to the sentence meted out by Judge Mira, Downey was originally expected to stay in prison until early November 2000. But by July, attorney Robert Waters was telling anyone who would listen that Mira had made legal and mathematical mistakes with Downey's case and in fact he should have been eligible for parole in February. He earned his fee at the start of August, when he convinced an appeals court Downey had served enough time to fulfil his mandated sentence, counting time in rehab and remand.

Downey was ecstatic at the news but knew he had a lot of work to do if he was to make it on the outside. It's all very well being a bad boy, but being an ex-convict? That was something Hollywood doesn't have to deal with very often. He left Corcoran, got into a waiting car and then changed automobiles so as to make the trip to his first post-prison 12-step meeting a paparazzi-free affair. After therapy and a fajita, he checked himself into Walden House, a Los Angeles drug treatment facility he had previously attended, having paid his required $5,000 bail. He loved being free. 'It definitely feels very pleasant,' he said soon after tasting fresh air. 'It's nice to be able to walk outside and not have to wear a uniform any more. Prison fashion is pretty limited.'

Waters spoke on his client's behalf, saying he was intent on 'putting his life back together and putting this behind him'. Meanwhile, publicist Alan Nierob added, 'I think he'll resume working as he was before he was incarcerated. His talents have always been in demand and I see no reason for that to change.' Downey was even more tenacious in his self-belief. 'It's amazing that anyone survives what they put themselves through. It's a tribute to the resilience of the human spirit,' he said. 'I know that I've been given yet another chance at straightening myself [out] after hundreds of failed attempts. But this time I've had a year behind bars to help me think my way out of my own nightmare. I'm pretty confident that finally I've figured out how to save myself.'

Downey was 35 years old. He was still broke. He had lots of people on his side, but many of them had been burned many times before by his lies and charming façade. 'I don't want to be a proponent of the system but certain ideals have changed for me,' he told *Details*. 'The idea of a victimless crime, it's an oxymoron. I can't say that someone who's involved in addiction only victimises themselves. It's not true. It's convenient and people run with that. I ran with that as a way to deal with it.'

Despite his experience, he was strangely belligerent about his time in jail. 'The threat of prison has been eliminated for me now,' he said. 'I know I can do time now. I can even go out and do stuff that makes what I did before seem tame.' But his sponsor Warren Boyd, a sober companion who was on call 24 hours a day to keep him on track was upbeat about the future. 'I don't like to make predictions, but I can tell you that the recovery that Robert demonstrates, the way he walks and talks, I've seen few people fail when they're like that,' he said. That was all very well, but would he be accepted back into the acting community? Who was going to take that chance?

David E. Kelley was one of the top writer-producers on American television, a veteran of *L.A. Law* who had turned series' creator and whose quirky legal show *Ally McBeal* had topped the ratings for two seasons, before beginning to tail off during its third. Now it needed a creative jolt and Kelley saw just what he needed in Downey. 'David Kelley took a big risk,' says journalist Ken Baker. 'Robert Downey Jr owes a lot to him.'

Kelley offered Downey half a million dollars to play lead actress Calista Flockhart's featured love interest during the coming series, initially signing him up for eight episodes, with a view to a longer-term deal. 'We knew he would have good chemistry with [Flockhart],' said *Ally* producer Pamela J. Wisne in *Details*. 'He agreed and it worked out well. The cast loves him, the crew loves him.' The casting coup was announced on 10 August and, before he knew it, Downey found himself on the Los Angeles lot of the show. He was to play lawyer Larry Paul, who Ally hires to do some legal work for her before falling for him. 'I think he's inspired people to go the extra mile,' said Flockhart, echoing the excitement of the cast members to have an Oscar nominee in their ranks.

To Downey's mind, it was a happy accident. 'TV is something new for me and I'm extremely grateful to have found this kind of a home and opportunity when a lot of people think I'm untouchable because of my past,' he said. The work days were manageable, close to home and fitted in with his recovery programme. There were even 12-step meetings on the studio lot. Indio was pleased his dad was playing a good guy. '[Indio's] really happy I'm playing a lawyer,' he said. 'He feels it'll make Daddy behave himself now!' And the money was great.

'It just smelled like a really good match,' said Kelley in *Entertainment Weekly*. 'Robert has this comedic tone that I thought was really organic to our show.' Downey particularly enjoyed his first day in 'court'. 'It was so nice to go into this fake courtroom,' he said. 'I immediately went up to the judge's chair. Nice view. A preferable perspective.' As with most people within the McBeal-verse, Larry was a bit of an oddball, though not as demonstrably as the rest of the characters. He's first introduced unpacking boxes in the office of Ally's therapist, who has left town without telling her, and ends up doling out some sage but tough advice of his own. From the off, he and Flockhart do have an undeniable chemistry, not an easy feat considering it rarely happened with the actress on screen. He looks handsome, coiffed, well tailored.

But perhaps the most interesting thing about Larry is the parallels he seems to share with his real-life portrayer. David E. Kelley is a notoriously prolific writer and was banging out the scripts from the moment he heard Downey wanted to do the show. It can't have been coincidence, the many attributes he gave to his creation, knowing his off-screen alter ego. There is plenty of opportunity for the actor to show off his innate charm, wooing the leading lady, displaying his lawyering skills – he even gets to sing a duet with his idol and former customer Sting in the programme's famous bar. But it's during scenes in the episode 'Tis The Season' that it's as if a mirror is being held up to his own life, when he talks about his guilt over being an absent parent. 'I'm ashamed I don't see him every day and I'm ashamed that he's grown up for the most part without his father,' says Larry Paul. As he begins to edge towards marriage to Ally and becomes more prevalent in the arc of the show, some of the lines are downright spooky, particularly when he has doubts over their relationship. 'Thing is, I don't really trust myself,' he says. 'I've failed as a father. I've failed as a husband. I would be lying if I said I understood what makes me fail. The biggest lie of all would be to say I'd never fail again.'

Larry went down a treat with *Ally McBeal* fans and critics alike. Websites sprang up praising the new relationship, with predictions for its longevity. 'Downey's portrayal of Larry Paul is one of the high points of current television,' wrote *Entertainment Weekly*. 'He takes the romantic byplay David E. Kelley has written for Larry and Calista Flockhart's Ally and runs with it . . . Downey's performance is a demonstration of the difference between film and TV actors. Though trained on stage, Flockhart has picked up the common TV habit of playing the lines, not the character; Downey has, as his very name suggests, brought her back to earth on a soft, thick – downy – cushion.'

A TV Star with Secrets

'I'm allergic to alcohol and narcotics. I break out in handcuffs.'

(2003)

'Robert really is a special guy,' says Dr Drew Pinsky, a celebrity addiction specialist who knows the actor. 'He gets under your skin. It does him a disservice, because it allows him to keep his relationships and manipulate people and keep the disease going, because he is such a wonderful guy.'

It's difficult to believe Downey would want to use drugs again. He had ruined two serious relationships, disappointed his son, upset his family, lied to his friends and eviscerated his bank balance. He had waded through kitchen waste and avoided violent retaliation in prison and sat through thousands of hours of recovery meetings and 12-step pledges. He had forgotten how many times he'd had to pee in a cup. He was an intelligent man, who promoted a healthy agenda. 'Right now I'm following a very strict routine, getting exercise, eating properly, getting a lot of sleep and living a very healthy lifestyle,' he said. 'I'm so incredibly well organised that I schedule everything to the last second.'

Surely he had the willpower to stick to his task? 'Willpower services the disease,' says Dr Pinsky. 'Addiction is a distortion of the motivational systems responsible for all drives like survival. In other words, your thinking, your volition, your judgement, your emotions all service a distorted motivation. The problem is, your brain will literally take you to the brink of death, because it biologically equates the drug use with survival itself.' One of the major problems Downey faced was his acquiescence when people asked him to work and his desire to do so. 'One of the most significant problems we have with celebrities is because they make so much money for people, they go back to work prematurely,' says Dr Pinsky. 'There's an ample supply of enablers. And they make so much money for people that as long as they continue to work, people let it slide. Anybody with a normal job would be pulled aside and told to get it together.' And as for Downey? 'I think he's so charming people didn't want to think he was in trouble. They wanted to think the best of him.'

'I think everyone is aware of how critical this stage in my life is because of what I've been through,' said Downey. 'No one who goes to jail for a year is anxious to go back. I know that studio executives might have some concerns because they need to sell a film to an audience and anything that threatens the box office is a liability. But I think the public is probably pulling for me and hoping that I get my act together and not fall back into my bad habits. So I really don't think my past is going to stand in the way of my work. On the contrary, I think it might make me that much more aggressive and responsible in pursuing as much work as I can get.'

'The genetics associated with addiction tend to be a very rich, intelligent, sensitive population of humans,' says Dr Pinsky. 'They also tend to be people who come from disruptive family systems that makes them interested in expressive things. It also makes them interested in being celebrities. Very few severe addicts have a straight road to recovery.'

Ally McBeal was going well. Outwardly, things were looking up. 'I find such great peace in getting my clothes out the night before work,' he said. 'I mean, to watch me, you would think I probably have OCD (obsessive compulsive disorder), but it's not really like that. It's meditation.' Nevertheless, even if Downey was publicly talking about how he was ready to move on, he knew it wouldn't be simple.

'Addiction is addiction and I'm an addict who has to fight for the rest of his life against the allure of substance abuse,' he said. 'Every day that I'm clean is a step in the right direction. But every day poses a risk that I can fall back and Hollywood is a palace of temptation. So I'm waging my fight against that backdrop, but I feel good about my life now, so I'm not worried. I just have to guard against that moment that might come in two days, two weeks or eight months from now when that urge comes back. That'll be the real test.'

And, true to life, privately it was all a sham. 'You put a Hugo Boss suit on a guy, clean him up a little, feed him his lines and he managed to perform like he isn't a drooling goo-goo,' Downey later admitted to the *Guardian* newspaper about his time on the show. 'I'm probably not the best person to ask about that period. It was my lowest point in terms of addictions. At that stage, I didn't give a fuck whether I ever acted again.' Nevertheless, by Thanksgiving 2000 Downey had finished production on his eight scheduled episodes and had signed up to more. Perhaps inspired by his performance in *Two Girls and a Guy*, his old friend Mel Gibson had been in touch and suggested they collaborate on a stage production of *Hamlet* in Los Angeles after he finished his television commitments, with Downey playing the lead role. Sensing an unmissable challenge, the actor agreed. Director Joe Roth wanted him for a role in the star-studded comedy *America's Sweethearts*.

But things don't always turn out the way you think they will, especially not when you're a substance abuser. 'It's a treacherous, cunning disease,' says Dr Pinsky. 'It can recur without any notice.'

'Uh, yeah, I'd just like to let you know that in Room 311 of the Merv Griffin Resort there is a man that is doing an ounce of cocaine and a couple of guns and is pretty upset. Thank you.' So went the 911 call to the Palm Springs police on the night of Saturday 25 November 2000. As the caller clicked off around half-seven, Downey was in his room – Room 311 – with a Californian performance artist nicknamed Cholla, a friend of a friend. She left minutes before the cops arrived at the complex and asked to search the actor's digs. They found no guns, but did uncover four grams of cocaine and sixteen Valium. One of the searching officers spoke to him, saying, 'Just because you are a movie star, that doesn't mean you can break the rules.' Downey replied, 'I'm not a movie star. I'm a guy with a drug problem.'

'He was co-operative and in our opinion under the influence of a controlled substance,' said a police spokesman. 'He was charged with that. He invited officers into the suite and we continued the search. Throughout the entire incident, he was compliant.' He spent the night in jail and was released the following morning on $15,000 bail. It had begun again.

Rewind back to the previous Wednesday and no one would have realised the star was about to have another public meltdown. He was depressed, no doubt about it – tired from working and going through a tough period with Deborah, who was threatening to finally divorce him. One friend said he was on the 'brink of destruction', distraught over the relationship with the mother of his child and because he wasn't able to spend the holiday weekend with Indio. He needed to get out of town, so asked his friend Mark Lawrence Miller, whom he had known since 1985, to come with him to the Merv Griffin Resort in Palm Springs about two hours east of LA. Clear skies, fresh air, peace and quiet. Miller wasn't keen. After all, it was the day before Thanksgiving, traditionally a big party weekend, and he would have preferred to stay in the city. But he saw that Downey needed some company, so they made their way there and checked into the $600-a-night suite. 'He was very friendly, very nice,' one of the staff told *Rolling Stone*, who found out he was on a four-day break from *Ally McBeal*.

The pair worked on their joint screenplay for a while, but Downey wanted to go out. Miller knew better than to lecture his friend. 'Robert will excommunicate you if you are just ragging on him like people in the AA programme do,' he said. Miller thought the best option would be a fully nude strip bar, not only for the distraction of the women, but also because California law dictates you aren't allowed to serve alcohol at an establishment that features completely naked girls. So Downey tried to disguise himself with a tatty blue cap and they headed out in a limousine to Showgirls in Cathedral City, about twenty minutes away.

Downey wasn't able to stay incognito for long. Soon word got round the club there was a celebrity in their midst and the star was happily chatting with his fans until he saw 21-year-old Kiley Ridge, an ex-employee of the club in with her big brother Mike to pick up her final wage packet. Downey liked what he saw and asked if she wanted to party with him that night. Ridge, a small-town girl who spent most of her youth in Florida, wasn't going to pass up what she considered to be the opportunity of a lifetime. And she wasn't going to keep quiet about it either. She bragged about her impending night of fun to Levi Castleberry, a Showgirls bouncer who fancied her. He was a bit jealous, but was keen to share the experience. First the party headed to Castleberry's apartment where he gave Downey a line of cocaine. The actor then asked for some baking soda and cooked up a small supply of crack, which they also smoked. Finally, the drugs ran out and they went to Ridge's house to pick up Valium. The vibe was getting increasingly antsy and Downey decided to leave by himself, but the others followed him back to his hotel room, before Castleberry headed out to a friend's place with a guy called Nick (who DJ-ed at Showgirls) to pick up another ounce of coke. Downey ordered room service, Miller returned with some strippers and everyone partied till the early hours, before the locals headed home.

He spent the following day relaxing, hanging out with some of the strippers he had met on the first night, as well as Cholla, who had been drafted in by Miller to help him make sure Downey didn't go too crazy. On Saturday, he was hanging out quietly in his room when he heard the knock on his door and found police standing outside. Most people believe it was Nick who called the cops, even though Castleberry had been angry about Downey's closeness to Kiley Ridge. Showgirls dancer Laura Burnett told *Salon.com* it was 'just somebody who knew [he] was there and wanted to make a big deal about it'.

As soon as people back in Hollywood heard, they were shocked. His uncle Jim Downey blamed the workload. 'It was not enough time for him to settle down and gather his strength,' he opined in *USA Today*. 'If you're as sensitive and fragile as Robert is, it's a set-up for disaster.'

His agent Ed Limato was upset. 'Those of us who love Robert – and there are many of us – are heartbroken,' he said. Rumours started swirling this wasn't his first relapse since getting out of jail just three months previously. One person said that a fortnight before it happened, Downey left Indio at home with an assistant while he went out to score drugs. His friend Tom Sizemore revealed not just that a group of actors had to pay for his attorney to appeal his conviction, but that he was using almost from the moment he was released. 'He was getting high day one [after getting out of jail],' he said to the *Chicago Sun-Times*. 'When you get out of jail and you're offered half a million bucks from David E. Kelley to do eight episodes of *Ally McBeal*, you go, "I don't have a problem". You go around saying lines with Calista Flockhart and then go buy some crack. It's very sad,' he added. 'But it's tough to be in the Hollywood world. People just give drugs to you if you're an actor. If Robert goes into a nightclub, he's doomed. Someone will give him drugs.'

He couldn't break the cycle. He also couldn't get a break from working. David E. Kelley and the Fox network were sympathetic to his plight, but three days later he was back on the set. 'He's concentrating on work and himself,' said Alan Nierob, his publicist. 'He's a recovering addict. Recovering addicts have relapses. He's working hard at his sobriety as he has for the last eighteen months.' He added, 'He was studying his lines yesterday to get back to work.'

Downey secretly met with his friend Mel Gibson at The Four Seasons hotel in Los Angeles where they had lunch and talked about what had happened. 'Robert is kicking himself,' said Gibson. 'Wouldn't you be? I know I would. Of course he is, but he'll be fine. He's a good guy. He's got a good heart. Obviously, I am very concerned for [him] but I don't judge him. I think it's something he's got to go through to get to the other side, but hey, we all fall.'

On 11 December he was charged with two felony counts of possessing cocaine and diazepam (the generic name of Valium) and for being under the influence of a controlled substance. He was scheduled to return to court for arraignment at the end of December. *Simpsons*' voice actor Hank Azaria was drafted in to replace him in *America's Sweethearts*. 'It's heartbreaking that this happened,' said Joe Roth in an interview with *The New York Times*. 'We're trying to sort it out now. We don't want to hurt him in any way, but we have to figure out what we'll do for our movie.'

Hamlet was put on the backburner. '*Hamlet* was actually on hold before Robert's recent arrest,' insisted Gibson, though few believed him. 'There's the actors' strike coming up so it's important that everybody get in there and make a living – particularly him, I think – so I wouldn't want to stand in the way of that. We figured we'll put it on hold a little while longer.'

It wasn't the only trauma for the *Ally McBeal* team. Calista Flockhart collapsed on the set, with stress over Downey's problems partly blamed. Downey had been flirting with her for some time and the pair were rumoured to be dating. On 27 December, Downey headed east for his arraignment. Ironically, the courthouse was in Indio, a small town 30 miles further inland from Palm Springs. He stood before Judge B. J. Bjork during a twenty-minute hearing dressed entirely in black. The press were everywhere; photographers and journalists crowded into the jury box in the small courtroom where his lawyer Daniel Brookman entered a 'not guilty' plea on his behalf. Brookman asked for a continuance until the following year but Bjork refused and the case was set in motion. He was hurried out the side door and jumped into a waiting car, but as soon as he came to an intersection, he was once again besieged by paparazzi. Finally he managed to get away. It was a hell of a way to end the year.

Awards and Arrests

'I had bigger fish to fry.' (2005)

Six days before Downey had returned to Indio, CA, he had received a nice surprise when his name was read out alongside five others, including Sean Hayes of *Will & Grace* and Bradley Whitford from *The West Wing*, as a Golden Globe nominee for Best Supporting Actor in a Series, Mini-Series or Television Movie. It was proof how quickly his portrayal of Larry Paul had captured the imagination of his peers and the public and was the first awards recognition he had received since *Chaplin* eight years previously. David E. Kelley's desire to reinvigorate the show and inspire it back to critical success was rewarded with a Leading Actress nod for Flockhart and a nomination for the programme itself in the Best Comedy Series category.

The house came down on 21 January 2001 when Downey's name was revealed as the winner. He was humble when he went up on stage to collect his trophy. 'I would like to thank David Kelley for creating such a great character,' he said. 'He said when he was writing it that it was like having a new toy. I will do my best not to get sent back to the factory.' When he went to the press room backstage he refused to take questions from the journalists, saying, 'I just want to share this with my fellow parolees, er, nominees. This really means a lot. I really appreciate the goodwill that comes from everyone.' He also told co-host Dick Clark: 'It's really meant the world to me that people have been so supportive and have come up to me on the street and said they're rooting for me. And something like this, to be acknowledged, is really good . . . All these things are esteem-building.'

He needed it. Two days after he scooped a Golden Globe, Deborah Falconer filed for divorce in a Los Angeles court. In *Madison* magazine in 2008, Downey said: 'I had largely unfortunate and occasionally wonderful philandering moments while I was in long-term relationships.' But no third parties were mentioned. After all they had been separated, though close, for years. She cited irreconcilable differences, and claimed for unspecified spousal support payments and custody of Indio, with Downey to have supervised visits. She more than anyone knew what was going on beneath the surface during the shooting of *Ally McBeal*. It appeared that enough was enough and it was time to move forward. Downey was understandably upset, but he had other pressing legal matters to attend to as well, returning to the Riverside Superior Court in Indio for a procedural hearing about the Merv Griffin bust. As a recidivist, he was facing a possible jail sentence of up to four years and had to provide his parole officer with weekly urine samples. In the event the case was postponed. His attorneys were working on an appeal claiming the search of his hotel room – and thus the discovery of the drugs – was unconstitutional.

To add to his problems, he was being sued by producers Terence Michael and Richard Finney, who revealed they had commissioned Downey and his dad to write a screenplay in 1996 and paid them

$250,000. According to Michael and Finney, the Downeys didn't deliver a proper script, rather a series of random episodes dubbed 'The Very Special', featuring waiters shouting at customers and other strands of 'anger and paranoia'. They agreed an out-of-court settlement.

Downey was busy at work. The Golden Globe was a sign his character was who the audience wanted to see and his screen time grew. This made him tired and unhappy, and he was taking two types of prescription drugs to combat depression. His friends often blamed his drug binges on periods of extreme stress. Many of them said the Thanksgiving bust was just one horrible holiday slip-up. They were wrong.

At 12.50 a.m. on 24 April 2001 Downey was arrested again. He was walking in an alley beside Washington Boulevard in Culver City, on the west side of Los Angeles. The officer who arrested him, Yvette Countee, didn't realise who it was at first, this strange man in black trousers and a green shirt. 'While speaking to him, I then noticed his speech was rapid, he interrupted me on several occasions and rambled on without any questions being addressed to him,' she said. 'I also noticed that while I was speaking with him, he constantly shifted his position and could not keep still. Based on my training and experience, I recognised the above stated symptoms to be indicative of a person under the influence of a stimulant.' She arrested him for being under the influence and Downey started explaining to her how he was on his way to get a taxi home. He said he hadn't taken any illegal drugs, but mentioned the pills he was taking for his depression. Countee didn't believe him. She asked him again if he had taken cocaine, but the actor insisted he hadn't.

Another policeman went to find the taxi and spoke to its driver, Paul Kalish. Kalish revealed he had picked Downey up at his home in Malibu and driven him to Culver City where he was told to keep the meter running while the star walked away into an alley behind a motel. Sensing he was running out of options, Downey told them he was visiting his friend Allan in Room 102 of the Baldwin Motel, situated a few doors away at 12823 Washington Boulevard. However, when the police knocked on the door, it was empty. Downey changed his story, saying his friend Allan Aleixo was in Room 116. *Albert* Aleixo was indeed in Room 116 of the Baldwin Motel and was rather unhappy to receive uniformed guests. It took him five minutes to open his door and when he did, it turned out he had tried to barricade himself in with a lightstand. Police Officer Horii asked him if he knew Downey, but Aleixo said he didn't and that he had been in his room alone all night.

The cops knew something was up. 'As Aleixo spoke to Officer Horii, he noticed that Aleixo spoke rapidly and incessantly,' said Officer Countee. 'He licked his lips as if they were dry, could not stand still [and] constantly fidgeted with his hands which were sweating, despite the cold temperature.' Officer Horii also caught a glimpse of Aleixo's hands, which were callused and covered in blisters. Police are trained to know this often occurs with people who regularly freebase cocaine, because they hold the boiling-hot glass pipe in their bare hands.

The cops took Aleixo and Downey to the police station, where the latter submitted a urine sample. They discovered Aleixo had an outstanding warrant against him, and at just after four-thirty in the morning, Downey's two parole agents Pedro Del Real and Abel Gonzales showed up to take custody of him. The story broke on the morning news and it took no time at all for Downey's pained mugshot to leak to the media. Del Real could have sent his charge back to jail, but instead he let him check into rehab. 'He is working hard at his sobriety and rehabilitation,' said Alan Nierob. 'He's in charge of his own destiny.'

Unfortunately, David E. Kelley had had enough. 'We are wrapping up the stories on the final few episodes of *Ally McBeal* for the season without him,' he said, which explains why the actor completely vanishes from the final show of the season. Downey remembered his television gig with mixed feelings. 'I wasn't unhappy doing the show but there was a director who pissed me off,' he said. 'I'd been out of prison for three months and I recall going into the dressing room, dialling 9 for an outside line and I remembered this drug-dealer's number. And when I finished work that day I quietly said "thank you" to this director whose guts I hated and got in the car provided by the salary I was making on the show and went out and that was it.'

Downey once again called lawyer Peter Knecht, but to represent Albert Aleixo. The police had failed to find any drugs on him and were waiting on the results of the urinalysis. 'A smart addict will keep his stash in a woman's purse with a lipstick, or even in the closet of his apartment, so that if someone does find it, an attorney has someone else to blame,' says Knecht. 'So the defendant can say, "Yes, I'm under the influence, but it's not mine." Then it's not possession.' But was Downey a smart addict? 'Oh, I wouldn't like to say,' he smiles. 'But he was arrested in Culver City and they didn't find any drugs, put it that way. A lot of the time, Robert would get lucky and the police would get unlucky.'

Back in 2001, Knecht told reporters the pair were friends and flatly denied Aleixo was a dealer, saying he was more like an 'older brother' to Downey. Now, he admits Aleixo was a drug pusher, but insists the arrest changed his life. '[Albert] has done a complete turnaround,' he says. 'He now helps run a drug facility. Some people can turn it around. He was always a sweet guy, so they made a good friendship in that sense. But the sad thing is in a situation like that, if one doesn't quit and the other does, they have to leave that person behind. I can't tell you who left who, but Al had no choice but to quit.'

Downey was also running out of choices. The California Department of Corrections stated almost immediately that prison wasn't likely to be considered for his Culver City infraction, especially since he was already ensconced in a treatment facility. 'He's not being treated more harshly nor is he being treated more leniently,' said a spokesman. Their goal was to get him clean. Six months in rehab was the more likely option.

The star had one major thing going for him. The previous November, Californian voters had gone to the polls and ratified the Substance Abuse and Crime Prevention Act – also known as Proposition 36 – a law scheduled to take effect from 1 July 2001. Essentially, this changed the current state legislation and meant that first- and second-time non-violent drug possession offenders would be given treatment rather than incarcerated. The threat of prison would only arise if they were charged a third time, or consistently failed to co-operate in quashing their addiction. The law was passed by 61 per cent of voters and Downey's case fitted right into it. He had committed his 'crimes' before the July start date, but even the prosecutors in his Palm Springs case were leaning away from a jail sentence. They could have enforced the rules otherwise, but since the electorate had already made their decision, they felt it more appropriate to comply with the changes. 'He definitely needs treatment. I think everybody across the board would agree to that,' said Riverside County prosecutor Tamara Capone. 'A guy like Downey, if he's popped on a new offence, the thinking is that Proposition 36 would take precedence because the idea is to divert to treatment,' prison spokesman Russ Heimerich told journalist Don Thompson. 'And frankly, why tie up another [prison] bed?'

When the urinalysis came back from the Culver City arrest, it showed cocaine in Downey's system, but rather than drag him back into court and because he was seeking treatment, no charges were filed. Downey was in and out of the Indio courtroom over the Merv Griffin incident until finally, on 16 July, he pleaded no contest to possessing cocaine and being under the influence. Since Proposition 36 was now official, Judge Randall White sentenced him to one year at a residential rehab called Wavelengths and three years' probation. He was also subject to random drug testing and had to pay a fine. 'We got the conviction,' said Tamara Capone. 'That was the most important thing.'

Judge White added: 'This is not a gift of the court. This is going to be hard work. It can provide tremendous benefit to you and to the public as well. But you are going to have to work at it.' He was warned that if he violated his probation any more times, he could be imprisoned for up to four years. Downey knew the price he would pay could be much higher if he slipped again.

Another Chance
and True Love

'I'm just a guy who knows he has a lot to be grateful for.'
(2008)

Under the terms of his sentence, Downey was allowed out for work purposes, which he did for one day in August when he shot the video to the new Elton John song, 'I Want Love'. Directed by artist Sam Taylor-Wood, the promo scored plaudits for its simplicity and innovation, which basically involved Downey wandering round a posh house lip-synching to the song in a single shot. It was a great piece of human art and re-ignited Elton's cool.

'I agreed to do it on a Tuesday, Robert said he'd do it on a Thursday. I flew out on Friday, we filmed it on Monday and it was on MTV the following Monday,' Taylor-Wood told interviewer Claire Carolin. 'You just know when something is going brilliantly, it has some kind of magic.' The film took sixteen long takes. When they finished, exhausted, Downey suggested they do an alternative disco version. He was quietly persuaded otherwise.

Downey stuck with the regime at Wavelengths, which was tough but fair. He was also photographed with a new girlfriend towards the end of summer 2001, a former fashion publicist

Downey Jr with frequent collaborator and friend James Toback on the set of *Two Girls And A Guy* (1997). The actor was just out of rehab when he took the role.

Ally McBeal creator David E Kelley offered Downey Jr the role of lawyer Larry Paul just as he came out of prison in 2000. His chemistry with Calista Flockhart spilled off-screen.

'He's turned out to be a really smart, intelligent guy,' says Downey Jr about his son, Indio.

Deborah joins her husband on the.U.K. set of *Restoration* (1995). During press for the movie, Downey shocked reporters with his peculiar and apparently drug-fuelled antics.

Happy families: Downey flanked by big sister Allyson and second wife Susan at the premiere of *A Scanner Darkly* (2006).

Chaplin off-duty. Director Richard Attenborough with his leading man on the set of the 1992 biopic. Diving headlong into the role, it earned the star his first Oscar nomination.

The star finds the Little Tramp's famous hat in *Chaplin* (1992). He went through rigorous training to perfect the slapstick stunts performed by the cinema legend.

Downey Jr was always contrite in court and it was all caught on camera thanks to *Court TV*. Here he is in Malibu being taken into custody (and off to jail) in 1997.

An accomplished piano player and singer, the star has contributed songs to several of his films and released self-penned album *The Futurist* in 2004.

While working at a New York restaurant in the 1980s, Downey Jr used to serve Sting peppermint tea. By December 2001 he was performing with him at a charity event in a Los Angeles drug clinic charity event.

Downey Jr scored a Best Supporting Actor Oscar nomination for playing an Australian thesp taking on the role of an African-American character in film-within-a-film *Tropic Thunder* (2008).

Downey Jr. joins the ranks of the greats by getting his hand and footprints immortalised in cement outside Mann's Chinese Theatre in Hollywood on 7 December, 2009.

The actor shows some heart reprising his role in *Iron Man 2* (2010). The film of superhero *Iron Man* (2008) and his alter ego Tony Stark made more than $500 million worldwide, the actor's first blockbuster. Director Jon Favreau credits his leading man with much of the character's dialogue.

With director Guy Ritchie on the set of *Sherlock Holmes* (2009). The super-sleuth sequel, already underway, is due into production in late 2010.

Susan Downey was convinced Matt Damon would win, but it was Downey Jr who scooped his second Golden Globe in January 2010 for his outstanding performance in *Sherlock Holmes*.

called Kristy Bauer-Jordan. Beautiful and blonde, he met her in a Hugo Boss shop and quietly dated her for a few months, weaning him back into the romantic fold. He was nominated for an Emmy for *Ally McBeal*, but this time lost out to his co-star Peter MacNicol at the ceremony in September 2001. He did some charity work, hitting the phones to convince Sting and Elton John to headline a show to raise money for the Hollywood Sunset Free Clinic. Later, he turned his attentions to the Musicians' Assistance Program, where he MC'ed a bash and introduced Deborah Falconer as a performer.

Finally, in July 2002 he was let out and ready to face the world again. There were no more chances, no more excuses. Gone were the days on the beach when he carried on locking himself out of his house. 'The locks had to be changed a few times,' remembers an old neighbour. 'He'd go to a local bar or café and we'd be there with the locksmith.' The neighbour would have to call Downey in the restaurant and get him to confirm with the locksmith it was OK to do his job. But that was in the past. It had to be.

It was tough for Downey. He continued to spend more than nine hours a week at Wavelengths of his own volition. He plastered Alcoholics Anonymous and Narcotics Anonymous paraphernalia around his bedroom, notes with words like Friendship, Prayer, Trust. One time he got so frustrated he kicked a hole in his wall. Next to it, he wrote 'I kicked the habit'.

He warmed back into work with roles in two short films. First he played an animal therapist in *Lethargy* (2002), a film directed by two USC students and co-starring Edward Burns. Then he went more high profile with *Whatever We Do* (2003), directed by actor Kevin Connolly and written by John Cassavetes' son Nick. He plays Bobby, a shady loudmouth who shows up at the house of his friends Tim Roth and Amanda Peet with a new flighty girlfriend (Zooey Deschanel). It seemed an odd choice for the actor, mainly because it involved him acting drunk and belligerent, a party image he was trying to shed. The film ultimately comes across as a middle-aged version of the Hollywood-centric TV show *Entourage*, which is ironic considering director Connolly was to star in it two years later. But watching the twenty-odd minute film and knowing where Downey was emotionally at the time, it's interesting to see him as the boozy, flaky loose cannon making sure everyone has a good time (and burning some bridges along the way). It's like stepping briefly into his past. At least, you hoped it was his past.

Shorts were all very well, but Downey needed something meaty to put him back on the Hollywood map. He was rumoured to be starring on stage over Christmas 2002 in the musical *Anything Goes* with Susan Sarandon (with whom he'd had a nervy and failed audition for *White Palace* in 1990) at the National Theatre in London, but it never came to pass. Instead, his old friend Mel Gibson came round to his house, made him a disgusting protein shake and dropped a bunch of tapes and a script in his lap. The tapes were a British BBC mini-series called *The Singing Detective* (2003), starring Michael Gambon and written by celebrated auteur Dennis Potter. The manuscript was a cinematic version of the story that Potter had always envisioned and adapted himself. It told the story of Dan Dark, a modern-day novelist who writes pulp detective stories. He's afflicted with a chronic case of the skin disease psoriasis, leaving him scabby, angry and unable to move in hospital. To take himself out of his misery, he imagines a world where he's a gumshoe involved in a case which links Dark's real-life wife, his childhood and his current situation. Oh – and the characters occasionally start miming to songs from the fifties. If it sounds esoteric, that's because it is. Ground-breaking when it appeared on the BBC in 1986, transferring it to the big screen in 2003 was a risk.

Putting Downey in the lead role was also troublesome for the insurance company bonding the movie. He had faced similar problems before, but with everything that had gone on in the intervening years, it was now at critical mass. Thankfully, Gibson came to the rescue. 'Basically, Mel was the insurance,' said director Keith Gordon, who knew Downey since they appeared together in *Back to School* and had since moved behind the camera. 'Robert was uninsurable at the time. The whole thing is really Mel giving a gift to someone he believed in as an artist.'

Gibson also appeared in the film as Dark's bald, bespectacled psychiatrist. 'He's an incredibly gifted actor,' he said of his pal. 'I've seen him [do] a lot of things and he's always great. But something like this is where he really gets to show what he can do.' One of the first challenges was to act beneath the layers of latex that made up his character's dry, lesion-covered flesh. It brought back memories of 'old' Chaplin, an experience Downey wasn't excited to emulate. 'They did things that have never been done with special-effects make-up before because I told them I would flip out if they didn't,' he said. 'And they believed me!' As the day wore on, Downey would play racquetball against the wall of the studio in full make-up for his daily exercise. The sweat would help the mask loosen up. 'But,' he recalled, 'there were food service people milling around and I'd just be like, getting my sweat on! I freaked some people out.'

The look created by legend Greg Cannom is tough to watch, but Downey pops through the layers of foam (although a body double stepped in for some of the long shots). It's the first flat-out angry man he'd played, a different role for him that wasn't entirely successful. You do get the sense of the seething bitterness Dark feels and it's tempting to equate it with the emotions Downey must have felt stuck in rehab: bored, annoyed, resentful and out of control. 'I'm kind of like this guy,' he said, while promoting the movie. 'Funny and charming, but pizza-faced and kind of gross and all about conspicuous consumption. This character's in the closet, in his worst nightmare of the disease and as a detective and then he comes out. I didn't understand what that meant because I hadn't gotten it yet personally that there's a fusion of denial and attachment. I've only recently made a departure from pessimism, so I was limited.

'I like doing hard stuff,' he continued. 'I'm good at hard stuff. It's the simple stuff that baffles me. You know what, I was a mess while making this movie. But when I saw it, all our bitching and lamenting was really for nothing, it turned out all right. We didn't have time for me to be precious about it. I had three things to do – be very still, very cool and be a man's man. I've done that tragic thing, that comic thing, but this was all new. The dance numbers, the singing stuff, scared the crap out of me. I always want a higher challenge and I'm always down for a good hard time, whether visiting studio lots or various serious institutions.'

'I've worked with actors who are more into the breaking down of the part, but Robert just kind of does stuff,' said Keith Gordon. 'And I don't even think he always knows how he does stuff. It's part of his mystery.' Downey does his best with the role – even if he does look slightly uncomfortable dancing on stage, in public no less! – but the movie ends up being a bit *too* meta. The original series was a seminal piece of work, but transposed to 2003 it feels arch, dated, a mess rather than quirkily natural. The music is excellent and the ambition is to be applauded. But while David Lynch pulls off this kind of material with ease, Potter's original intention to explore his own mind (he was afflicted with psoriasis in real life) through a number of hours is the right one. The cinematic *Singing Detective* is the very definition of a noble failure, but for the star it was an important step in his recovery and another reminder to the world of his on-screen gifts. The film was shown at the 2003 Sundance Film Festival in January, along with *Whatever We Do*. While the film received mixed reviews, his performance generated awards buzz. He appreciated the goodwill. 'I think it's empathy,' he said. 'I've never had the hesitation to do whatever it is I'm doing in public. I was raised that way. If you're partying, don't try and hide behind a closed door. Which isn't necessarily a good thing. When I was growing up it wasn't about trying to appear conservative, it was about being who you want to be and if you pay for it you pay for it. So what? Which is really a kind of macho egotistical idea. Not everyone is out to slash you in this town. Everyone's so fearful they're going to appear as who they really are. If I had to look back on it I wanted to appear as I was. If I tried to keep it all under wraps, I wouldn't have got much help. I have every reason to be proud of [*The Singing Detective*]. I'm not a pathetic waste of life presently.'

Susan Levin certainly didn't think so. When she had met him on the set of *Gothika* (2003) in the first half of 2003, she thought he was a bit weird and initially rejected his advances. She had been a producer for three years already and witness to enough set romances to realise most of them didn't survive the wrap party. Levin was a short brunette Jew, with a huge dollop of Hollywood beauty. She knew she wanted to be in the film business from the age of twelve and had focused more on her career than worrying about getting married, running marathons in her spare time and limiting her partying to the odd glass of red wine. After moving to Los Angeles from Illinois, she graduated from the University of Southern California and after three years at New Line Cinema was hired by Joel Silver, the notoriously bellicose producer behind the *Matrix* movies. She started out in development for his horror franchise spin-off *Dark Castle*, graduating to co-producer. *Gothika* was her first shot as a fully fledged producer.

She assembled quite a cast. Halle Berry was hot from winning an Oscar and playing a Bond girl; Penelope Cruz was beginning to gain traction in her American career thanks to a relationship with Tom Cruise and some astute choices. And then there was Robert Downey Jr. The film's insurance company was holding back 40 per cent of his salary until the shoot but Levin knew he was a talented actor. However she was smart and sophisticated, had a proper job. She didn't date the help.

Except Downey wasn't going to let her get away. In the past, he had tried to shy away from short women with brown hair – women like his charismatic, but flaky mother, who was short and brunette. Nevertheless, he'd been inexorably drawn to the brown-haired Sarah Jessica Parker, but then swapped to the Amazonian Deborah Falconer. But he saw something in Levin he couldn't resist. They struck up a relationship and quietly got more and more serious. '*Gothika* was like this,' he said. 'Go to Montreal, fall in love, play squash, tell the person you've fallen in love with that you're in love with them. Have her say, "Don't talk to me until we're done shooting," play squash. Oh yeah, shoot the movie.'

Downey had plenty of downtime on *Gothika* anyway, which he used to ride bikes around the picturesque city and visit the Biodome with Indio, now nine. In the spooky thriller he played a psychiatric doctor trying to treat Berry after she murders her husband and then tells police she can't remember committing the crime. The film has flashes of quality, but ultimately wastes its talented cast. Downey plays the straight man for once (though director Mathieu Kassovitz tries to throw in some red herrings), but story strands are left unanswered and the twist is predictable. Rumours of a tense set were exacerbated by an incident in which Downey and Berry were struggling in a scene and the latter's arm was accidentally broken. Downey was mortified, but Berry pushed on regardless. 'I'm so glad that I was sober when [her arm broke] or everything on Earth would be my fault,' he said. 'It was just a really weird thing because things had been so tense on the set for days before. Things were getting really wild and I was really shaken up and I was nervous that someone was going to get hurt and I'd been expressing that. So when it happened I felt two things – a) I was right and b) what I couldn't have imagined was that it would've been at my hands that it happened, so I don't know how to explain it.'

Yet while it's nice to see Downey administering the doctoral advice rather than receiving it, the only memorable part of the film was the fact he had found the woman he wanted to spend the rest of his life with. She says she knew it was the real thing after three months. Aware that their daughter always made considered decisions, her parents were ecstatic, despite Downey's history. Impetuous as ever, he proposed to her on her thirtieth birthday, 6 November 2003. He got the ring, made from diamonds and a rare African sapphire, from his old manager Loree Rodkin (who had since become a jewellery designer) and hid it among various other presents. With tears in her eyes, Levin said yes, with some immutable conditions. He must stay sober and drug-free. Downey couldn't agree fast enough. 'Basically you know when you're done,' he said. 'It doesn't mean you couldn't pick it up and start over again, but it's kind of like a square peg in a round hole at this point.

'Love is great therapy,' he continued. 'If I had just gotten into recovery and become a total recovery robot and not had a girlfriend for five years, I would probably still be pretty happy and all right. But everyone gets what formula they need.' He loved Levin's attention to detail, her ability to multi-task, her desire to just *look after him*. The couple celebrated their engagement with a trip to London. Still, staying clean was a constant battle. 'I believe that once your brain is no longer hijacked by these substances and you have enough time away from them to realise, it's kind of like battle fatigue,' he said. 'You're in there and every day the shells are coming down and that becomes reality to you. I am at war. Now I feel I don't want to go back and have to get out of that situation again. When you're in that situation and want to get out, you have to realise you're not the best version of yourself. You're at a serious disadvantage.'

He had two big roles under his belt and a new fiancée, but it wasn't all good. The money he earned from *Gothika* and *The Singing Detective* was used to pay off debts and he was named in a defamation lawsuit brought by Charles Bell, otherwise known as Figueroa Slim, his former cellmate. Bell was asking for $100,000 after Downey called him a 'recovering pimp' who 'talks to satellites' in a magazine interview. Bell claimed the quotes were intended to 'increase the sinking ego' of Downey and 'increase the public's opinion of him'. The star also hit problems when the producers of the new Woody Allen film *Melinda and Melinda* couldn't get insurance for either him or his planned co-star and friend Winona Ryder, who had recently been busted for shoplifting. Allen professed to be outraged by the incident, but Downey was angry, especially after it came out in public. 'It's not that they couldn't get insurance for me, it's that they did the best they could but they waited several weeks before they started to inquire as to the insurance situation,' he said at the time. 'There was no way it could have been possible because there was no lead time. With *Gothika*, they sorted it out before they offered me the job.'

Nonetheless, he tried not to let it get to him, even threatening briefly to retire. 'Believe me, I'm not so desperate to be an actor and keep acting,' he said. 'If it got to the point where it wasn't worth it, I'd go. Maybe I'd have regrets, but there's a lot of ways to enjoy your life. You don't have to keep being in the Hollywood scene, there are a lot of things I could do.'

He often suggested that he might pursue alternative careers. It seemed to come up whenever he was nervous about whether he was on the right path. He craved success and knew he could act, but the insecurity was always there. 'I write, I compose, I can write for films, I can happily involve myself in fund-raising,' he said. 'I can go to as many colleges that would have me do little stints there working in the theatre department and I'd see what it was like in Prague. I'd study Czechoslovakian history and I'd go to Europe and Asia and go be a citizen of the world. What's more exciting than that?'

Of course, the difference between him and most other stars was that he really could do other things than emote lines written down for him in a script. At Levin's urging, he finally got around to completing an album of songs, some of which had begun to form fifteen years previously, at his friend Jonathan Elias's music studio in New York. He named it *The Futurist* and it was one of his most personal achievements, 'because it's so autonomous', he said. It wasn't the first time he had recorded music. He had actually recorded an album before he went to Corcoran, at the studio of his longtime friend and musician Moogy Klingman. The latter, who had played with Todd Rundgren and Eric Clapton, also produced it, but it remained unreleased. Downey had written and performed the title song on his father's film *Too Much Sun* as far back as 1990, then composed 'Snake' for the *Two Girls and a Guy* soundtrack. And that doesn't count the impromptu songs, like 'Carla' in *Friends & Lovers*, for which he was uncredited. He had also appeared on two *Ally McBeal* compilation albums with the show's resident chanteuse Vonda Shepard, singing 'Every Breath You Take' and 'White Christmas' among others. In fact, he was featured so prevalently on the *McBeal* album that he was scheduled to do some promotion for it at the Virgin Megastore in Los Angeles. He had to cancel 'due to unfortunate circumstances' according to an Epic Records press statement – it was the day he got busted in Culver City.

Downey was even a frequent subject for other people's material. At least five other artists have recorded songs *about* him. Marissa Levy penned a folksy paean after realising she didn't have a fitting track to open her very first show. 'My set list was a lot of slow, mellow songs,' she says. 'I realised I didn't have a song to really get the crowd going and needed to write something funny to make the audience laugh and get into it. I looked around my dorm room where I had about half a dozen posters of Robert and decided to write about it. A few of my dorm mates sat in the room and helped me come up with outrageous things to say about him. I think it took about 30 minutes.' But she wasn't prepared for the reaction. 'It became kind of a cult classic,' she says. 'I was forced to play it at every show. I still get a lot of requests to play it and people love to sing along to it. I don't know if it's funny now that he's cleaned up his act and people don't know who *Ally McBeal* is or that he was even on that show. I did write a follow-up called '(Wanna Be) in Rehab with You', which was a love song to the messed-up, but it never really took off. I do have some friends out in LA who kind of know him, but I'm not sure they're ballsy enough to play it for him!'

There's also a death-metal song by Killwhitneydead called 'Starring Robert Downey Jr as "The Addict"' and one by Swedish group Southside Stalkers. 'I read an interview with him in a magazine where he said, "Looking back now, I can tell I was wrong," about his drugs use,' says Sparrow from the band. 'That was the first line we wrote. I had been to rehab briefly that summer and my friend and I had a text conversation every day with her saying, "Have you seen Robert Downey Jr yet?" me replying "no" and her saying, "Then you have to stay one more day." My band-mate Indy wrote the tune, it's a happy song. Our fans love it and it's the song we've sold the most copies of on iTunes. We haven't tried to tell him, we're too shy for that. I was afraid there would be some angry Robert fans, but there's none yet. The fans that have contacted us about the song have only been positive about it, especially when they hear the story behind it.'

The Futurist was a different proposition. Named as he said because 'essentially to me, it means I'm not as I was before', he got the chance to redo Charlie Chaplin's 'Smile', a version of which he had performed for the film that he never liked. But the majority of the ten tracks on the album were original songs he wrote himself or co-wrote and then recorded with friends. He insisted none of the tracks were written in prison, despite being in the jailhouse band, but admitted there was a sense of autobiography. However, he was keen for people not to be too literal about the songs, some of which were mooted to be about his split from Sarah Jessica Parker and his subsequent troubles. 'Some of the lyrics might have originated from a period of heartbreak,' he said. 'But when I actually wrote songs like "Broken" and "Details", it's really more about characters. Every one of the songs is influenced by my experience, but I hope it's a little obscured.'

Downey was being disingenuous when he said the album was more about stories than autobiography. Especially when he more or less chants the Serenity Prayer on 'Broken', one of the mantras adopted by the various Anonymous groups, or talks about how he thinks a mother would be unhappy with her daughter falling in love with a 'Man Like Me'. The latter opens the record and is by far the most impressive of the ten tracks. The music incorporates elements of Sting and even Phil Collins, while the lyrics showcase a Bernie Taupin vibe. They're often reminiscent of Downey's chaotic rhymes during his phase as a public performance poet.

His raw, untrained voice strives for the languid phrasing of Norah Jones or Harry Connick Jr, but often he is trying too hard, oversinging the words to a point where his pronounced American accent takes on an almost comical tone. There are flashes of class, however. 'Little Clownz' goes for stop-start jazziness and is enjoyable, making it all the more annoying that the vast majority of *The Futurist* sounds like a new-wave mix CD with an A-list frontman.

The intuitive verve he showed on the *Ally McBeal* albums demonstrates how successful the pairing of his voice and some quality songs could be. Or how great he would have been as sleazy lawyer Billy Flynn in the film version of *Chicago*. What's particularly interesting is just how soppy it is, revealing musical aspirations more suited to the Easy Listening section of HMV than the rock and roll arena. He's never hidden his AOR leanings (apart from as a teen with the cool kids in New York), but it's hard to reconcile the hard-partying, music-loving agit-boy with such middle-of-the-road tastes. Maybe the album was just one of the ways to prove his transformation. He's undeniably talented – his piano-playing is beautiful throughout and there's genuine soul frequently emanating from his mouth. But mostly you wish his Beck-esque musings were coupled to tunes with real depth.

'I adore music,' he said. 'Though the album didn't really get the support from my label. But then if I was a label and I looked at what I'd got – Destiny's Child or the guy from *Ally McBeal* – then OK, fair point. But I've no intentions of giving it up.'

Generally, the reviews weren't kind. 'The musical backdrop is so predictable that it doesn't allow him a single fold to his voice behind, resulting in a set of bare, warts-and-all performances,' wrote *Slant* magazine. 'One of the songs is titled "5:30", but I'd put *The Futurist* at about three in a karaoke bar, long after the hot shots have finished their nightcaps and at the precise moment when the shy guy in the corner has finally worked up the nerve to sing to a nearly empty room.' *Entertainment Weekly* gave him a D grade, saying, 'Unfortunately, this dribbly effort lands him in the same category as Don Johnson circa 1987. Snarling away . . . Downey displays neither a supple voice nor the ability to at least keep the beat. And actors wonder why we tease them when they try to sing.' *Rolling Stone* and *Details* magazine were more positive, noting the influence of Elton John and arguing the record showed 'beautifully evocative flair'. And Allmusic.com said: 'The results are largely laudable . . . Vocally, Downey has a unique sound that falls somewhere between the melancholy twang of Bruce Hornsby and the soulful grit of Joe Cocker – think Bruce Springsteen doing a cabaret night.'

Downey was proud of what he'd done, but also had reservations. 'Clearly I have some hesitation in being an actor who puts out an album,' he said. 'No way would I ever get to express myself musically if I wasn't an actor of ill-repute. So, yeah, I'm a little uncomfortable about it.'

Deborah Falconer was another who was pleased with *The Futurist*. When they had been married, music had often been their only way of communicating when she tinkered about in her husband's home studio. She had since got quite a following around Los Angeles and was playing several shows. Listening to her lyrics was tough for Downey because they frequently referred to Falconer's heartbreak and he knew it was a veiled reminder of their time together, particularly the moments he had let her down. But she was glad he had finally managed to commit his long-held musical aspirations to disc. She also realised it was time for a change. They would always have Indio and she had witnessed his commitment to sobriety (though she had been duped before). But he was engaged to a new woman and she had been living with celebrated session drummer Victor Indrizzo. Their divorce was finalised with a petition in Los Angeles court on 26 April 2004. Downey, who had previously joked that Falconer was 'a girl who is still wondering why I won't sign the divorce papers' was finally ready to move on. It was a strangely muted end to a tumultuous relationship.

Downey married Susan on Saturday, 27 August 2005 at six-thirty in the evening. Keanu Reeves and Sting were among the guests who sat on white benches while the couple said their vows under a gazebo in the upstate New York town of Amagansett at the swanky Windy Dunes estate. The star – who now sports a Suzie Q tattoo on his left arm – couldn't wait to marry his fiancée but was riddled with nerves all day. He tried to calm himself down by going for a swim with his son and doing a half-hour of kung fu. The rehearsal dinner the night before had been at the East Hampton Point restaurant, but he hadn't been able to eat on Saturday, drinking water instead. He wore a dark suit, but couldn't resist harking back to his fashionista past with a flamboyant purple scarf. Susan wore a stunning floor-length gown, her gently curled hair topped by a long veil. As they walked back down the aisle as husband and wife, his unabashed smile was wider than it had been in years.

'She will be Mrs Downey for the rest of her days on Earth if I have anything to say about it,' he said. 'My wedding ring means everything to me. I had it inscribed with the Latin for "until the wheels fall off" and I mean that.'

He was 40 years old and his new life was just beginning.

Proving Them Wrong

'She's a great cheerleader for me.' (2008)

The newlyweds honeymooned in the south of France. Their choice wasn't completely arbitrary. After three days, they travelled to England to do press for Downey's new film, *Kiss Kiss Bang Bang* (2005). 'I think it's supposed to go on for a while,' he said of his honeymoon, just after arriving in Britain. 'She's my boss, my wife, my obedient slave and servant – for about three seconds a year – so it's supposed to go on for a while.'

They had just been boyfriend and girlfriend when Susan came home with the script one day, written by Shane Black, the scribe behind *Lethal Weapon* and *The Last Boy Scout*. Coincidentally, Black had bumped into Downey many years earlier at a supermarket on Sunset Boulevard and the pair had discussed working together. It took more than a decade for that conversation to come to fruition. Susan loved the script and when he kept on hearing her laughing in the other room, Downey asked to take a look. The film was written by Black as a homage to the detective stories he read as a child. The writer was renowned for his buddy films and on the surface this was no different, teaming an LA cop with a New York actor on the trail of murder. If only it were that simple. Val Kilmer played the cop, nicknamed Gay Perry because, well, he was. Downey signed on as Harry Lockhart, a petty thief who inadvertently wins an audition and is flown to the West Coast to do research for the role, getting caught up in death and (his own) dismemberment along the way. Witty and scathing, with a healthy dose of action, the movie ends up as a bizarre and winning combination of social commentary, detective story and farce. It was the best film Downey had been in for years.

'I'm like Harry in that I came to LA and was a little naive, immediately disillusioned,' Downey said while promoting the film. 'I was chasing my tail and trying to do the right thing and was a little bit stupid. Or irresponsible, which is the same thing I guess. Harry is a guy who wakes up when the neon lights go on – and I've had some experience with being nocturnal myself.'

'[Harry's] a guy chock-full of schemes that sputter and die almost as often as he puts his foot in his mouth,' said Black. 'Harry is a perpetually unlucky guy, yet he's a cock-eyed optimist. He's never really learned the lesson that if you try something over and over and you keep failing, you'll probably continue to do so. Harry just keeps slamming headlong into the same wall, but somehow never loses his youthful enthusiasm.'

It was a gruelling shoot, filming for 37 nights downtown. At one point, Downey even found himself hoisted onto a crane and dangled over the Long Beach freeway. He became immediate friends with Kilmer in whom he saw a kindred spirit. Kilmer remembered him frequently regaling the cast and crew with party stories. Downey also saw a lot of himself in Black, who ended up making his directorial debut on the film. 'I think it's a combination of Shane and I,' said Downey of Harry. 'Save for the fact I was asked not to return to several stores I worked at in New

York because I had a problem with sticky fingers. Then I came out to LA, a New York kid pretending to be an actor and was eventually taken seriously, unlike Harry. Then I got into all kinds of trouble and at the end of the movie decided to stay, grateful for what I had.'

Kiss Kiss Bang Bang let him cut loose, show off the comedic chops and loose style he hadn't exercised on screen for a long time, though he admitted, 'I've been living a comedy in my private life for some time.' Looking to find his way back into more mainstream fare, it was a fantastic opportunity. 'I think it's a great part,' he added. 'But I will agree that I think it also happens with people in relationships – and situations – that you [would] have been able to enjoy Morocco, say, if you weren't getting out of a bad marriage. You know what I mean? I think you wind up doing the stuff you were supposed to do, largely at the time you were supposed to do it. Look, even bad years are pretty good years, I think. Everything is kind of OK if you think about it. Nobody has West Nile virus or is dealing with any life-threatening viruses at this point, right?'

Robert and Levin (who would quickly change her surname to Downey) were living a chaotic existence. Susan produced the film under the Silver Pictures banner and Robert admitted it was tough sometimes to be dating the boss. 'I get a little uptight sometimes as we have to communicate a lot,' he said. 'Our relationship is high-maintenance because we spend less time together than you might want to so we need to communicate a lot and when we don't maybe that's the thing we need to do. I get a little crabby when I'm making a movie, get a little self-centred. I think I'm not high-maintenance but maybe I am. It's not like I'm any more extraordinary a nightmare than she's used to!' He knew that his tumultuous past – and the fact he had never really been in a hit film – meant he had to work especially hard. 'I'm not in a position like some of my peers where they lay back and wait for a role that suits their proclivities,' he said. 'I don't have that luxury just yet. I've got to really work my ass off. My karma has been to be in movies that almost work, don't work, or are OK.'

But whereas in the past he had thrown himself headlong into everything, he was now able to take a step back, be more self-aware about his life and his career. 'Making the jump from $40,000 to $70,000 a year is a big deal,' he said. 'Making the jump from $70,000 to $140,000 you'd think would be a bigger deal, but it actually creates more stress for people. At a certain point you have to think how much more of your life do you want to enjoy and how much are you sacrificing by how much harder you have to work. So now I tend to look at things as like, "Am I going to be stronger, wiser and gladder if I shoot a certain movie?"' He remembered a role he had tried to get playing a cancer victim and his thoughts just prior to the audition. 'I thought I should go into the meeting with a shaved head,' he said. 'But I didn't do it. Hopefully I won't have to resort to that, because inevitably you go to the waiting room and there's a dozen guys with shaved heads.'

Kiss Kiss Bang Bang turned out to be a family affair in more ways than one when Indio was cast as a younger version of his father's character. He and Falconer had discussed their son following in his dad's thespian footsteps, but his ex 'damn near castrated me on the spot'. Luckily for her, while Indio did a good (if brief) job in the movie, he didn't show any signs of wanting to continue. 'He's a natural and all that,' said Downey, 'but I think his whole demeanour is wrong for it. Instead of imagining that you need to go and be the centre of attention, or you have to go and make a bunch of money, or you have to have successes and failures, he said, "Why don't you just cut out all the garbage and figure out how to get happy?"'

Indio was actually much more interested in playing his guitar and was beginning to explore putting a band together. Despite the dysfunction of his upbringing, with two parents high on drugs or alcohol at various points of his young life, he had turned into a saner person than either his mum or dad put together. 'He's turned out to be a really smart, intelligent guy,' said Downey in 2009. 'I think most fathers when you ask if they mean it or not, they will say they are proud of their kid. It's not cool to say you aren't. But I mean it. I'm so proud of him.' He realised his substance abuse had involved a lot of lying, particularly to his loved ones. 'Alcoholism never just involves one person, you can't just be alone in your room drinking yourself to death,' he admitted. 'The crappy part of it is the people you enlist to keep your secret. Alcoholism involves the people that were around you. It's not like someone just decides "I'm going to drink myself to death". This isn't even advice, it's just a fact. When people say the only person he or she is hurting is himself, I get really mad.'

Downey and Susan moved into a modest place, which was dotted with scripts and socks. 'I'm really a domestic guy,' said Downey. 'I like the kitchen to be together. I like picking the right colours for the duvet and I like the towels in the bathroom to rotate. I love to co-ordinate the flowers in my home. I like to maintain continuity. I like things nice at home.'

He thought harder about directing. He had so many ideas and it was something he had considered for a long time, ever since he directed that play back at Stagedoor. He was writing again and felt he could use the things he'd learned from the directors he admired like Robert Altman and James Toback, Michael Hoffman and Oliver Stone. He had never been one to shy away from opinion on a set either. When he was filming *U.S. Marshals*, with Stuart Baird, he constantly insisted his character Special Agent Royce was darker, but to no avail. 'It's a big fucking pissing contest,' he said of stepping behind the lens. 'I'll probably want to direct something I've written.'

Asked what kind of helmer he'd be he replied, 'A monster. I have a happily split personality, so on the one hand I would like to induce [the cast and crew] to feel that they were going where they'd never gone before. And at the same time you know they don't know how to do [it] as well as you could do it. I would not stop until they got it right. I'd probably be a bit like Chaplin. I'd probably be a fucking basket case about the details.'

He added, 'I swear to God if I was directing a movie, people would be slitting their throats. But I don't want to say that because, when I direct, if someone offs themselves, I don't want to be held responsible.'

He thought long and hard about a futuristic science-fiction idea he had called 'The New Math', but his desk was filling up with scripts people wanted him to act in and the lure was too strong. He took a small role in 2005's *Good Night, and Good Luck* (2005), George Clooney's biopic of legendary journalist Edward R. Murrow. He played the crucial part of Joe Wershba, a reporter who is married to a co-worker but has to hide it from his bosses. He's also the one who nabs the scoop that encourages Murrow to take on Senator Joseph McCarthy and his anti-Communist witch-hunt. He got to meet the real Wershba, who during his career won two Emmys and was nominated for a Pulitzer Prize.

It was a welcome change of pace. 'The character is a very simple, straightforward, hard-working guy, which is kind of like what I am now,' he said during filming. 'It's a little bit boring, but it's perfect and respectable.' He also lent his voice to the animated TV sitcom *Family Guy*, at the urging of his son, who was a huge fan. He played Patrick, Lois Griffin's long-lost brother who has spent decades in a mental institution, for a good reason as it turns out – he likes to murder fat people. Indio was over the moon.

He was finally getting a chance to give something back, to repay the loyalty so many had shown to him. 'I've done jobs that I knew weren't really any good for my career but were going to help a friend of mine because they were starting off as a director,' he said. 'I've gone out of my way and helped an actress get a shot at a role and I've had no motive with her. I wasn't trying to sleep with her, her dad wasn't someone who could do me a favour back.'

He had met author Dito Montiel in 2002 through their mutual friend Jonathan Elias. Montiel had recently written *A Guide to Recognising Your Saints* (2006), a tough memoir about growing up in Queens, New York during the eighties. Initially hanging out with local junkies and criminals, he was 'adopted' by various members of the era's in-crowd including Andy Warhol, poet Allen Ginsberg and photographer Bruce Weber. It was an incredible story and Downey liked it. 'They came to a reading I was doing at Book Soup in Los Angeles and Downey was like, "You wanna make a movie out of this?"' recalled Montiel. 'I think he liked the idea of working on something from scratch.' Downey considered directing it, but found himself caught up with acting work. He gave Montiel an office, hooked him up with producer Trudie Styler (Sting's wife) and began the four-year process of bringing the project to the big screen. The actor had often been involved in the creative machinery of his films, but never to this extent. He became a co-producer, signed on to play Dito as an adult and worked on the story whenever he had free time. Eventually, he ceded directing duties to Montiel himself.

'Dito and I are, first and foremost, friends,' he said. 'Ultimately, my job as producer on this movie was having Dito's back. If he became obsessed with one approach or another, my role was to say, "Go explore it".' On screen, Downey plays a fictionalised version of the author who travels home to visit his dying father, only for the neighbourhood to spark old memories.

'He came to the set thinking it was about a guy who comes back to his neighbourhood and realises everyone from his past is a loser,' said Montiel. 'That's not what it's about at all, but I never told him that.' In the end Downey's performance is insular and refreshingly threadbare, which pleased Montiel. 'He said he would try a Queens accent or something, which got me really worried!'

Despite good reviews and a clutch of awards, including the Special Jury Award for Best Ensemble Performance and the Dramatic Directing Prize at the Sundance Film Festival, *A Guide . . .* was a bust at the box office. That wasn't news to Downey, who was used to reading poor box-office numbers. Sure, he wanted to be in a smash-hit film, always had, but the way his life was now it was about building a career, creating a portfolio. The hits would come, he was sure of it. 'Years ago people would say to me, "I think your best work is ahead of you," and I used to think, have they seen *Chaplin*? How dare they talk to me like that?!' he said. 'But they were right. I'm really enjoying my work right now. If this is a part of my story – and it is a story when we are dealing with someone who has been around as long as I have and put themselves and their public at large through all these roller-coaster moments – then this is the part of the story when I have my comeback.'

But at the same time, he grew increasingly cross with people bringing up his drugs period and recovery. He had made that promise to himself to be more serious, but, like Val Kilmer recalled, he couldn't help himself telling tall stories from the past. He was used to being the guy everyone crowded around, listened to, laughed with. Would he still be that person without chemical help?

He dipped into Disney fare with the transitory Tim Allen fantasy *The Shaggy Dog* (2006), but altered states played an integral part in his next film, *A Scanner Darkly* (2006). Adapted by writer/director Richard Linklater from a novel by Philip K. Dick, Downey plays James Barris, a friend of Bob Arctor (Keanu Reeves) and a Substance D addict. Set in the near future, Substance D is a highly addictive and available drug made from a blue flower that causes cognitive breakdown and paranoia. Ironically, he spent the shoot with friend (and fellow on-screen huffer) Woody Harrelson eating raw food and doing pilates. The complex narrative follows Arctor as he changes identity, going undercover to dig out the drug's manufacturer.

Downey provides loquacious support. He developed a unique mnemonic system to remember his torrents of dialogue. He wrote it all out as a stream of consciousness, then broke it down into more easily absorbed acronyms. 'If I don't have a process, I have no way of knowing anything,' he said of learning the part. 'The last three or four films I've done *combined* didn't have as much dialogue as I had in the first three days on this movie.' He shot the film in the middle of 2004, but its unique style of animation (which Linklater tested in *Waking Life*) meant the technicians essentially painted over the live footage with their computers. The method meant an eighteen-month post-production period, but also allowed for a more organic shooting style. Just before filming started, the star tried to cut his hair himself and screwed it up, much to the amusement of his wife. No matter – the animators were Vidal Sassoon in the edit. 'I thought it was probably the strangest script I ever read,' he said. 'But I really loved my character. He reminds me of those propeller-head guys you knew in high school who knew how to take apart a bike and put it back together and other freaky stuff.'

He had frequently traded on his verbosity but, like a lot of the best actors, Downey's truly transparent moments on screen happened when he was silent – the steely intensity when he decides to make *The Great Dictator* in *Chaplin*, the sense of worthlessness when he begs his father for help in *Less Than Zero*, the look of shock when his hand is eviscerated in *Natural Born Killers*. The making of his next film, *Fur: An Imaginary Portrait of Diane Arbus* (2006), required him to go beneath prosthetics yet again, playing Lionel, a man covered head to toe with hair. As well as a different-looking performance, it was a different-*sounding* one too, with Downey's voice much more contained. In Steven Shainberg's bizarre biopic inspired by Patricia Bosworth's biography, he was the muse of the eponymous avant-garde photographer who committed suicide in 1971. Coincidentally, Arbus's husband Allan was an old friend and frequent collaborator of Robert Downey Sr, having appeared in *Putney Swope*, as well as *Greaser's Palace* and *Too Much Sun*, which Junior had small parts in.

'Robert's eyes speak,' said Nicole Kidman, who played Diane and with whom, as usual with his leading ladies, he generated a taut chemistry. 'He doesn't really even need dialogue. And I think that's unusual for him because a lot of the time when he's performing – and he has said this himself – he's verbose. But in this film he's left with very little to say, just his heart and his presence.' The pair got on famously – 'easy on the eyes, too, in case you hadn't noticed,' he said – finding their way together through an ambitious attempt at revolutionising the biopic by Shainberg, who had scored critical cachet for his erotic drama *Secretary* (2002) starring Downey's pal James Spader.

Lionel was based on a real-life 'freak', who the film-makers found in an old book during their research, and was brought to life with the help of special FX guru Stan Winston. Never a fan of effects make-up, Downey made sure no one talked to him for the first half-hour of each day, was left alone for an hour at lunchtime and told the director he had to be told when they were going to finish first thing in order to preserve his sanity. Prosthetics are hard enough for a normal person, but it's difficult to imagine what it was like for a hyperactive persona like Downey to sit for two hours having layers of foam rubber glued to his face even before he shot a frame of film. He didn't want to be a diva but he knew the rules protected him from losing his temper, something he had never done on a set. The hirsutism did have some positives however, particularly when it came to the scenes where he is de-haired. 'At the end of the film it behoved me to look emaciated,' he said. 'And it was not a problem because on the whole shoot, eating was like an exercise in irritation.'

'I had no interest in portraying the conventional sad, lonely, isolated freak,' says Shainberg. 'Lionel is sexy. He's a man, a strong man, and I wanted the relationship between him and Diane to be wonderful. So Lionel had to have some beauty to him. What I did want was tenderness, sensitivity, unpredictability, surprise and love. And all that is Downey. With the soulfulness of his eyes, the elegance of his movement and his sheer inventiveness. When we finally saw Robert in his full make-up, with the hair and the look created by Stan Winston, his humanism came through. Robert was still there – we knew everything was going to be OK.'

'Downey Jr is not just his usual great value; he is spellbinding,' said *Empire* magazine, just part of the unanimous praise for his performance. 'Those dark eyes penetrate through his pelt, exerting a supernatural charm that makes a memorably erotic love scene believable and affecting.' The *Los Angeles Times* was equally effusive. 'Downey, for the most part using only his soulful, yearning eyes and a silky, urbane voice, creates a man no one could resist,' it wrote.

Fur . . . was never intended as a blockbuster, but it died without trace, despite the art-house kudos *Secretary* had generated. But Downey was steadily putting in performance after performance proving himself to be better than he had ever been. Plus he now had what a thousand actors dream about – emotional depth. He had always been a technically gifted, instinctive actor, someone who leapt off the screen. But he could do it so easily. And sometimes you could see that in his work, when it became apparent he wasn't completely immersed in the character. He was still great to watch, but there was a sense of ironic detachment almost, as if he were diving into the role and, rather than plunging into it, was bouncing off the surface. But rehab and prison and divorce and – well – everything had changed all that. The self-directed edict he announced to himself after *Chaplin*, the one about never doing something that wasn't completely right, about 100 per cent commitment, was at last coming true. Because he was part of his own life. You could see every storyline in his own comedy-drama etched on his face, in every laughter line, wrinkle and fleck of grey hair. It was all there. And ready for him to use.

'You got to live into it,' he said self-reflectively in 2008. 'I really got some time. I swear to God I'm going to make you proud. I'm really going to earn this. It's like that final scene in *Saving Private Ryan* when Tom Hanks says to Matt Damon, "Earn this".' He felt a mishmash of emotions about his previous achievements, but rarely analysed it too deeply, instead focusing on specific memories. 'Dewy, handsome, sexy, drunk, I don't know,' he said about stumbling across the earlier entries in his filmography. 'Tired. That dog almost bit my knee off. That was a fun day. God, I ate too much rice before lunch. That type of stuff.'

He may have been trying to pull away from talking about his 'troubled past', but he didn't make it easy for the press by playing a louche boozehound – who also happened to be a journalist – in director David Fincher's detective yarn *Zodiac* (2007). 'I would never have drunk those sissy drinks,' he said about his character's cocktail tendency.

In inimitable Fincher (*Fight Club*) style, the film was an intricately researched, atmospheric procedural about the hunt for the Zodiac killer in seventies San Francisco. Downey played Paul Avery, a world-weary hack who teams up with cartoonist-turned-writer Robert Graysmith (Jake Gyllenhaal) to investigate and publish the story of the famous murderer who sent letters to the local newspaper and outfoxed the police, sending the city into paroxysms of fear. The case was never solved and Avery's pivotal position in the story gradually fades until he ends up drunk, but still mercurial, on a houseboat divorced from the action. Downey barely features in the second half of the movie, but manages to leave his footprint on the negative. 'I did some research,' he says. 'I don't want to say I didn't care. I am going to say I had other concerns. Some people do a ton of research and then you're like, "Wow, that's really impressive. You suck in the scenes! But your research was fantastic." I'd rather not suck in the scenes.'

The director is a notorious taskmaster, renowned for doing a lot of takes. Though he may have complained – or at least taken his foot off the gas – in the past, this time Downey was prepared to step up, against his better judgement. 'I would like to do two takes a day,' he said. 'That would be my personal preference. And then do a lot of ass-slapping, *USA Today* reading and kung fu ass-kicking. But sometimes you got to suck it up and sing for your supper 65 times.' The multiple set-ups meant he didn't have time to dwell on the similarities Avery had with his own boozy past. He even managed to let a little love back into his heart for the media who had supported him, then plagued him, then pitied him and were now beginning to show their appreciation once again. 'It is easy to misplace,' he said of his rediscovered respect. 'It's very tenuous, very fragile.'

Becoming a father is a big moment for an actor. Not a real-life dad, a cinematic one. Downey had played one before, notably in *Chaplin*, but 2007's *Charlie Bartlett* was really the first time he played a character whose interactions with his children are key to the story. He had always been seen as something of a man-child, an adult with the kind of youthful exuberance normally reserved for teenagers. But he was 41 years old now and rather than running around the school halls, he was playing the principal – a disenchanted, booze-loving teacher who finds himself in a battle of wills with a new student (Anton Yelchin). Cocky and wealthy, young Charlie has been expelled from several posh establishments and eventually finds himself in regular high school. He soon starts a business selling prescription pills to the student body, attracting the attention of Principal Gardner and his strong-minded daughter (Kat Dennings).

Early on in the production Downey confided in the director Jon Poll that the most difficult thing to believe was that he was old enough to play a character with a daughter in high school. He was not immune to the irony of being the antagonist fighting against someone he may well have been cast as if it had been made in the eighties. 'We all talked about how I would have been Charlie Bartlett twenty years ago,' he said. 'But that's part of what makes the relationship between Charlie and Gardner so interesting. You know, every wild guy's secretly a square and every square is secretly a wild guy.' Watching the two face off, it's easy to imagine Downey in his high school pomp talking his way out of situations with teachers, roles reversed. And, like Downey, Charlie isn't your usual troubled kid – there are more deep-seated family problems and a keen intelligence permeating his desire to rebel. 'Of course he brings a lot of real-life stuff to the part,' says Jon Poll. 'His character has a lot of issues but it's refreshing to see Robert come in and do that.'

Even more ironic is that on the cusp of middle age, the star had also become a role model. Not for his off-screen behaviour (though that probably inspired some people), but as a movie veteran with twenty years' experience behind him. His young co-stars loved not just his ability, but his attitude on the set. The way he would talk with the young kid of the family who owned the actual house that was doubling as Gardner's home in Canada. 'It was really one of the first experiences that I had where I would consciously sit and learn from someone,' says Yelchin, who was seventeen at the time. 'His range and his understanding of the freedom he has as an actor are so eye-opening. Watching him experiment with what he wanted to do and finding the right thing was so incredible. Robert is in his own category of actors, with the way he approaches the characters he does and the way he uses his body.'

Dennings adds, 'He's really smart and cool and it turned out we have a lot of funny, obscure stuff in common.' She gave him various nicknames, including Taps McGee and Mr Short Tie. She watched in awe at some of his acting techniques. Playing drunk, he realised he need to be off-balance, so he spun himself around just before every take, causing him to stumble realistically. More insightful is her take on their parent–child relationship, which shares similarities with his real-life role as Indio's dad, especially as the film progresses and he starts to mentally unravel. 'I think Principal Gardner is really a pretty cool dad and he and Susan have a good relationship, but then he starts becoming unhinged,' she says. 'She loves him a lot but she's not sure how much she respects him right now. It was very interesting to me the way that both Charlie and Susan are in this position where they're acting more mature than the adults in their lives, even though they also really need those adults.'

Downey didn't need to worry about Indio, though he was about to enter the world of music, hardly the most sheltered place to be. The kid had toyed with acting, appearing in his school production of *As You Like It*, but music was always his first love. When Downey had tried to rehearse with him, he was more concerned about finding more tracks to listen to and cull influences from. He got together with some friends to form The Jack Bambis, a funk-rock band whose oldest member was thirteen and whose drummer was a mere nine. They wrote their own songs and started to play some shows, quickly building up a celebrity fanbase. Red Hot Chili Peppers frontman Anthony Kiedis declared them his favourite live act of 2006 and they opened for Pearl Jam. Playing the blues with his fingers like one of his heroes Jeff Beck, it looked and sounded like Indio had found his calling.

'Half the time with my kid I just feel like I'm the schmuck who drives the mini-van,' said Downey, who has a tattoo of the word Indio on his right arm. 'I think like any parent of a teenager, I'm struggling to stay current, see if anything is changing with him, see if he feels emotionally healthy, see if he looks like there's anything that needs to be addressed. And also manage the fact that he needs to have fire lit under his ass to meet the status quo scholastically. We horseplay or take a walk and I'm sure he'd rather be with his friends half the time, but there's that little gap where his social life hasn't come together so he might as well hang out with me for a minute. There's those moments where I have my little Saturday nights with him. And because things are so busy and life is not easy, whether it's going well or not going well, it's just less exhausting when it's going pretty well. You see those little windows of enjoyment and you really look forward to them. It's revitalising.'

Which was good, because his entire being had had a makeover. Life with Susan was perfect, living in a rented pad in Brentwood, a neighbourhood on the Westside of Los Angeles. Susan didn't exactly control his life, but was certainly integral to how he lived it, a different set-up from the more Lone Ranger tendencies he had shown in the past, even during his relationship with Deborah Falconer and Sarah Jessica Parker. Susan interviewed Steven Shainberg when Downey was considering *Fur* . . . just to make sure it was suitable. He had a tendency to bring out the co-dependent side in anyone – which went all the way back to his schooldays – and he shared this with his wife. They talked deep into the night about anything and everything. He let himself be laid open more than he ever had before. For perhaps the first time ever, he knew what it was to experience true openness and honesty. After all, actors lie, right?

She constantly told him he should be looking for more mainstream parts, scoring that blockbuster role, working within the system then dipping his toes outside to do the odd thing he was really passionate about. She kept an eagle eye on him, calling or texting him to make sure everything was OK. He was smitten. 'I like the challenge of it, to tell you the truth,' he said. 'It's nice. During some point in the challenge if you suddenly say, "Great challenge, wrong person", that would suck. But I got the right girl.' Their house became about order. His wife kept her clothes colour-co-ordinated in her closet. Downey kept a small grey bag on him that held his essential items (Camel cigarettes, most importantly, as well as a host of vitamins, herbal supplements and assorted lotions). He couldn't believe how domesticated he had become. His younger self would have been appalled. The twenty-something who presented *The Last Party* would have been shocked to see the picture of him and his wife with George W. and Laura Bush at the White House proudly displayed in his kitchen. Of course, his new 'conservative' existence sat alongside a reminder of his old one, courtesy of what he dubbed 'The Wall Of Shame' – a board on the wall featuring embarrassing pictures of himself in a variety of past lives. They spent most of their time curled up together on the sofa, watching movies like *The Queen*.

Much of his new balance had to do with martial arts, which he attacked with a vengeance. He had dabbled in various disciplines before, but when he got out of rehab for the last time in 2002, he called Eric Oram, an LA-based Wing Chun teacher. Wing Chun is a form of kung fu dating back hundreds of years. 'For me, it was just a way in,' Downey said in 2007. 'It was a way to commit to something that is inevitably at times just massively humiliating.' Oram – a rock-solid bald man who Downey has said looks like actor Colin Farrell – wasn't just any teacher. For a start, he told his new pupil that if he ever fell off the wagon, he would terminate their relationship. Downey had to call him Sifu (teacher). And he was going to feel it, *really* feel it. Wing Chun mixes aggression with relaxation, balance and structure, and is characterised by short-range power and deflecting techniques. Downey was ecstatic when he received a black eye while sparring and deep down felt it gave him more in common with his father, who had been an excellent boxer in his youth and had never seen his son as the fighting sort. As well as keeping him in shape, Downey found a spiritual connection within the form too, training up to five times a week.

Oram came to his wedding in 2005 and his presence on the actor's film sets became a contractual pre-requisite. 'I had no idea the academy I joined has a complete system that permeates every aspect of your life,' said the actor. '[Eric] is a direct descendant of the man who was Bruce Lee's instructor. So it's kind of like I thought I was going to be in the Navy Reserves and all of a sudden, I'm like a Green Beret. I'm like, "This is not right", but it's exactly what I needed. Something really comprehensive and specific with a bunch of people who are not interested in your personality. Or charm.'

He confessed, 'I would love to do a great movie in which there is martial arts and work in China. But I wouldn't want to do it just to get my rocks off. There is also something to be said for really keeping what is a personal and spiritual endeavour for you off the screen.'

Finally: Superstardom

'You have a billion-dollar box-office year and you start
wondering if there isn't more to you. Maybe I'm
more than I thought? Nope!' (2009)

It must be weird, being 43 – having been in the business since the
age of five – and getting a phone call telling you for the first time
your film has grossed half a billion dollars at the box office. It
must be even stranger to get another call from the film company
telling you to expect delivery of a top-of-the-range Bentley to say
thank you for helping to make them rich. And all this for a role
that required you to audition for the first time in sixteen years.
Life's funny sometimes . . .

Iron Man (2008) first came into being in 1963. He was created
by comics legend Stan Lee, who wanted to challenge himself by
coming up with a character who would go against the thinking of
the era. It was at the dawn of hippies and free love. Lee came up
with a multimillionaire capitalist arms manufacturer/inventor,
though he did have a taste for the ladies. As with any Marvel
Comics hero, the details of Iron Man and his alter ego Tony
Stark's origins have been finessed over the years, most notably in

light of the change in enemies from his conception (Vietnam) to the modern day (the Taliban and Al-Qaeda). But the basic story remains the same. Stark was born on Long Island and was soon picked out as a child genius. He went to MIT at the age of fifteen to study electrical engineering and soon became one of the pioneers in his field. After his parents die in a car crash when he's 21, he takes over his father's company, turning it into one of the foremost multinational corporations in the world and making himself rich. After a weapons demonstration goes awry, he is captured (by the Vietnamese, or in the First Gulf War or the war in Afghanistan depending on which year's comic you are reading) and severely injured by a bomb, leaving bits of shrapnel around his heart. His fellow prisoner is a Nobel Prize-winning physicist who builds an electromagnet to stop his heart being pierced and together they are forced to make a weapon for the baddies. Instead, he builds a suit made of iron and escapes (though his physicist buddy dies during the fracas). Realising he has something special, he goes home and refines the suit, ultimately becoming a superhero.

Hollywood likes superheroes. They get audiences into the cinema. What's more Marvel, the company behind *Iron Man*, had had some success putting 'actors' rather than 'movie stars' in their films, from Hugh Jackman in *X-Men* to Tobey Maguire in *Spider-Man*. Studios had been trying to get an *Iron Man* film off the ground since 1990 (he appeared in cartoon form on television in 1981), when Universal pitched it as a low-budget movie. Comic books weren't in vogue then and the project languished in development hell while various screenwriters, actors and directors attached themselves then left. Self-confessed comics geek Nicolas Cage considered the role at one point, as did Tom Cruise. In 1999, Quentin Tarantino was approached to write and direct, but the deal never materialised. The rights changed hands several times, with endless scripts being tossed in the recycling bin. It got close to pre-production twice when *Buffy the Vampire Slayer* creator Joss Whedon was suggested and then when Nick Cassavetes (who wrote *Whatever We Do*) became attached. Two of *Spider-Man 2*'s writers, Alfred Gough and Miles Millar, handed in drafts, as did *X-Men* scribe David Hayter. But all to no avail. In November 2005 the rights reverted back to Marvel and the following year they announced the movie would be their first effort as an independent studio.

They hired Jon Favreau to direct it. Favreau had started off in Hollywood as an actor, before writing his own breakthrough pic *Swingers*. He had since moved behind the camera, firstly on small movies like *Made*, before graduating to blockbuster fare like *Elf*. Two writing teams were hired – Mark Fergus and Hawk Ostby, who were best known for the Oscar-nominated *Children of Men* and Hollywood journeymen Art Marcum and Matt Holloway – and they set about writing a version each, which Favreau then combined and refined. Pledging to treat the film as if it were a low-budget indie, he got input from a series of esteemed comic-book writers, to make sure it was as authentic as possible, with the right balance of respect for the fans and exposition for the average punter. And then he went looking for his Iron Man.

Downey really wanted the role. 'I turned 40,' he said later from the set. 'I said, "If I'm going to do something like this, I'm running out of time." The more I thought about it, the more appropriate it seemed . . . but I couldn't stop thinking about it. There's a real sense of honour and honour's something I've come to know a little bit about.' He reckoned Tony Stark's back story had echoes of his life. He had empathy with the mythology, even if he felt Tony's coolness outplayed his own. He had been a fan of comics as a kid, tending to go for the more out-there ones like *Fabulous Furry Freak Brothers*, but he also enjoyed the more traditional *Sgt.*

Rock. Several other actors were considered, including Sam Rockwell and Clive Owen. But Downey had been to see *The Matrix* at the cinema with Tobey Maguire and was jealous of Keanu Reeves. Then Maguire himself had gone on to be Spider-Man. He had even hung out with Bruce Willis, who played a more down-to-earth superhero type in *Die Hard*.

Downey wanted his turn. He campaigned for the part and Jon Favreau thought he was a great option. 'We didn't want to just go with the safe choice,' he said. 'The best and worst of Robert's life have been in the public eye. He had to find an inner balance to overcome obstacles that went far beyond his career. That's Tony Stark. Robert brings a depth that goes beyond a comic-book character who is having trouble in high school, or can't get the girl.'

Downey agreed to go in for a screen test, the first time he had done it since *Chaplin*. Susan could see how much he wanted the job. She thought it was the most committed he'd been to a part since playing the Little Tramp. He had three weeks to prepare for his one-hour audition. The actor spent the whole time practising his lines, coming up with new stuff. He worked out hard. 'I felt that if I was ever going to do a movie like *Iron Man*, I had to do it quickly before it became embarrassing being the guy in tights with a flabby body,' he said. When he stood in front of the camera in a dark suit and loosened black tie, he was ready. He had grown the beginnings of a goatee and was in good shape. The camera rolled. Rarely have his eyes looked so intense on screen. Shrugging off his actorly tics, he spoke in a low voice, playing well within himself, making the crew laugh with the odd throwaway sentence. He was low key, direct and quiet.

By the end of the 60 minutes, Favreau knew he had his man. 'He wasn't the most obvious choice from the studio's point of view,' says Favreau. 'But Marvel gave me the freedom to cast the best person for the role.' He said that, but convincing the higher-ups was a little trickier. Luckily they too saw in Downey many of the qualities Tony Stark embodies. 'He is flawed, but also brilliant, funny, extremely talented and likeable,' said producer Kevin Feige. 'Tony Stark is a figure that is famous and has a lot of notoriety both positive and negative,' added Favreau. 'His face has been bannered in newspaper headlines many times before he ever becomes Iron Man. He's been involved in weapons manufacturing for years but suddenly realises the ramifications of what he does for a living. It's like waking up one day and realising you're the bad guy when you always thought you were one of the good guys.'

Swap munitions for acting and they could have been talking about either man. Feige allayed the fears of his superiors and Favreau called Downey to tell him he had the job. He was over the moon. 'You tend to get offered better stuff when you're not crazy,' he joked on set. 'I kind of feel like you get the jobs you're supposed to get. I don't want to be too naive or altruistic about the whole thing, but I think as often as not that's the case.' He had his potential franchise. But though comic-books nerds knew all about him – and Marvel received more female fan mail than for any other character in their canon – it wasn't a slam dunk. He was definitely a second-tier superhero. And then there was Downey's lacklustre box-office history. They had plenty more work to do.

It was fitting that the majority of filming took place on soundstages in Playa Vista, Los Angeles. They were originally part of the studio owned by Howard Hughes, the template Stan Lee had used for Tony Stark. Downey showed up looking buffer than ever. He was lifting weights five times a week and taking the supplement creatine to build muscle. 'About a year ago, I decided that I really want to put on some size,' he said during filming.

'It was really about survival for me and all the hard work in preproduction wound up giving me the strength to do the movie.' Jon Favreau was impressed – and glad, because the physical requirements of the role were going to be tough. 'Robert really went the extra mile and trained heavily to make his body look the way it should to play a superhero,' he said. Downey was keen to push himself further than he had done in a long time. 'I want to be fearless, but I don't just want to do that in the box,' he said. 'You know you are doing it because it's risky.' Nevertheless, he was aware of how the outside world might perceive his casting, especially the famously picky geeks. 'These days, with the media or your own ego blog, they can be like, "Oh, can you believe he's doing that?"' he said. 'It's a tricky little deal.'

He needn't have worried. People across the board were happy when they heard the news. Downey couldn't believe it. It was the best reception he had ever had. 'I can't even express how much I love that choice,' said film spy website *Ain't It Cool News*. 'And when the franchise finally gets into some of Tony Stark's darkest hours, when he faces down his own demons in the second film or the third, can you imagine how much soul Downey can bring to it?'

That's right; like any great superhero, Tony Stark has a dark side. And what does this gazillionaire genius have to worry about? Alcoholism. Always a fan of liquor, at one point during the saga, after a flurry of mishaps, Stark becomes an alcoholic. He conquers it, but then is tricked by his colleague and relapses, loses his company and becomes a homeless alcoholic. Not very family-friendly stuff. The film-makers chose to ignore this dangerous side of his personality for the first instalment, concentrating instead on his womanising and playboy attitude. The closest we get to booze is him holding a Scotch on the rocks while careering through the desert in a Humvee. Downey didn't think this facet of his character was essential, he saw it more as an outward reaction to Stark's basic narcissism.

But these story decisions – and the potential arc for a so-called franchise – were all crucial. Through the development process there had already been multiple villains and plots. And Downey wanted to be a part of it. He set up an office next to Favreau's and worked with the writers to hone the script. Much of the dialogue was created in rehearsals (with one of the writers watching the actors workshop the scenes), while a lot of it was done on the spot during shooting. It was what Downey loved the most, only this time he was doing it with a $180 million budget. It was dangerous. Though Favreau made sure he had top-notch behind-the-scenes talent to work on the more action-orientated sections of the film, the movie relied on audiences liking and feeling a kinship with the central character. And unlike Spiderman's alter ego, Peter Parker, who's just a geeky kid, Stark is a babe-magnet billionaire genius without, it seems, a worry in the world. The creative team pored through the material and settled on an origin story they hoped would satisfy all sections of the audience. You'd see how Iron Man got his name, meet his friends and put him up against one of his famous foes, but not try to cram too much into one film. It was a risky ploy.

One of the key sequences was the first half-hour of the film when Tony is captured and held by terrorists in an Afghani cave, where he forges the first Iron Man suit and creates the prototype for his electromagnetic heart. For production designer J. Michael Riva, having Downey around proved beneficial. 'Robert, who has had some first-hand knowledge of what it's like to be held captive, brought some of his own very revealing ideas to the cave dressing that made our job easier and gave it authenticity,' said Riva. 'Things like how to make tea with a sock and how you make a backgammon set out of nothing.'

Inevitably with the baddies being from Afghanistan (though they aren't shown to be aligned with a specific group), the story edges into political territory, especially given Tony's day job as an arms dealer to the US military. Though he was probably the only person on set to have gone to both parties' conventions, it wasn't an area Downey was entirely comfortable with. 'I don't see this as a bunch of limousine liberals trying to slip one past the bad guys,' he said. 'I'm seriously pro-American. I don't mean that in a blind or gung-ho way. I love travelling, but when I come back and see our flag, I could cry every time. But the good news is that if it gets too heavy I can say, "Dudes, it's a comic-book movie, will you relax?"'

What he was far more concerned about was the suit. There were several versions of the costume, which transformed from a crude cumbersome version built in a terrorist's cave to the sleek red and gold outfit splashed across Marvel pages. And they weren't even touching the more recent comic incarnations like the one that was sentient and ended up sacrificing its own life to save its creator, or the one that sprouted liquid-like from its maker's pores. Downey had never been very good at this stuff. His favourite films to work on had always had as few costume changes as possible. Yet here he was, about to embark on months inside restrictive panels of fibreglass and various other materials (though much of *Iron Man*'s action would also be crafted inside a computer).

At first, he was excited. 'The first half-hour of being in the Iron Man suit is like being in the coolest Halloween costume ever,' he said. 'You're putting the suit on and you catch a glimpse in the mirror and you go, "That's right, Grandma would be proud".' That wasn't to last. The original armour, known as the Mark I suit, weighed 90 pounds. 'I'd been training for all these years and thought I was pretty tough, but the first time I put on the Mark I suit, I almost had a personality meltdown,' said Downey. 'Even having one that's ergonomically designed and I'm number one on the call sheet, it's hard not to have my spirit broken after wearing it for twenty minutes.' Keeping the suit as a practical effect – one that is performed on camera, rather than added using digital technology – was one of the things Favreau pushed most for. Often Downey couldn't see what he was doing because he ended up trying to look through the nostrils of the six-foot-five-inch model. He equated it to driving with a blindfold on.

He spent much of his time on the motion-capture stage, performing for a bank of computers who would translate his movements into on-screen action. He wanted to do more of the action, not stand around on a bare stage with a blue or green screen behind him. He rarely got to go around shooting at people and here he was, with access to Iron Man's trademark hand repulsor rays, and he wasn't getting to use them. 'One of the reasons [the film] was interesting to me is that I've always been a more fierce and game guy than I might have been given credit for,' he said. 'It's not like I felt I had to go out and prove what a butch guy I am or anything, but I love this stuff. I love hardware. I love fighting and guns! I have an appreciation for things that your average eight-year-old loves. Except I can back it up a little better than an eight-year-old.'

When it came time to do the stunts, he pushed his body as far as it would go. It was, after all, a Wing Chun-trained temple now. 'Robert kept wanting to do more and more of his stunts and I had to keep reining him in,' said the film's stunt co-ordinator Thomas Robinson Harper. 'He had taken the baby steps in preparation for one of the bigger pulls and one night we pulled [his harness] so hard his feet went above his head.' But Downey didn't mind. He had committed himself to the film and wasn't going to let go. The crew appreciated his devotion to them in trying to make the finished product as good as it could be. He spent much of his time wandering around the different departments, learning how the other parts of the movie were being put together. For the comic-book fans among them, they recognised the same loyalty Tony expects and receives from his confidants, his assistant Pepper Potts or best friend James 'Rhodey' Rhodes.

Marvel's gamble paid off. The film was a critical smash, as well as being a commercial blockbuster. From the party in his private jet, through the daring escape from his cave prison and on to the flights through the city, *Iron Man* is a buoyant, exciting and intelligent action pic. The supporting cast are great, particularly Jeff Bridges as Tony's shady colleague, and Gwyneth Paltrow is enjoyable as Pepper. The latter had only signed on when Downey personally called her house to ask, shocking her real-life husband Chris Martin from Coldplay.

Downey is magnificent in the lead. He looks his age, but in a way that suggests he has seen and experienced life. His transformation from glib businessman to man-on-a-mission feels natural and uncontrived. And he pulls off the comedy – 'Give me a Scotch, I'm starving'; 'Let's face it – this is not the worst thing you've caught me doing?' – with aplomb. Sneak-peek footage that had been shown at the Comic-Con convention in July 2007 in San Diego had gone down a treat in front of 6,500 fickle fans, so the film-makers had an idea they were on to something. Downey was on the set of his next movie when he heard about their convention success and was thrilled, but even he didn't expect it to pull in $100 million in its opening weekend. It was beyond their wildest dreams. Downey had turned 42 while making it and was just 43 when it reached cinemas. He *finally* had a hit film and he wanted to savour it. He, Favreau and Susan sneaked into some midnight screenings in Los Angeles and watched rapt as the audiences soaked it up. Susan in particular had never seen anything like it.

People started buying Iron Man dolls with Downey's likeness, Tony appeared in political cartoons. Downey started hatching possible sequel scenarios, using the long-haul flights to promote the film around the world as brainstorming sessions with his director. Marvel announced *Iron Man 2* and *3* almost instantly. Youngsters who had no idea that he had ever been Charlie Chaplin or one of Bret Easton Ellis's drug addicts queued up to scream his name.

It was bizarre. The mass-market adulation he had hoped for had taken more than more than a quarter of a century to arrive. When he had done *Chaplin*, he had half-expected it to happen, the same kind of thing that happened to young actors like Megan Fox or Shia LaBeouf after they did their 'big' film in their twenties. Immediate fame, superstar patronage, the promise of forward momentum and happiness, a firm, mapped-out course. That had never really happened for him. He hadn't read the scripts when they came in, just checked the cover page, saw who the director was and his potential co-stars. If he liked what he saw, he said yes. Simple as that. The creative experience of *Chaplin* and its Oscar-nominated aftermath hadn't been replicated and he had sought acceptance elsewhere, another outlet for his artistic energies. But it was different now. He had a path and he had someone to join him on his journey. He had ploughed everything into convincing the powers-that-be that he was worth a shot, had thrown himself into the process, and for once the audience's wallets had agreed with him. When magazines chased him up to congratulate, he was surprised. 'I genuinely never thought I'd be having this conversation,' he said. You'd be forgiven for agreeing with him.

Sobriety was paying off. He felt that *Iron Man* would be the film to put the nail in the coffin of his past, to turn the media and nay-sayers on to his success rather than his failures. 'It's all just so last century,' he said in late 2008. 'It's like certain weird things have become an elixir for public consumption.' His days of making fun of his past, publicly anyway, were over. 'I've always thought that clarity was better,' he said about his new life. 'I was out of touch with reality, I thought that I was doing exactly what was best for me. I think people are always doing what they think is the best thing for them, it's just nobody understands. Particularly if it's outlandish.' He remembered back to those pivotal moments when he officially chose to stop using drugs. Susan says she met the person she dubs 'Darth Vader' once just after *Gothika* wrapped and quickly said 'he' couldn't be seen again. Downey recalls driving around his Venice neighbourhood in Los Angeles, his car weighed down by drug paraphernalia – pipes, glass stems and nitrous oxide – when he was pulled over by a policeman. He was finally off probation, but it could still have spelled a serious amount of jail time. The cop told him to fix his number plate. It was an incredible let-off. A couple of days later, around 4 July 2003, he was driving up the Pacific Coast Highway on his way to a friend's wedding. His gear was with him. Suddenly he was struck by the chance he had been given. He doesn't know *exactly* what it was, but something or someone told him the time had come. 'It takes a lot of effort to get out of control again, so if you don't start shit you don't wind up getting in that powerless situation,' he said. 'I think I was just lucky.' He stopped at a Burger King, then went to the edge of the ocean and threw the drugs away. 'It takes a lot of denial to keep going,' he added. 'Like the rave has been done for four days and you're still there hearing music in your head. It's not real, but I could also say that I celebrate every single thing that's happened.' Still, he found it wasn't the last time the police would take an interest. Such is the life of an ex-con. Once an officer pulled him over just to look in his eyes, convinced he would see dilated pupils. 'I was like, "I did not do anything,"' he remembered. "He says, 'I just wanted to smell your breath."' He is looking at my eyes. He just wanted to see if I was loaded. He wanted to be the cop who gets to say, "Yeah, you look really good on TV, but I'm going to cuff you."'

Downey knew he had got out just in time. 'Nowadays, if I was doing what I was doing five years ago I'd be fucking finished, as evidenced by some friends of mine, who shall remain nameless, that are fucking done,' he said in 2008. 'I'm no better or worse an actor, but there was just this kind of deadline where people were like, "We don't stand for this any more."'

He continued, 'I have become more Harrison Ford about the whole thing. I'm separating my life and my career. I get a kick out of being in the public eye and it feels like my real life because I spend so much time in it. But I have this aesthetic distance now too, because I know about the dangers . . . I know how unhealthy my self-love and my desire to be in the spotlight have been. It's all about becoming rooted in the mundane, in the day-to-day stuff. Life is 70 per cent maintenance. I'm learning the business of building a life.'

He relished the normal, like going out to dinner at the Chateau Marmont with friends, who marvelled at how great he was doing. '[Susan] was just cool,' says *Two Girls and a Guy* producer Chris Hanley. 'She cancelled out all his issues. I saw him once without her and he was jittery. When I saw him again with his wife, it was like, this is it, he's going to get through it all.'

Downey tried to give up cigarettes, using a nicotine inhaler Susan hoped would work. When she went off to Canada to produce two movies, he kept a small team around him, including Eric Oram and his lawyer Tom Hansen, whose house in Wyoming ski resort Jackson Hole he had once almost burned down. At home, he was looked after by two crucial cogs in what became known as Team Downey, Christine Mammolito and Jimmy, his assistant. Jimmy Rich was the cousin of a professional American footballer, the co-best man at his wedding and the guy who looked after the minutiae of his life. Chief among them was bagging up Downey's pills for the week, a cluster of herbal supplements, ones to feed his brain, others to help cure a stomach ache or a cold. That wasn't to say the star never cut loose, it was just in different ways from before. He would drop Indio off at school, then dance wildly in his car to Toots and The Maytals, the only man in the world to enjoy the morning run.

The world was Downey's oyster, but he threatened to kill his newly minted superstardom with a film he had shot just two weeks after leaving Tony Stark behind. *Tropic Thunder* (2008) was an idea hatched by actor and comedian Ben Stiller back in 1987 when he had a supporting role in Steven Spielberg's *Empire of the Sun*, set in a World War II POW camp. 'At the time, all my actor friends were doing Vietnam films like *Platoon* and *Hamburger Hill* and going off to fake boot camps for two weeks,' said Stiller. 'Then during interviews, they would say, "This boot camp was the most intense thing I have ever experienced in my entire life and we really bonded as a unit."' An idea began to form about a group of actors starring in a big-budget Vietnam War movie who end up getting in over their heads. Not only would it be an action film, but a satire of Hollywood pomposity and thespian overzealousness. The project languished for years while Stiller got famous and finally he decided to revisit it, teaming with Justin Theroux and Etan Cohen to write it.

The eventual rather complicated plot was thus: five actors descend on the jungle to shoot the most expensive war movie of all time, called *Tropic Thunder*. The director, tired of their whining, takes them out into the bush to try and create a guerrilla feel to filming. However, they inadvertently stumble onto a gang of local drug dealers who try to kill them. Believing this to be all part of the director's ploy (even after he has been blown up by a landmine), they stay in character and end up going face to face with a real enemy, thinking they are still shooting the film. The whinging stars are a parade of witty archetypes. One is a fading action star (Stiller), one a heroin-addicted comedian (Jack Black), one a rapper looking to break into films (Brandon T. Jackson) and one a neophyte performer having his big break.

And then there's Kirk Lazarus. Lazarus was originally written as Irish, an award-laden thesp with method sensibilities, lampooning people like Daniel Day-Lewis and their decision to spend months as a cobbler in Italy to prepare for a role. But there's a twist. In the film within the film, Lazarus is playing a character called Lincoln Osiris. Who's black. Lazarus is white. Not to be put off, he visits a controversial clinic in Singapore and has his skin dyed. '[Lazarus] seriously sees this as his next great acting challenge,' explained producer Stuart Cornfeld. 'When Lazarus reports for duty on set, he *is* Lincoln Osiris and he refuses to drop out of character at any time throughout the movie.' It was an idea filled with potential risks, not least that whoever Stiller got to play Lazarus (and in turn Osiris) would be accused of dressing up in blackface.

'I didn't know how it was going to play,' said Stiller, who also directed. 'I knew what our intention was so you have to trust your instinct and go in and commit to what you're doing, knowing that on the other end of it you'll see how it works and then you deal with that when you get to the point where you have a movie cut together.'

Though Downey was yet to become a megastar thanks to *Iron Man*, there were no other names in the frame when Stiller and co. came to casting. They approached Downey, who was wary at first. 'I kind of initially got mad,' he said when the film was released in August 2008. 'I was like, "Fuck Ben Stiller, he's going to call me up and say I want to do a great big movie with you, but I want you to have the highest risk factor and I want to maybe put you up to ridicule and have people hate you for doing something that you should have known was wrong to do."' This could wind up having been a really terrible idea for me personally and for the movie if we don't execute it properly." But then he started thinking. He began to realise it wasn't racist, but rather a brutal piquing of the narcissism he was all too aware of. How far-reaching can someone's narcissism go, he thought. 'To me it's like the ultimate crossover,' he said. 'Someone who's a basketball star who says I really want to be a catwalk model and they don't know what to do and the clothes don't fit, but they do it anyway.' He was reminded of an incident earlier in his career when a co-star felt the vibe on set wasn't the way he wanted it, so started trying to encourage the rest of the actors to break from the shoot, put on animal masks and run about with each other, getting in touch with their primal instincts. Downey laughed it off. 'I don't need to dress as a reindeer,' he said. 'Who taught you this garbage?'

Tropic Thunder also felt strangely cyclical. His father had made the racially progressive *Putney Swope* 40 years previously. Now here was his chance to add something to the debate. 'You check your gut and you say, "Do I feel like the universe is going to support this?"' he said. 'Kirk's heart is in the right place. The way it's portrayed is self-deprecating. He has literally gotten so into the role that he cannot get out of it, even when there's no indication they're making a movie any more. Certain of us actors have gone that method route at times, but only up to a point.'

Downey was in. Exhausted but elated from *Iron Man*, he travelled to Kauai, where the production designers turned the picturesque island into a dense war zone. Many of the locations were a long drive from civilisation. Fresh from having sand blasted in his eyes and sweating in a fibreglass suit, the remoteness was tough for Downey to grasp at first, exacerbated by the two hours he spent in the make-up chair every morning. 'It didn't seem like there was any good reason why we should be shooting here,' he said. 'We could've just gone off the side of a major thoroughfare somewhere and made it look like this.' But as the thirteen-week shoot wore on, he began to start feeling the same kind of camaraderie that Stiller's war-film actor buddies had got. '[It was] so complete in its realism and isolation. It was so tough and so knee-deep in mud and rain,' he continued. 'Oftentimes when you go into those situations or locations you think it's going to be hell, but this was a very enjoyable purgatory.'

During rehearsals, Lazarus became Australian rather than Irish, giving Downey the opportunity to revisit the accent he had impressed Steve Dunleavy with in *Natural Born Killers*. Also, he said, he could improvise better as an Aussie. The film-makers frequently relied on co-star Brandon T. Jackson, an actual African-American, to tell them if they were going too far. One day, Downey blurted out the N-word. It was a clever moment, but Jackson was unconvinced, telling his director it was one step too far. They cut it. However, Jackson was impressed by Downey's performance. He too had had initial reservations, before seeing how committed the star was to his character.

'If he had held back, or had said, "Maybe this is too offensive", it wouldn't have worked,' said Stiller. 'He got so into it and he was so clear about what his intention was as the character. I think that confidence is what makes the audience feel OK with it. And it was important that Brandon's character was always there just sort of saying what an audience member might be saying.' Downey isn't a fan of broad comedy, so for him it was about treating Lazarus/Osiris like he was in a drama. 'As far as I'm concerned I didn't tell a joke for three months,' he says. 'I was just wearing a mask and having an experience.'

Playing the part had an odd effect on him however. Scenes

with him 'staying in character' were written into the script – as Lazarus says, 'Man, I don't drop character till I done the DVD commentary' – but Jackson witnessed some of that mentality bleeding into the actor's performance. Downey said he couldn't be bothered to get that deep into his role, but Stiller said, 'I remember Robert being very mean to me at certain times. I think we all got along, but it was funny, Robert in character had this freedom when he was being Lincoln Osiris, because he was so not himself and he had the freedom to shout out stuff. It was almost like a Tourette's thing where he would shout out and curse at people. He could say whatever he wanted and get away with it in character, which he does in the movie too. It was the funniest thing listening to Robert do that. He would do it all the time on set.'

Downey did get away with it. When filming was completed, Stiller took it to the National Association for the Advancement of Coloured People (NAACP) and a few African-American journalists and showed them what he'd put together. They weren't offended. Even when the first photo of Downey in his make-up hit the press, the controversy was more media-concocted than genuine. Nonetheless, the star got more than his fair share of journalists who hadn't seen the film asking him how he could do a film in blackface. He got tired of trying to explain the context, focusing instead on mocking the artistic community. 'The whole film is based on the idea that what [actors] do at some level is offensive and who we are, at some level, is despicable and pathetic, which is the truth and not the truth,' he said. 'But the part of it that is the truth is entertaining.' Downey and the film did get in some trouble, but it wasn't racial. Instead, the premiere was picketed by disabled people's rights groups, who objected to a plotline in the film in which Ben Stiller's character Tugg Speedman plays a mentally challenged boy called Jack in a desperate bid to win an Oscar. But, as Lazarus tells him, you never win an award if you go 'full retard'.

The use of such language caused outrage and organisations such as the American Association of People with Disabilities and the National Down Syndrome Congress called for a boycott, despite the film-makers' retort that they were making fun of actors who go to any lengths for glory, not the disabled.

The hullabaloo didn't affect *Tropic Thunder*'s success. When it came out in August 2008 a mere three months after *Iron Man*, it made more than $110 million at the worldwide box office. Downey had gone from having no hits to two smashes in a row. What's more, the role that could potentially have destroyed him was getting some of the best reviews of his career. 'Downey Jr is the unquestionable star,' said the *Daily Telegraph*. 'He not only embraces the absurdity of his character, but takes it to such an extreme that he becomes weirdly real and affecting . . . the scenes in which he, in all earnestness, bickers with [Jackson] over which of them is blackest, or chides Speedman for using the phrase "you people", are as rich in their multi-layered takes on racial niceties as anything since the first Ali G series.' *Empire* magazine agreed, announcing Kirk Lazarus as 'up there with the comedy greats'. They noted the fine balance between laughs and offending people saying, 'It's a testament to Downey Jr's meaty acting chops that Lazarus's jiving makes you wince without ever feeling genuine discomfort . . . and Downey Jr convinces us completely that Lazarus is such a twit that his self-absorbed concerns with the craft leave him unable to understand that his performance is just deeply wrong.'

In fact, so successful was Downey's portrayal that the film's distributors decided to back him as a possible Oscar contender for Best Supporting Actor. It was a startling twist considering *Tropic Thunder* was supposed to be skewering the awards process and Lazarus was a five-time Oscar winner. The promotional campaign even featured several ads asking voters to consider

Lazarus for his performance in 'Satan's Alley', one of the mock trailers that begin the movie. Downey thought it was hilarious. 'The funny thing is I was playing an Oscar-crazed weirdo whose every motivation was somehow geared towards accolades,' he said. 'It's about time narcissistic, accolade-seeking idiotic actors were formally recognised. It's been a long hard road for us all.'

The film in which he played an Australian playing a black man turned out to produce his second Academy Award nomination, as well as a nomination for a British Academy Award (BAFTA) and a Golden Globe. He was facing tough competition – the late star Heath Ledger was widely considered the number-one choice for his portrayal of the Joker in *The Dark Knight*. Come 22 February 2009 at the Kodak Theatre in Hollywood, Ledger did indeed win the Oscar posthumously (as well as the Globe and the BAFTA), but Downey didn't mind. He walked down the red carpet to screams of 'I love you, Iron Man!' from the crowd, many of whom had come out just to catch a glimpse of him. He repeated his fears about the character. 'We were always on some level wondering if people would misunderstand our intention,' he said. Thanks to him, they hadn't.

Sober & Happy

'That's the great thing about Hollywood – memories are short.' (2009)

Downey's mother Elsie always worried that her son's early success, the fact it seemed to come to him so easily, prevented him from growing emotionally. At least that's what she said before his endless bouts with rehab and jail cells. He had enough humility to last a lifetime – and he had acquired most of it in the public eye. So the box-office bonanza of *Iron Man* and *Tropic Thunder* – the moment he changed from regular leading man, or character actor in a leading man's body, into a flat-out, bona fide megastar – came when it was supposed to, after he had paid his dues, faced his demons, even literally served his time.

'You can fuck up your career in five minutes,' he said. 'Whereas it takes a little longer than five minutes to get it back.' He had taken up smoking again during filming in Kauai, so was trying to wean himself off again. Mum was now living down the street and would swing by on occasion to swim in his pool. As his career ratcheted up, he became ever more aware of how she conducted the business of acting, being dedicated to the vision, but not running in all guns blazing.

He'd been watching *Putney Swope* too, on his computer, experiencing his father's work anew. There were some things that could never be fixed, but thanks to therapy and sheer bloody time, their relationship was as good as it had ever been. Downey Sr cropped up as an actor in the films of various younger directors who appreciated his work – in Paul Thomas Anderson's *Magnolia* and *The Family Man* by Brett Ratner, who had hung out with Downey Jr and Anthony Michael Hall in New York as a youngster. But his directing career had stalled with the documentary *Rittenhouse Square* in 2005, though art-house cinemas were increasingly putting on seasons of his earlier films. The triumph of *Tropic Thunder*, however, had led him to consider updating his seminal achievement. He was also happily married again, to a music producer and writer called Rosemary Rogers, author of the book *Mother-Daughter Movies: 101 Films to See Together*, which she had written with her own daughter Nell Rogers Michlin. Downey had been best man when they wed in May 1998, taking a leave of absence from the halfway house he was living in at the time (with a sober companion) to attend the ceremony, which was held at Rogers' sister's apartment in Manhattan and presided over by a Roman Catholic priest.

Downey was also on great terms with his sister Allyson, who lived on the East Coast and had come to the premiere of *A Scanner Darkly* with him. Allyson had been through an equally tricky time, though out of the spotlight. She had been through a variety of jobs and dabbled with the family business, acting in a couple of movies. One, *1999*, also featured a pre-stardom Jennifer Garner, while *Funny Valentine* – which was filmed in New York and released in 2005 – had Downey's best friend Anthony Michael Hall in the lead role. '[Hall] suggested we meet her and audition her,' says Jeff Oppenheim, the latter film's writer/director. 'She has a natural sense of timing, a playful, self-deprecating style and a quiet, inquisitive pause to see how you register her wit.' She worked one day on the picture as one of the women answering a personal ad two of the main characters have posted for their friend (Hall). 'Allyson comes in dressed in an ultra-conservative skirt suit that a nun might wear to try and blend in at a school dance,' says Oppenheim. 'She sits down and does her bit as this rather overzealous woman looking for a man to father her child. She slowly builds to this screeching protestation. She was amazing and terrifying at the same time. The entire crew was trying not to ruin the shot by laughing out loud. When the assistant director yelled cut you heard everyone bust out laughing. That was one of my favourite days on set. It really was a celebration of female comic genius.' Ironically, the film features a homage to the director's favourite star Charlie Chaplin, allowing Hall a chance to play the character his best friend had won an Oscar nomination for. 'There is a whole Chaplin fantasy in the film done in black-and-white,' says the director. 'Michael and I worked a lot in rehearsal on his Chaplin and I think both of us had questions and thoughts on the film. So there was a natural segue to talk of Robert's marvellous portrayal of this comic genius. [Allyson] spoke of Robert with great love and affection and I recall our conversations were more about their relationship than his work, although I know she thinks highly of his work.' While she obviously showed aptitude for acting, writing was where her heart was and she started working on an anthology of short stories. But like her sibling, early middle age appears to suit her. She went through a blonde phase, then returned to brunette. By the time she showed up with Downey at his premieres, she looked glowing and happy.

Meanwhile, after *Tropic Thunder*, for Downey it was exactly like Susan predicted. Work within the mainstream and then go off and do the passion project in between. In April 2008 he started shooting *The Soloist* (2009), a prestige film that was English director Joe Wright's follow-up to *Atonement*. It was a uniquely

Los Angelean story. Almost exactly three years previously, *Los Angeles Times* writer Steve Lopez had been desperate to find material for his column in the paper one day, when he had stumbled across a homeless man called Nathanial Ayers. He got talking to him and it turned out Ayers was a Juilliard-trained musician, who after being diagnosed as mentally ill lost his way and ended up on the streets. Lopez started writing about his friendship with Ayers and the work he did with Lamp, a homeless charity whose mission is to re-house street people.

'Readers got very involved in the story and began rooting for Mr Ayers,' said Lopez. He received hundreds of letters and emails, as well as musical instruments from people showing their support for his subject. He turned Ayers' story into an acclaimed book, which in turn was snapped up by Dreamworks. Oscar winner Jamie Foxx was signed to play Ayers, while Downey took on the role of the journalist. 'He is the film's Everyman,' said Wright. 'Steve is someone who's never been able to commit to other people and he goes into this relationship thinking he can save Nathaniel, but actually it's he who's changed by the experience in the end. Robert was able to bring a great humanity and a fierce intellect to that.'

Though Downey looked nothing like him, he started trying to get into his real-life alter ego's head, asking to look in his clothes cupboard and trying to interview him. Lopez refused. He felt it would be wrong for the actor to do an impersonation. After all, in the film script, the reporter was written as being divorced. In real life, he was happily married. For Downey, it was more about thematic links than copying. Instead, he tried to come up with an alternative, starting with the idea that 'movie Steve' should have short hair. 'Next thing you know, [co-star Catherine] Keener's shaving my head in our first day of rehearsal with a number two blade,' he recalled.

It was a tough gig for Downey, who had to dampen down his usual proactive acting habits. 'Joe Wright said it was really important that I do next to nothing and listen a lot,' he said, 'which is very counter-intuitive.' The director did encourage his improvisation skills, though. 'There are scenes in there that he wrote, or I wrote, or we wrote together,' said Wright. 'He improvised a lot on the day, the day before. The thing was to keep making sure he was on story, if you like. Although sometimes you're like, "That's such a good line I've got to have it in there", you know?'

Downey marvelled at Foxx's ability to interact with the homeless extras, as they hired Lamp members to provide the movie's background support. In between takes, Foxx would hold impromptu movie quizzes, handing out cash prizes to those who got the right answer. For Downey, it was more a case of there but for the grace of God go I. He had worked with disadvantaged people before, lending a hand to The London Shakespeare Workout, an initiative to teach acting in prisons, which he did under the radar. But though he was loath to admit a film had changed his outlook, it was difficult not to be affected while he was sitting on the downtown Los Angeles set at half-four in the morning, watching the extras peel away to try to find somewhere to sleep. 'It's not like I need a movie to get my head right and I would take umbrage at the idea that there was some lesson I had to learn,' he said. 'It was just this sense of how little direct contact I'd had with so many of [the] things I thought I was sure of. This last year I've done these big, fun showy movies and I think [*The Soloist*] was just what the cosmos ordered for me,' said Downey. 'To do something about humanity and humility and tolerance. [Joe] spoke about how he wanted to pepper the cast with actual members of the Lamp community. It was a fantastic leap of faith that this was somehow going to work out and we'd all interact and get along and simultaneously shoot a movie about this story – and yet we did.'

Originally intended to be released during the awards season, the film was held back until April 2009 in the US (and September in the UK). 'Budget issues' were put forward as the reason – the likelihood of Downey potentially going up against himself in *Tropic Thunder* in the Oscar race was a more likely explanation. Continuing his excellent chemistry with his female co-stars, the boyish charm he displayed in so many of his early films was finally becoming a more openly roguish sexuality, helped by the salt-and-pepper hair and gradually more crinkly eyes. It was a welcome addition to his armoury. Joe Wright summed up his current state effectively, while also managing to intuit something about the person he used to be. 'He's an extraordinary man,' he said. 'There's so much character, there's almost too much character for one person, for one brain. He self-medicated for a reason. It must be very, very difficult to live inside that mind. It's a beautiful mind, there's a lot of energy in it and it's a million different ideas, thoughts, references, per second. And it's fascinating and you have to hold on to his shirt-tails basically, really tight and try not to let go!'

There are some benefits to having a spouse in the film industry. Just two years after feeling bereft for not having the chance to be in a franchise, one day Susan mentioned a name to her husband. Sherlock Holmes. The English sleuth, created by Arthur Conan Doyle, was looking at a cinematic comeback. Columbia Pictures were developing a comedic version of the character, potentially starring Sacha Baron Cohen and Will Ferrell as Holmes and Watson respectively. But Susan was involved in a more serious take on the stories, one that turned the deerstalker-wearing, pipe-smoking detective into a bad-ass action hero.

The idea had been hatched by producer Lionel Wigram, who had been thinking for years about how to present a fresh side of

Holmes. Going back to the books, he discovered Doyle actually wrote about the pair's scuffles with the bad guys and saw a way in – a modern, physical account of the traditionally cerebral literary icon. He put together a comic-book-style treatment which was snapped up by Warner Bros, who got Susan and her producing partner Joel Silver involved. They had just worked with *Lock, Stock and Two Smoking Barrels* director Guy Ritchie on his film *Rocknrolla* and thought he would be the perfect person to shepherd the project. Initially, Ritchie thought about casting young actors to play the lead duo. But with *Iron Man* earning half a billion dollars worldwide, Downey was now a bona fide box-office superstar. Whereas the announcement of the actor as Tony Stark caused a few ripples amongst those who thought he spelled financial poison, now companies were chomping at the bit to sign him up. But Downey was now facing a different kind of pressure. Before, his film's failures hadn't been blamed on him. But if Sherlock didn't work, the 'sophomore slump' argument was an easy one, especially since he was guaranteed a huge pay packet. Downey remained publicly defiant. 'Scared? I don't get scared anymore,' he said. 'I just get busy.' Holmes intrigued him, especially the persona Ritchie and his writers were creating. As well as being a detective who spent his downtime fighting in illegal bare-knuckle boxing matches, his verbosity and almost manic depressive mindset rang true. Susan certainly saw the parallels. 'The eloquence of Holmes, his use of language, seems to come very naturally to Robert,' she said.

'[She] said that when you read the description of the guy – quirky and kind of nuts – it could be a description of me,' said Downey. 'When he feels he's not inspired or motivated by some creative charge, he'll fall into a state where he barely speaks a word for three days and when he's engaged, he has incredible amounts of energy, super-human energy.' It's the kind of attitude that several of Downey's friends and collaborators pinpointed as the reason for his drug use. Ironically, of course, Sherlock Holmes is a notorious drug addict, as evidenced in one of the best previous Holmes movies, *The Seven Per Cent Solution*. 'It was never a high enough percentage for me, kind of a weak, tepid solution,' laughed Downey. 'But this is a PG-13 movie and even if it wasn't, if you go back to the source material he's never described as being some strung-out weirdo.' In the finished film, there's a barely-noticeable reference to it, though inevitably it was at the forefront of many of the questions Downey was forced to face from the journalists while promoting it. 'We thought it would be irresponsible to not make reference to it,' he said.

When Susan put his name in the mix for the role, he went to her office and had a glimpse at some of the ideas Ritchie was putting together. He was hooked. Ritchie too fell in love with the idea and the story was altered slightly to fit an older actor. Downey went to Claridge's Hotel in London to woo Jude Law personally to play Dr Watson, who was portrayed in the script as a war veteran about to leave 221B Baker Street to get married, much to the consternation of his partner. Law, whose second job on TV was playing a stable boy in one of the episodes of the classic Jeremy Brett series, agreed and it was full steam ahead.

Before he knew it, Downey found himself playing another superhero, only this time it was an intellectual one, rather than someone in a metal suit. 'The more I look into the books, the more fantastic it becomes,' he said. 'Holmes is flighty and very much living in his head and in the case.' He saw the character as a progenitor of the crime procedurals that littered the television schedules – *CSI* and *NCIS* in Victorian times. He particularly empathised with Holmes's investigative side. Susan didn't see much of the detail-orientated observationist in her husband, but more of a psychologist's ability to read people. He was brilliant, she said, at 'breaking down other people's irrational psychotic behaviour. I think he's masterful at understanding the inner workings of people's heads.' Downey agreed with the specificity of his skills. 'If someone is off the rails, or behaving erratically, I can probably tell you exactly what is going on,' he said. 'If there's been contact with law enforcement, I can tell you probably where they are located and what their thought process is. I could guess the contents of someone's urinalysis probably within a quark.'

Downey started training, running drills with Eric Oram, who was hired as a consultant on the film. Doyle had written about his hero's affinity with baritsu, a fictionalised version of the martial art Bartitsu, which combines self-defence, boxing and stick fighting. He lost weight, 'helped' by a parasite he contracted promoting *Iron Man* in Japan, which made him ill for three days. 'I started losing weight and thought to myself, "Hey, this is a nice jump-start!"' he said in *Rolling Stone*. 'No one ever tells you in Weight Watchers like, "Contract a parasite in Japan and then run with it!" They say, "Starve yourself and be miserable and work out too much . . ." It just gave me a nice little head-start with the first five pounds and then I kept going until I was so thin, I felt as though I may float away and give people tours of the local area from 500 feet up!'

He went to Malibu to see one of the world's foremost Holmes aficionados, Leslie Klinger – a co-trustee of the so-called Baker Street Irregulars, a group of experts from around the world who meet once a year in New York to talk about Sherlockiana. Downey's only previous experience of Holmes was watching *The Hound of the Baskervilles* and reading a couple of the short stories (Conan Doyle wrote four full novels and 56 self-contained short stories). '[Klinger] gave me a bunch of rare books which I proceeded to highlight,' admitted Downey. 'I'm going to have to say my kid did it!' Having locked himself away for a weekend to read everything, he, Law and Ritchie started getting into the nitty-gritty of the story. 'Guy, Jude and I would get together and have a proper bit of food,' he says. 'I realised that doing the civilised approach gets you miles ahead. It's not just like that ugly American thing like, "OK, let's go. Scene 71. We'll have coffee in here after we have a breakthrough." It's like, "Oh, this sounds lovely. These apricots, are they for me?"' Mugging up on his English accent, he headed to the UK for the shoot.

It was a relatively easy affair, with a different Conan Doyle quote on the call sheet each day. They shot in London, Liverpool and Manchester, before transferring to Brooklyn, New York for some of the interiors. 'I consider myself a worker amongst workers and that's what suits me,' said Downey, who enjoyed the fact the British crew didn't treat him any differently just because he was suddenly one of the hottest movie stars around. Susan was there as the production's den mother and during lunchtime they would all sit in someone's trailer; Downey would usually go off on a riff and make everyone laugh. Similar to *Iron Man*, he was heavily involved in the creative process, assisting with casting (Mark Strong as the baddie and Rachel McAdams as the love interest for starters) and frequently adding lines to the mix, often phrases or quotes he remembered from Doyle's originals. He jokingly called Law 'Hotson', because of his handsomeness, and loved it when Ritchie would gee up the set when it came time for physicality. That machismo occasionally spilled in front of the camera. During one fight scene on the docks, stuntman Robert Maillet accidentally punched Downey on the chin, knocking him down. The star graciously came in the next day and gave his on-screen nemesis a bottle of champagne.

The intention had always been to avoid the stereotypical images of Holmes, so the deerstalker and cape were ditched in favour of cool overcoats, period sunglasses and a fedora picked out by the star. 'He never wore a cap except maybe once for a minute, but even then it was described differently,' he said. 'And the long pipe was just something that William Gillette [a theatre actor who played Holmes more than 1,300 times in plays and defined the iconic look] used to not obscure his face on stage.' They went for a mix of genres – *Withnail & I* while the pair were formulating plans in the office and *Butch Cassidy and the Sundance Kid* when they were out and about. Once again, onlookers marvelled at his onscreen chemistry with his co-star, only this time it was between him and Law, their relationship hinting at a homoerotic undercurrent much like Guy Ritchie's earlier films. The director himself would never admit to it, but his star was happy to acknowledge the vibe. 'They're talking about Jude and I like we should be doing romantic comedies together or something,' he said. 'But this film is not a comedy, it's a love affair of sorts.' They were having such fun that although it was premature (despite the film being planned as part of a franchise), they began to debate future films – travelling to America, introducing Holmes's arch-nemesis Moriarty. The competing Will Ferrell project drifted into development hell.

Downey's version was released to much fanfare on Christmas and Boxing Day 2009 around the world, relying enormously on the star's name in its advertorial push. A waxwork of his likeness graced the platform at Baker Street Underground Station in London. He was given the honour of imprinting his hands and feet in front of Mann's Chinese Theatre in Hollywood, a welcome and deserved tribute, but one which now always seems to coincide with the recipient's new film lending it an unfortunate air of promotional puff. Elsie Downey joined her son on the dais, looking on proudly in a baseball cap as he stood waving to the crowds, his hands orange with cement. *Sherlock Holmes* opened on more than three and a half thousand screens in the US, taking over $60 million on its first weekend. By the end of December, it had reached $100 million worldwide. It broke the single-day box-office record for 25 December, taking in $24.9 million. Reviews were mixed, unsurprising particularly in Britain where Guy Ritchie had become something of a critics' punching bag. *The Times* called it 'boisterous, unabashed fun', while the *Guardian* accused the director of managing to 'steal hours of precious time belonging to cinemagoers everywhere for his latest silly escapade.' However, even those who disliked the film – or simply felt it was a typical action blockbuster which could have been set any time and featured any two leading characters – responded to the interplay between Downey and Law. Their spirited banter sustained the slim plot, which required little or no deduction. Then there was the device coined on set as Holmes-A-Vision, a slow-motion sequence designed to show Holmes mapping out and winning a fight in his mind before it had even occurred. Utilised, no doubt, to show cinematic flair, it was symptomatic of a film seemingly designed to slip from the viewer's memory the moment he or she left the auditorium. *Iron Man* needed no such spin.

Nevertheless, $100 million at the box office in less than a week is a mighty achievement. The icing on the cake came when Downey scooped Best Actor in a Comedy or Musical at the 2010 Golden Globes, a shock all round. Susan was so convinced Matt Damon would win in Steven Soderbergh's *The Informant!* she told her husband not to bother preparing a speech. Luckily, his riotous 'anti-acceptance' proved one of the highlights of the night. 'I really don't want to thank my wife because I could be bussing tables at the Daily Grill right now if not for her,' he said. 'Jesus, what a gig that'd be.' He didn't get the same attention from the Oscar Academy, when the nominations were announced a few weeks later, although the film was nominated for Best Art Direction and Best Score. But Downey didn't have much time to breathe. He was now the man upon which two cinematic sagas were based, joining Harrison Ford and Christian Bale as double 'franchisees'. He said he was happy just to flit between the two until he was 'forcibly retired', and admitted, 'I wouldn't want to launch anything else.' A mere few months after *Sherlock Holmes* conquered the box office, he was back playing Tony Stark in *Iron Man 2* (scheduled for release in April 2010). Film insiders put his fee at a staggering $25 million.

'We set ourselves up for this one by having Tony say he was Iron Man last time,' he said at San Diego's Comic-Con in July 2009, where he was treated like a god. 'So you have an origin story, at the end of which you give away the one trump card that usually every other trilogy or franchise doesn't. I think we got a lot of brownie points for that because it was somewhat unexpected. So how do we keep doing the unexpected? I think we just look deeper into what it would be like if you were that guy and that had happened to you and you said you were Iron Man.' The answer? 'I said, "I would probably need a drink!" And I would probably also be really high on myself and feel like I had it all going on. I would feel invincible, but would also know that pride comes before a fall.' It would have been easy for the film-makers to rest on their laurels. After all, the first film was such a smash that the sequel would have a guaranteed audience. Downey wasn't having it. Coming off the back of the bare-knuckle brutality of *Sherlock Holmes*, he encouraged the stunt team to get even grittier than before and involved himself even more deeply in the process. And, along with Favreau, they tried to echo the tone of early Bond films – serious but playful.

'Jon and I are naturalists – not saying that we collect butterflies and discover new species – but we like playing things like they might really be happening,' he said. 'As an audience member, what I love is films where I suspend my disbelief and I can imagine – because they've convinced me just well enough – that this could really be going on. That's why I love films like *The Matrix* or

Jurassic Park, because they're kind of within the realm of possibility.' Gwyneth Paltrow returned as Pepper Potts, while Terrence Howard was replaced as Rhodey by Don Cheadle. As the villains, one of Favreau's original ideas for Tony Stark, Sam Rockwell, came on board as our hero's business rival Justin Hammer. And playing Ivan Vanko – also known as Whiplash – was another actor who had recently enjoyed a career renaissance, Mickey Rourke. Rounding out the ensemble was Scarlett Johansson playing Natasha Romanoff, the alter ego of superhero Black Widow. 'It was amazing,' says Johansson of her experience working with Downey. 'How you kind of watch his train of thought go all the way round and then come back to the centre. More than anything, I just love to interact with that kind of energy, it's fun. It's fresh and exciting and I think the two of us really were able to bounce off of one another.'

Plot details stayed under wraps, but Downey promised exploration into the wider Marvel universe following the (semi-) surprise cameo by S.H.I.E.L.D. leader Nick Fury (Samuel L. Jackson) at the end of the first movie. 'Obviously,' he added, 'there's some sins of the father stuff going on, because Ivan/Mickey is kind of saying he sees me for who and what I am and he is going to take me to school.' He equated it to *Jaws 2* – 'Just when you thought it was safe to go back in the water!'

He loved going back to Tony. 'I was in the elevator last night and there were some guys going up to the club on the roof of this hotel,' he said. 'And they say, "Man, you play Tony Stark, that's so smooth. You were so cool." And I was like, "Excellent".' He had grown up around kids he thought were cooler, actors he thought were cooler. He had watched Steve McQueen, Paul Newman and Marlon Brando on the big screen.

Now he *was* them.

The Next Chapter

With the *Iron Man* films and *Sherlock Holmes*, plus his pick of other projects, Robert Downey Jr could now conceivably be called the biggest movie star in the world. He has filmed the comedy *Due Date* by the director of 2009 blockbuster *The Hangover*, about a man who must hitch a ride cross-country to see his child being born, which is due out in late 2010. Susan has gone independent and set up a production company with her husband, negotiating a first-look deal with Warner Bros. In January 2010, the London Film Museum launched a Chaplin exhibition featuring some of his movie costumes, while his Holmes outfits are also on display. Bret Easton Ellis is reportedly writing a sequel to *Less Than Zero* in which Julian is very much alive. It's also rumoured Downey to play Edgar Allan Poe in a biopic of the writer. *Sherlock Holmes 2* has been fast-tracked and is set to go before cameras in late 2010. And that's even before *Iron Man 3* and *The Avengers*, the planned match-up of all the heroes in the Marvel universe. It's safe to say his dance card's pretty full, which, after all, has always been the way he likes it.

But is that true any more? He can do whatever he wants and it doesn't look like that holiday's coming any time soon. It's probably just the insecure actor in him, the guy who realises just how lucky he is, just how many times he has flirted with disaster and come out the other side, seemingly unscathed and still employable. He's still only just 45. It's not like he can retire. Only that's what he's been saying in the press, throwing around statements suggesting he will hang up his iron boots and move on. But at the same time he's saying, 'I think about rock stars and they always say they're going to retire by this or that age. And then I think about other guys who had double franchises and I think the thing is if the material is still good and if you still love working with the people you get to work with, then why not? As long as what you're working on is feeding you more than it's draining you, everything's cool.'

There's no doubt he has plenty of other things he would like to do: those scripts he's been working on since rehab; his directorial aspirations; more music. He's even been considering following in the footsteps of someone like Sundance Film Festival founder Robert Redford, a legacy that benefits the greater good. On 21 January 2010, Downey Jr met with Senators Mark Leno and Abel Maldanado, along with other key legislative staff to discuss prison reform and prisoner re-entry initiatives in a bid to bring down California's 70 per cent recidivism rate. It's just one political issue he knows too much about. First stop, though, appears to be making a brother or sister for Indio ('The ultimate artefact of our love. In a onesie,' as he described it to *Esquire* magazine in November 2009). It makes sense. Everything's in place. They finally bought a house – a luxurious triplex with a warehouse door, where the window of the couple's bedroom looks into their rooftop pool. And Susan has settled into the role of step-mother, never trying to force it and subsequently building a strong, organic relationship with her husband's 16-year-old son.

'I bumped into [Downey] in a clothing shop in Malibu a while ago,' says his former lawyer Peter Knecht. 'It was over from the cinema which was playing *Iron Man* and behind us was the Malibu courthouse. He started to reminisce and I said to him, "Wow, man, do you see where we are standing? Look at the difference. Look at how far you've come." He smiled at me and nodded his head. He went for dinner afterwards and insisted on taking me in there to meet all the people he was having a meal with and introduced me as the best lawyer in the world. I'm not surprised he has done as well as he has done now. He has the ability and the determination and even when he was on drugs he had the ability to function and act. He could withstand all that and he is a man who has lived with triumph and disaster. He has been to hell and back and he deserves the success he has. There were a lot of people that hated him, because he was a drug addict. But there are a lot of people who hate Obama too. You can't win every battle. It's all how you react to the emotion and he always acted cool. He is still a young man and we don't know what the future holds for him. It could be the fall and rise of Robert Downey Jr and then the fall again. It could continue like that – the rise, the fall and so on. It's been my experience in the 40 years I have been out here practising law that if a person is seriously addicted, the only way you can say he is cured is if he doesn't go back to drugs before he dies. Very few people make 100 per cent recovery. You are playing against the house if you are seriously addicted, you have to have some severe motivation. It all depends on what lies ahead for Robert, in the form of tragedy, disappointments, divorces, death of loved ones and career fall-backs.'

Ah, the elephant in the room. Will he be able to stay clean? So far, the signs look good. It's been eight years. He's happier romantically than he's ever been. 'Between the two of us, we've got the whole package,' he said of his marriage in 2008. 'She tells me flat out, "You know the thing that most people don't understand is that there can only be one rock star in every relationship. Fortunately, I don't want to be a rock star.'" He's rebuilt his relationship with Indio. He's on good terms with his ex Deborah Falconer and he's reconciled his differences with his family. Plus, of course, there's Tony and Sherlock funnelling millions into his bank account.

'In lots of ways, Robert was really lucky to have got caught by the law,' says his *Danger Zone* director Allan Eastman. 'He was pretty far gone based on his behaviour and getting jailed a couple of times forced him to get clean. I'm sure coming out the other end of it, Robert's intelligence recognised what a close-run thing it had been and how much he had fucked himself up. We are all very lucky not to have lost him, like Gram Parsons, Jimi Hendrix or River Phoenix. It makes total sense to me that, having gotten clean, Robert would understand what had happened and never let it happen again.'

Looking at him now, the huge star beloved by kids, it's difficult to reconcile that with the man he was, which was essentially a car crash – the Britney Spears or Lindsay Lohan of his generation. But because he did it before the explosion of blogs and web gossip (the *National Enquirer* was still the go-to cheap tabloid), he managed to avoid complete humiliation on a cultural-permeation level. Not only that, but as a man he seemed to fare better when his drug use was reported in the media. It seemed almost macho, whereas with girls it's unladylike.

He continues to charm audiences and journalists. Look at the glowing profiles by writers who were won over by the sheer force of his personality. He's a genuinely nice guy, and that's great. But once in a while, it's worth delving beneath the nice-guy exterior. Like his high school friend Chris Bell said, Downey is a man who is good at hiding the parts of himself he doesn't want anyone else to see. Sometimes his magnetism and coolness sweep up his interviewers in a wave and, like the hair that covers his face in *Fur . . .* , we get to see what's on the surface, not what's behind it. Sure, they ask about jail and drugs – but they let him get away with vague answers. Hopefully, that's not the case here.

Ultimately then, it's probably best, as with most actors, to look at what you see on screen in the dozens of performances he has given during, would you believe it, 40 years in the business (thanks, Dad). In *Wonder Boys*, as Terry Crabtree, he leans over to another character and says, 'Sometimes, subconsciously, a person will put themselves in a situation, perhaps even create that situation in order to have an arena in which to work out an unresolved issue. It's a covert way, if you will, of addressing a problem.' The apparent parallels between his cinematic personas and Downey in real life have been talked about a lot here. But it's oddly poetic that one of his creations speaks a line that sums up so perfectly the majority of his filmography. *Saturday Night Live* – the youthful desire to goof around with his friends. *The Pick-Up Artist* – a young, successful actor with access to the feminine riches that endows, but who is already ensconced in a long-term relationship. *Chaplin* – the mark of a man who has never been truly tested in his chosen profession and needs something that will make him put it all on the line. *Two Girls and a Guy* – a chance to show the world he's the best in the business. And *Wonder Boys* itself – playing a man who hasn't had a professional success in five years. The list goes on.

Yes, this is a journalist comparing Downey's real life with the one he performs on screen. It's something actors hate, because they always say there's aesthetic distance, that it's lazy to assume what someone is like in front of a lens is what they're like in the flesh. That, they say, is why you call it acting. And that's true, at least to the extent that when someone plays a killer, it doesn't mean they're going to go out and murder someone, or when someone else plays a lawyer, they have a secret desire to defend the needy. But all actors, just like the rest of us, use what they have within themselves to be the people they have to be from day to day. For an accountant, that's mathematical skill and attention to detail. For an actor, that means reaching inside and taking strands of their personality or experience and translating it into the character they have been chosen to portray. No actor lives in a vacuum, especially not Robert Downey Jr. It's not a failure to have played different versions of yourself, particularly when you're one of the more fascinating people on this planet.

And so we arrive at our finale. There's been the first act – the origin story. Then the second act, culminating in spectacular disaster – a man facing seemingly un-winnable odds. Luckily, this story has a happy ending. At least it does so far. It's highly unlikely Downey's going to be retiring any time. It's simply not in his character. 'My motto creatively is if you see fear, head for it,' he has said. 'And the best way to absolve myself of that consuming sense of foreboding about a creative venture, is get busy. If you're not busy preparing something, you should be scared.'

Downey doesn't want to be scared any more. It's taken a while. But finally he knows what he wants. 'I used to be so convinced that happiness was the goal, yet all those years I was chasing after it, I was unhappy in the pursuit,' he said. 'Maybe the goal should really be a life that values honour, duty, good work, friends and family . . . maybe happiness follows from that.'

Acknowledgements

This book would simply not have been possible without dozens of people's help. And here's my chance to thank all of them (hopefully!).

On the pastoral side, Christina – for her constant support, strategic nagging and life-saving back rubs; Laura for her honesty; Benno for his enthusiasm; and the rest of my friends and family for their unfailing politeness whenever I whinged about deadlines or begged off engagements to write.

For the actual writing of the book: many of you have chosen to remain anonymous and will of course remain so here, although you were incredibly generous with your time and resources. Thank you for everything. Many thanks also to: Malcolm Croft, who liked the idea in the first place; Hannah for her pursuit of the truth, even when it preferred to stare at her legs in a mini-skirt, and for not laughing at a no from the Guttmeister; Anwar Brett for not messing up the sheets and all the bumph; Ian Allen for his assiduous editing; Erik Filkorn for his openness and phe-nomenal Facebook skills; Andy Dougan and his access to Dickie; Allan Eastman, whose life I envy; Alan Metter – a mensch; Cathy Moriarty; the effervescent and insanely busy Chris Bell; Chris

Hanley, the most intellectual film type I've ever met; Dr Drew Pinsky (even though you weren't supposed to); the British Library for its big desks and reading rooms; IMDB Pro – you rock; Sparrow from Southside Stalkers; Marissa Levy; Sa'id Mosteshar; Jeff Oppenheim; mckellen.com; Mike Lobell; Josi Konski; Associated Press; Stuart Kleinman, who set the ball rolling and pointed me towards Downey Sr; the genii at Downey Unlimited and The Institute For Robert Downey Jr Studies; Adrian Turner; Kristin Gallagher, right place right time; John Young and his great pub; Peter Knecht; Ken Baker; Tom Schiller; James Robert Parish; Steve Dunleavy; George Dreher; Toni Basil; the Stagedoor crew – Deren Getz, Dina McLelland, Jeff Blumenkrantz and Richard Allen; for the help and advice – Melanie Bromley, Sophie Vokes-Dudgeon, Colin Paterson, Eloise Parker, Sandro Monetti, Elliott Wagland, Jamie Riordan and Fenton Bailey. And finally, for the crucial words, I owe you all HUGE – Adam Tanswell, Rosa Gamazo, Jane Crowther (kudos too for your editing skills), Richard and Holly at Viva Press, my alma mater the Press Association, Tony Horkins, Damon Wise, James Swanwick and Crocmedia, Izumi Hasegawa and Hollywood News Wire.

And finally Robert Downey Jr – who is probably dreading this book (but somebody was going to write it), considers me an arsehole and thinks I should have waited for the one he will finally get around to writing. It's been a pleasure. I hope this brings back some fond memories, and if it encourages one more person to buy *Kiss Kiss Bang Bang* or *Less Than Zero* on DVD, it's been worth it.

Filmography

Pound (1970)
Plays: Puppy.
Cast: Lawrence Wolf, Elsie Downey, Stan Gottlieb
Director: Robert Downey Sr

Greaser's Palace (1972)
Plays: Uncredited.
Cast: Toni Basil, Albert Henderson, Michael Sullivan
Director: Robert Downey Sr

Up The Academy (1980)
Plays: Uncredited.
Cast: Wendell Brown, Ralph Macchio, Antonio Fargas
Director: Robert Downey Sr

Baby, It's You (1983)
Plays: Stewart
Cast: Rosanna Arquette, Vincent Spano, Joanna Merlin
Director: John Sayles

Firstborn (1984)
Plays: Lee
Cast: Sarah Jessica Parker, Christopher Chollet, Peter Weller
Director: Michael Apted

Deadwait (short, 1985)
Plays: Unknown
Cast: Donnie Kehr, Leslie Durnin
Director: Sam Hurwitz

Tuff Turf (1985)
Plays: Jimmy Parker
Cast: James Spader, Kim Richards, Paul Mones
Director: Fritz Kiersch

Girls Just Want To Have Fun (1985)
Plays: Uncredited
Cast: Sarah Jessica Parker, Helen Hunt, Jonathan Silverman
Director: Alan Metter

Weird Science (1985)
Plays: Ian
Cast: Anthony Michael Hall, Ilan Mitchell-Smith, Kelly LeBrock
Director: John Hughes

Back To School (1986)
Plays: Derek
Cast: Keith Gordon, Rodney Dangerfield, Terry Farrell
Director: Alan Metter

America (1986)
Plays: Paulie Hackley

Cast: Zack Norman, Michael J. Pollard, Richard Belzer
Director: Robert Downey Sr

The Pick-Up Artist (1987)
Plays: Jack Jericho
Cast: Molly Ringwald, Dennis Hopper, Harvey Keitel
Director: James Toback

Less Than Zero (1987)
Plays: Julian
Cast: Andrew McCarthy, Jami Gertz, James Spader
Director: Marek Kanievska

Johnny Be Good (1988)
Plays: Leo Wiggins
Cast: Anthony Michael Hall, Uma Thurman, Paul Gleason
Director: Bud Smith

Rented Lips (1988)
Plays: Wolf Dangler
Cast: Martin Mull, Jennifer Tilly, Dick Shawn
Director: Robert Downey Sr

1969 (1988)
Plays: Ralph Carr
Cast: Kiefer Sutherland, Winona Ryder, Bruce Dern
Director: Ernest Thompson

That's Adequate (1989)
Plays: Albert Einstein
Cast: Tony Randall, Jerry Stiller, Susan Dey
Director: Harry Hurwitz

True Believer (1989)
Plays: Roger Baron
Cast: James Woods, Margaret Colin, Kurtwood Smith
Director: Joseph Ruben

Chances Are (1989)
Plays: Alex Finch
Cast: Cybill Shepherd, Ryan O'Neal, Mary Stuart Masterson
Director: Emile Ardolino

Air America (1990)
Plays: Billy Covington
Cast: Mel Gibson, Nancy Travis, Lane Smith
Director: Roger Spottiswoode

Too Much Sun (1990)
Plays: Reed Richmond
Cast: Allan Arbus, Laura Ernst, Eric Idle
Director: Robert Downey Sr

Soapdish (1991)
Plays: David Seton Barnes
Cast: Kevin Kline, Sally Field, Teri Hatcher
Director: Michael Hoffman

Chaplin (1992)
Plays: Charlie Chaplin
Cast: Kevin Kline, Diane Lane, Paul Rhys
Director: Richard Attenborough

Heart And Souls (1993)
Plays: Thomas Reilly

Cast: Tom Sizemore, Charles Grodin, Alfre Woodard
Director: Ron Underwood

The Last Party (1993)
Plays: Himself
Cast: Bill Clinton, Roger Clinton, Robert Downey Sr
Director: Mark Benjamin & Marc Levin

Short Cuts (1993)
Plays: Bill Bush
Cast: Chris Penn, Julianne Moore, Matthew Modine
Director: Robert Altman

Hail Caesar (1994)
Plays: Jerry
Cast: Anthony Michael Hall, Bobbie Phillips, Leslie Danon
Director: Anthony Michael Hall

Natural Born Killers (1994)
Plays: Wayne Gale
Cast: Woody Harrelson, Juliette Lewis, Tommy Lee Jones
Director: Oliver Stone

Only You (1994)
Plays: Peter Wright
Cast: Marisa Tomei, Bonnie Hunt, Billy Zane
Director: Norman Jewison

Richard III (1995)
Plays: Lord Rivers
Cast: Ian McKellen, Annette Bening, Nigel Hawthorne
Director: Richard Loncraine

Home for the Holidays (1995)
Plays: Tommy Larson
Cast: Holly Hunter, Dylan McDermott, Anne Bancroft
Director: Jodie Foster

Restoration (1995)
Plays: Robert Merivel
Cast: Meg Ryan, David Thewlis, Sam Neill
Director: Michael Hoffman

Danger Zone (1996)
Plays: Jim Scott
Cast: Billy Zane, Lisa Collins, Ron Silver
Director: Allan Eastman

One Night Stand (1997)
Plays: Charlie
Cast: Wesley Snipes, Ming-Na Wen, Kyle MacLachlan
Director: Mike Figgis

Two Girls And A Guy (1997)
Plays: Blake Allen
Cast: Heather Graham, Natasha Gregson Wagner, Angel David
Director: James Toback

Hugo Pool (1997)
Plays: Franz Mazur
Cast: Alyssa Milano, Cathy Moriarty, Malcolm McDowell
Director: Robert Downey Sr

The Gingerbread Man (1998)
Plays: Clyde Pell

Cast: Kenneth Branagh, Embeth Davidtz, Robert Duvall
Director: Robert Altman

U.S. Marshals (1998)
Plays: Special Agent John Royce
Cast: Tommy Lee Jones, Wesley Snipes, Irene Jacob
Director: Stuart Baird

In Dreams (1999)
Plays: Vivian Thompson
Cast: Annette Bening, Aidan Quinn, Paul Guilfoyle
Director: Neil Jordan

Friends & Lovers (1999)
Plays: Hans
Cast: Stephen Baldwin, Danny Nucci, Alison Eastwood
Director: George Haas

Bowfinger (1999)
Plays: Jerry Renfro
Cast: Steve Martin, Eddie Murphy, Heather Graham
Director: Frank Oz

Black And White (1999)
Plays: Terry Donager
Cast: Brooke Shields, Elijah Wood, Mike Tyson
Director: James Toback

Wonder Boys (2000)
Plays: Terry Crabtree
Cast: Michael Douglas, Tobey Maguire, Katie Holmes
Director: Curtis Hanson

Auto Motives (short, 2000)
Plays: Rob
Cast: Allison Janney, James Cameron, Michael Imperioli
Director: Lorraine Bracco

Lethargy (short, 2002)
Plays: Animal therapist
Cast: Edward Burns, David Gelb
Directors: David Gelb & Joshua Safdie

Whatever We Do (short, 2003)
Plays: Bobby
Cast: Tim Roth, Amanda Peet, Zooey Deschanel
Director: Kevin Connolly

The Singing Detective (2003)
Plays: Dan Dark
Cast: Katie Holmes, Jon Polito, Robin Wright Penn
Director: Keith Gordon

Gothika (2003)
Plays: Pete Graham
Cast: Halle Berry, Penelope Cruz, Charles S. Dutton
Director: Mathieu Kassovitz

Eros (segment *Equilibrium*, 2004)
Plays: Nick Penrose
Cast: Alan Arkin, Ele Keats
Director: Steven Soderbergh

Game 6 (2005)
Plays: Steven Schwimmer

Cast: Michael Keaton, Grffin Dunne, Ari Graynor
Director: Michael Hoffman

Kiss Kiss Bang Bang (2005)
Plays: Harry Lockhart
Cast: Val Kilmer, Michelle Monaghan, Corbin Bernsen
Director: Shane Black

Good Night and Good Luck (2005)
Plays: Joe Wershba
Cast: George Clooney, David Strathairn, Patricia Clarkson
Director: George Clooney

A Guide To Recognizing Your Saints (2006)
Plays: Dito Montiel
Cast: Shia LaBeouf, Melonie Diaz, Dianne Wiest
Director: Dito Montiel

The Shaggy Dog (2006)
Plays: Dr Kozak
Cast: Tim Allen, Spencer Breslin, Kristin Davis
Director: Brian Robbins

A Scanner Darkly (2006)
Plays: James Barris
Cast: Keanu Reeves, Winona Ryder, Woody Harrelson
Director: Richard Linklater

Fur: An Imaginary Portrait of Diane Arbus (2006)
Plays: Lionel Sweeney
Cast: Nicole Kidman, Harris Yulin, Ty Burrell
Director: Steven Shainberg

Zodiac (2007)
Plays: Paul Avery
Cast: Jake Gyllenhaal, Mark Ruffalo, Anthony Edwards
Director: David Fincher

Lucky You (2007)
Plays: Telephone Jack
Cast: Eric Bana, Drew Barrymore, Robert Duvall
Director: Curtis Hanson

Charlie Bartlett (2007)
Plays: Principal Nathan Gardner
Cast: Anton Yelchin, Kat Dennings, Tyler Hilton
Director: Jon Poll

Iron Man (2008)
Plays: Tony Stark/Iron Man
Cast: Gwyneth Paltrow, Terrence Howard, Jeff Bridges
Director: Jon Favreau

The Incredible Hulk (2008)
Plays: Tony Stark
Cast: Edward Norton, Tim Roth, Liv Tyler
Director: Louis Leterrier

Tropic Thunder (2008)
Plays: Kirk Lazarus/Lincoln Osiris
Cast: Ben Stiller, Jack Black, Tom Cruise
Director: Ben Stiller

The Soloist (2009)
Plays: Steve Lopez

Cast: Jamie Foxx, Catherine Keener, Tom Hollander
Director: Joe Wright

Sherlock Holmes (2009)
Plays: Sherlock Holmes
Cast: Jude Law, Rachel McAdams, Mark Strong
Director: Guy Ritchie

UPCOMING

Iron Man 2 (2010)
Plays: Tony Stark/Iron Man
Cast: Gwyneth Paltrow, Don Cheadle, Mickey Rourke, Scarlett Johansson
Director: Jon Favreau

Due Date (2010)
Plays: Unknown
Cast: Alan Arkin, Jamie Foxx, Zach Galifianikis
Director: Todd Phillips

TELEVISION

Mussolini: The Untold Story (1985)
Plays: Bruno Mussolini
Cast: George C. Scott, Gabriel Byrne, Gina Bellman
Director: William A. Graham

Saturday Night Live (1985-86/1996)
Plays: Various/Host
Cast: Randy Quaid, Anthony Michael Hall, Terry Sweeney
Director: Dave Wilson

Mr. Willowby's Christmas Tree (1995)
Plays: Mr Willowby
Cast: Stockard Channing, Leslie Nielsen, Steve Whitmire
Director: Jon Stone

Ally McBeal (2000-2002)
Plays: Larry Paul
Cast: Calista Flockhart, Jane Krakowski, Peter MacNichol
Director: Various

Family Guy (2005)
Plays: Patrick Pewterschmidt
Cast: Seth MacFarlane, Alex Borstein, Seth Green
Director: Sarah Frost

MUSIC

'Too Much Sun' – *Too Much Sun (1990)*
'Snake' – *Two Girls and A Guy (1997)*
'In My Dreams' – *The Singing Detective (2003)*
'Broken' – *Kiss Kiss Bang Bang (2005)*

The Futurist (album, 2004)

Bibliography

BOOKS

Actor's Director: Richard Attenborough Behind the Camera by Andy Dougan (Mainstream Publishing, 1995)

The Hollywood Connection by Rayce Newman (S.P.I. Books, 2004)

Killer Instinct: How Two Young Producers Took on Hollywood and Made the Most Controversial Film of the Decade by Jane Hamsher (Orion, 1997)

Entirely Up to You, Darling by Sir Richard Attenborough & Diana Hawkins (Century Hutchinson, 2008)

Smoking in Bed: Conversations with Bruce Robinson ed. Alistair Owen (Bloomsbury UK, 2001)

Projections: Hollywood Film-makers on Film-making 10th ed., Mike Figgis (Faber & Faber, 2000)

Before They Were Famous: In Their Own Words by Karen Hardy Bystedt (Stoddart, 1996)

The New Breed: Actors Coming of Age by Karen Hardy and Kevin J Koffler (Henry Holt & Co.,1988)

Live from New York: An Uncensored History of Saturday Night Live by Tom Shales & James Andrew Miller (Back Bay Books, 2003)

Toxic Fame: Celebrities Speak on Stardom by Joey Berlin (Diane Pub. Co., 1996)

The Film Director as Superstar by Joseph Gelmis (Martin Secker & Warburg Ltd, 1971)

Brat Pack Confidential by Andrew Pulver & Steven Paul Davies (Batsford, 2003)

Good, Bad & the Famous Sherman by Len Sherman (Lyle Stuart, 1990)

Kiefer Sutherland: The Biography by Laura Jackson (Piatkus Books, 2008)

Mel Gibson: Man On A Mission by Wensley Clarkson (John Blake, 2005)

Winona Ryder: The Biography by Nigel Goodall (Blake Pub., 1998)

Sam Taylor-Wood by Michael Bracewell, Jeremy Millar and Claire Carolin (Hayward Gallery Publishing, 2002)

Film Voices: Interviews from Postscript, ed., Gerald Duchovnay (State University of New York Press, Albany, 2004)

ARTICLES

Tracks of His Years, *Sunday Herald (Scotland)*, 17 April 2005, by Graeme Virtue

The Sobering Life of Robert Downey Jr, *New York Times Magazine*, 19 October 2003, by Mim Udovitch

The Star in Cell 17, *Vanity Fair*, by Steve Garbarino, 2000

Robert Downey's Last Party, *Detour*, February 1999, by Steve Garbarino

My Kind of Guy, *Premiere*, February 1998, by James Toback

Robert Downey Jr, Playboy Interview *Playboy*, December 1997, by Michael Fleming

The Father of the Man, *Movieline*, June 1997, by James Toback

Trampled, *Premiere*, January 1993, by Cyndi Stivers

Single White Males, *New Republic*, 7 September 1992, by Michael Lewis

Robert Downey Jr's Weird Science of Acting, *Rolling Stone*, May 1988, by Lynn Hirschberg

Scarcely out of their teens, Sarah Parker and Robert Downey play house in Hollywood, *People*, 3 September 1985, by Gioia Diliberto and Hilary Evans

The Bad and The Beautiful, *Interview Magazine*, September 1985, by Margy Rochlin and Jonathan Roverts

Coming Up – Robert Downey, *US Magazine*, 19 May 1986, by Sheila Rogers

Face to Face, *In Fashion*, January/February 1987, by Camille Soriano.

What's Up with Robert Downey Jr?, *WOW*, August 1987

Kid Controversy; Robert Downey Jr, *Elle*, November 1987, by Joyce Carus

Spotlight: Downey's Up, *Vanity Fair*, March 1988, by Stephen Schiff

Up-Close with Robert Downey, *Modern Screen*, April 1988, by Ivy M. Miller

Robert Downey Jr succeeds in show business without really trying, *YM*, October 1988, By Stephen Schaefer

Cover Story: Robert Downey Jr & Virginia Madsen, *In Fashion*, October 1988, by Camille Cozzone.

Acting – Or Just Acting Up?, *Mademoiselle*, November 1988, by Laura Morice

Insight; Up and Downey, *Elle*, by Eugene J Patron

Woods a true believer in prodding co-stars, *Chicago Sun-Times*, 20 August 1989

Critical Acclaim, *Hero*, 1989, By Nicki Gostin

Arresting Appeal – Partners vs. Crime, *Harper's Bazaar*, February 1989, by Betsy Borns

Robert Downey Jr – A Natural Tease, *Glamour*, March 1989, by David Denicolo

Cinema Scion, *Interview Magazine*, April 1989, by Kenneth Turan

Hollywood's Newest Golden Boy, *Premiere*, April 1989, by Phoebe Hoban

Junior High, *Sky Magazine*, June 1989, by Eugene J. Patron

Robert Downey Jr Acts Like An Adult, *Sassy*, July 1989, by Christina Kelly

Best Friends: Robert Downey Jr and Judd Nelson, *Mademoiselle*, September 1989

Star Poetry – Sonnet Boom, *US Magazine*, 13 November 1989, by Andrea R. Vaucher

20 Questions – Robert Downey Jr, *TV Hits*, Special edition, 1990

Where style meets substance: Upside Downey, *Vanity Fair*, August 1990, by Kevin Sessums

Robert Downey Jr A – Z, *Young Americans*, August 1990

Red and hot right now . . . The delightful upswing of Robert Downey Jr, *Cosmopolitan*, September 1990, by Kirk Honeycutt

Robert Downey Jr gets his kicks – on screen and off – with pyrotechnics, *Video Software*, November 1990, by Bob Strauss.

Ups and Downeys, *Interview Magazine*, November 1990.

Fly Guy, *Sky Magazine*, December 1990, by Dan Yakir

Junior High – Robert Downey Jr, *The Face*, January 1991, by Sheryl Garratt

Something In The Air, *Film Review*, January 1991, by James Cameron-Wilson

Beyond Therapy – Robert Downey Jr, *Blitz*, January/February 1991, by Jeff Yarbrough

Welcome to Air America, *Empire*, February 1991, by Anne Thompson

Profile: Downey Time, *Mirabella*, February 1991, by Trish Deitch Rohrer

Idol Thoughts About Chaplin, *Women's Weekly*, August 1991, by Paul Dougherty

20 Questions, *Playboy*, August 1991

Young Hollywood – Rockin' Robert, *Movieline*, March 1991, by Steven Rebello

Charlie's Angels, *Film Review*, March 1992, by David Aldridge

Robert Downey Jr – The New 'Little Tramp', *Movie Extra*, April/May/June 1992, by Lynda Leftwich

A Right Charlie?, *Sky Magazine*, December 1992, by Adam Sweeting

A new and improved Robert Downey Jr, takes on the role of a lifetime and grows up in the process, *Harper's Bazaar*, December 1992, by Kathy Bishop

It's the tramp! It's the great dictator!, *Mirabella*, December 1992, by Peter Haldeman

Robert Downey Jr is Chaplin (on screen) and a Child (off), *The New York Times*, 20 December 1992, by Jamie Diamond

On the set: Ladies and The Tramp, *US Magazine*, January 1993, by Bob Spitz

What a Tramp!, *GQ*, January 1993, by Johanna Schneller

Party On – There's got to be a morning after, *Paper*, September 1993, by Angela Matusik

Robert Downey Jr – Natural Born Talent, *Cosmopolitan*, January 1994, by Frank Sanello

Upside Downey, *W*, September 1994, by James Fallon

Love Connection, *Tribute*, October 1994, by Jim Slotek

Downey Jr's Roman Holiday, *Film Review*, January 1995, by Judy Sloane

Bawdies, Rest, and Motion, *Premiere*, January 1995, by Philippa Bloom

Irrepressible, Irresistible Robert Downey Jr, *Cosmopolitan*, March 1995, by Nancy Mills

Gettin' Downey, *Detour*, March 1995, by Jim Turner

Downey to Earth: 'Home for the Holidays' star touches base, *Toronto Sun*, November 1995, by Bruce Kirkland

Upside Downey, *Details*, February 1997, by Sam Slovick

Robert Downey Jr, *Syracuse Herald America*, 29 November 1987, by Steven Rea

Less Than Zero role disturbed Downey, *Chicago Sun-Times*, 4 November 1987

Downey makes most of Less Than Zero, *Chicago Sun-Times*, 1 November 1987, by Bob Strauss

Chaplin, *Salina Journal*, 6 January 1993

Restoration star headed to the dogs, *Alton Telegraph*, 18 February 1996, by Scripps Howard News Service

Natural Born Killers, *The New Yorker*, 8 August 1994, by Stephen Schiff

Jack Of All Roles, *Logansport Pharos-Tribune*, 7 July 1991, by Bob Thomas

Robert Downey Jr gets into spirit of comedy, *Syracuse Herald-Journal*, 8 August 1993, by Doug Brode

Downey returns to work on Ally McBeal set, *Albany Times Union*, 29 November 2000

Downey posts bail, back on Ally set, *Chicago Sun-Times*, 30 November 2000, by Kelly Carter

The Scene, *Winnipeg Free Press*, 30 November 2004

More than skin deep, *The Guardian*, 8 November 2003, by Jon Wilde

The Iron Man Effect, *Entertainment Weekly*, 8 May 2008, by Adam B. Vary

The Wizard Q&A: Robert Downey Jr, *Wizarduniverse.com*, 23 March 2008, by Danny Spiegel

Why Robert Downey Jr is a spiritual opportunist, *Time*, 16 April 2008, by David Carr

Downey Jr sued for defamation, *WENN*, 7 April 2003

The Man Who Wasn't There, *Rolling Stone*, 21 August 2008, Erik Hedegaard

Robert Downey Jr biography, *Tiscali.co.uk*, by Dominic Wills

Robert Downey Sr, *Philadelphia Citypaper*, 24 April – 1 May 1997, by Daisy Fried

Filmmaker Robert Downey talks film outside the mainstream, *Daily News, Huntingdon, PA.*, 23 December 1975

Sting surprised to be served by Downey Jr, *The Hindustan Times*, 7 November 2006

Parker speaks out on Downey Jr's drug addiction, *The Hindustan Times*, 16 March 2005

Sarah Jessica Parker on stardom, dating (Nic Cage, JFK Jr, Matthew Broderick) and the baby she'd love to have, *Redbook*, 1 July 1996, by Bernard Weintraub

I rose from the ashes, *Parade*, 20 April 2008, by Dotson Rader

Ex, drugs and rock and roll, *Talk*, February 2002, by Holly Millea

Downey, Falconer divorcing after 12 years, *AP Online*, 28 April 2004

Downey But Not Out, *The Age*, 26 November 2006, by Stephanie Bunbury

Robert Downey Jr takes one day at a time . . . , *Newsweek*, 12 February 2001, by Ana Figueroa

The Smoke Clears, *Salon.com*, 30 November 2000, by Amy Reiter

Sizemore talks about how he hit bottom, *Chicago Sun-Times*, 21 May 2001, by Cindy Pearlman

Hitting Bottom, *People*, 14 February 2000, by Kyle Smith

Bad Weekend in Palm Springs, *Rolling Stone*, 10 May 2001, by Evan Alan Wright

News Lite, *Daily News L.A.*, 18 October 1997

Hitting Bottom, *People*, 19 August 1996, by Tom Gliatto

Downey arrested for trespassing, *Daily News L.A.*, 18 July 1996, by Associated Press

Robert Downey: Flirting With Disaster, *Entertainment Weekly*, 9 September 1996, by Dana Kennedy

Downey Jr gets three years on probation, *Chicago Sun-Times*, 7 November 1996

Downey leaves prison, goes directly to rehab, *Reuters*, 5 August 2000

Downey to attempt life of sobriety, *Associated Press*, 4 August 2000

Downey busted, back in rehab, *Associated Press*, 25 April 2001

Ally McBeal star sentenced, avoids jail, *Associated Press*, 17 July 2001

Actor will get fresh start with new law, *Journal-Tribune, Marysville, OH*, by Don Thompson

Downey likely to receive six months of treatment, *The News, Frederick, Maryland*, 26 April 2001, Associated Press

Downey Jr fired from Ally McBeal following latest arrest, *Aiken Standard*, 25 April 2001, by Anthony Breznican

The Daily On Downey, *The Boston Globe*, 28 December 2000, by Michael Saunders and Jim Sullivan

Film star's unusual releases; Downey's privileges raise L.A. Sheriff's hackles, *The Washington Post*, by William Claiborne

Robert Downey Jr's Hell Behind Bars, *The National Enquirer*, by Michael Glynn

Downey to be released to work on movies, *Norwalk Reflector*, 4 March 1998

Downey has Hollywood's sympathy, *The Milwaukee Journal Sentinel*, 14 December 1997, by Amy Wallace and Robert B Welkos

Mr. Clean: married, sober and on the road to career salvation, Robert Downey Jr pulls no punches, *W*, 1 March 2007, by Kevin West

The Genius Of Junior, *In Style Australia*, May 2007, by Mike Goodridge

Robert Downey Jr marries girlfriend, *People*, 29 August 2005, by Katy Hall

The quiet one: may God bless and keep Robert Downey Jr and if you're up there we're not kidding this time, *Esquire*, March 2007, by Scott Raab

The Man With The Irony Mask, *GQ*, May 2008, by Matthew Klam

Times Of Tyson: James Toback's Heavyweight Documentary, *Blackbookmag.com*, 20 March 2009, by Steven Prigge

Robert Downey Jr: The Second Greatest Actor In The World, *Esquire*, December 2009, by Scott Raab

Public Lives, *The New York Times*, 12 May 1998

Index